A ROUND *the* WORLD WITH A KING

By WILLIAM N. ARMSTRONG

A MEMBER OF THE CABINET OF KALAKAUA, THE LAST KING OF HAWAII

D1720257

MUTUAL PUBLISHING

ISBN 1-56647-017-X

Cover design by Mark Abramson, Zen Jam

First Printing May, 1995

Printed in Australia

Mutual Publishing
1127 11th Avenue, Mezz. B.
Honolulu, HI 96816
(808) 732-1709
Fax (808) 734-4094

CONTENTS

INTRODUCTION by Glen Grant

A Royal Girdle About the Earth: King Kalakau's Tour Around the Spencerian World

CHAPTER I

CHAPTER II

CHAPTER III

CHAPTER IV

CHAPTER V

CONTENTS

CHAPTER VI

CHAPTER VII

CHAPTER VIII

CHAPTER IX

CONTENTS

CHAPTER X

CHAPTER XI

CHAPTER XII

CHAPTER XIII

CONTENTS

CONTENTS

CONTENTS

CHAPTER XXI

CHAPTER XXII

CHAPTER XXIII

CHAPTER XXIV

CONTENTS

CHAPTER XXV

CHAPTER XXVI

CHAPTER XXVII

CHAPTER XXVIII

CONTENTS

A ROYAL GIRDLE ABOUT THE EARTH: KING KALAKAUA'S TOUR AROUND THE SPENCERIAN WORLD
by Glen Grant

King Kalakaua's departure from Honolulu harbor aboard the steamer the *City of Sydney* on January 20, 1881, was attended by a fanfare of music, *mele*, and dance, as sweet-scented flower leis were heaped about the necks of the royal suite. From Punchbowl Crater's fort, a twenty-one gun salute thundered over the town, followed by the strains of "Auld Lang Syne" and "Hawaii Ponoi" played by the Royal Hawaiian Band. As the *City of Sydney* maneuvered through the harbor channel, wailing was heard from the king's subjects who had gathered on the shore. Aboard the steamer bound for San Francisco, King Kalakaua and his suite could hear the plaintive cries of farewell until they had reached the open sea. His Majesty had commenced what would be the first circumnavigation of the globe by a monarch.

The King's decision to make a tour around the world was first announced to his cabinet on January 11, 1881. After several politically strife-torn months during the summer of 1880, His Majesty probably viewed the extended, nine-month journey as a welcome relief from the trying affairs of state in his island kingdom. Having been elected king during a hotly contested campaign in 1874, Kalakaua had learned to maneuver the often treacherous waters between the powerful, predominantly American foreign interests that controlled the kingdom's sugar-based economy and the prerogatives of a Polynesian sovereign. In August 1880, those waters nearly drowned the monarchy following the King's appointment of Italian newcomer Celso Caesar Moreno to his cabinet as minister of foreign affairs. The foreign business interests of Honolulu viewed Moreno as a smooth-talking confidence man who had inveigled his way into the royal confidence. At angry public meetings, the King's judgment of character was denounced as Moreno's questionable past was exposed and vilified. With a strong taste of the political banter which would mark his reign in the 1880's, Kalakaua finally acquiesced to the protests of those men who would eventually topple his government. Moreno was dismissed from office as His Majesty began to contemplate a recuperative journey around the world.

The purpose of the tour was ostensibly to promote immigration to Hawai'i from the many nations of Asia and Europe that were on the King's itinerary. With the native population seriously in decline, the sugar plantations were sorely in need of steady, stable, cheap labor. The importation of young men of a "cognate race" to work in the sugar fields would also serve another purpose: to bolster and repopulate the Native Hawaiian race. As climbing mortality rates from foreign illnesses and epidemics had decimated the native population, the birth rates had also declined. The infusion of new, vigorous races compatible with the Hawaiians, it was hoped, would reverse these seemingly inexorable trends.

Recognizing the expense of a world tour if a full royal entourage were to be included, it was decided that Kalakaua would be accompanied by only two government officials: Chamberlain Colonel Charles H. Judd and Attorney General William N. Armstrong. Promoting Armstrong to a minister of state, Kalakaua also designated the Attorney General to be the Royal Commissioner of Immigration. Included in the royal suite was a multilingual valet named Robert, who in actuality was a German Baron Von Oehlhoffen. Although Robert had a drinking problem which on occasion would embarrass the suite, he proved helpful as a translator during the European portion of the tour.

At a farewell banquet for the King hosted on January 14 by his cabinet ministers, Kalakaua revealed his expansive frame of mind—his inclusive vision of the multicultural kingdom over which he ruled. "Around this table are gathered people of many nations," he began. "In common with my predecessors, I desire the best welfare of all who gather under our flag in my dominions, and I believe that you who come from other lands, bringing with you the wealth, enterprise and intelligence of those lands, sympathize with me in my desire to protect my native Hawaiian people, and strengthen my nation." Two days later, His Majesty repeated this theme when he addressed his native people at Kawaiaha'o Church. Noting the need to recuperate, he saw his world tour as a way to regain the health of his people through the introduction of foreign immigrants.

Another, more personal, reason behind this attempt to wrap the "royal girdle around the earth" was the king's great intellectual curiosity about the nations of the world. As the new biography by Helena Allen stresses, Kalakaua was indeed a "Renaissance King." The son of Hawaiian *ali'i*, chiefs Kapaakea and Keohokalole, Kalakaua was born in 1836 in Honolulu, one of four siblings who were to leave to Hawai'i a legacy of royal grandeur, music, dance and devotion of leadership. Leleihoku, the brother of Kalakaua, was an accomplished musician who died when he was only nineteen years old. His sister Princess Likelike married Governor Archibald S. Cleghorn, a Scotsman with a strong loyalty to the monarchy. Their daughter, Ka'iulani, was destined to be named the heir apparent before her early, tragic death in 1899 at the age of twenty-four. Kalakaua's other sister, Princess Lili'uokalani, was to reign during her brother's absence on his world tour and would ascend to the throne following his death in 1891. The last ruling monarch of the Hawaiian kingdom, Lili'uokalani was illegally overthrown by American business interests, with the assistance of U.S. Minister John Stevens and American military troops from the USS *Boston* on January 17, 1893.

With other high-ranking children, Kalakaua attended the Chief's Children School under the tutelage of the American Protestant missionaries Amos Starr and Juliette Montague Cooke. The Cookes provided an excellent English language instruction under strict discipline. Exposed to the study of history, geography, literature, religious studies and science, Kalakaua blended his Polynesian heritage with an insatiable desire to learn about the scientific, intellectual and spiritual progress of other civilizations. The men and women of art and intellect, such as Robert Louis Stevenson, who had the opportunity to meet this Hawaiian king were invariably impressed with his quick intellect, expansive background and good-natured humor and creativity. As a Mason, His Majesty was linked to the internationalism of this ancient organization and, through his own secret Hale Naua society ("House of Wisdom"), Kalakaua integrated ancient Hawaiian religious belief with scientism and spiritualism. His ardor for technological advances resulted in the electrification of his palace, and one of the first installations of a telephone in Honolulu was between the Palace and the King's boathouse. Even on his deathbed, Kalakaua utilized the new Edison "talking-machine" to record a last message to his people.

To journey around the world, meeting the monarchs and heads of state of Asian, African, European and American nations, observing the ways of life of these many cultures, would be for the King a personal fulfillment of his profound, lifelong curiosity to see for himself those places known only through books or journals. The Chief Justice of the Hawaiian Supreme Court, Charles C. Harris, perhaps touched upon this deeper royal motivation when he noted in an unflattering tone that the king "has gone for no object whatsoever, except the gratification of his own curiosity, which may be said to be object enough."

The excitement His Majesty experienced in seeing the many faces of the globe was continuously revealed in the letters he wrote home to his sister Lili'uokalani. In one letter dated May 22, 1881, Kalakaua wrote that after visiting "Rangoon, Singapore, Hongkong and Shanghai so familiar to us during our school days in our geography, strange that I should live to be able to see them, has been a complete wonder, not only to myself but to the Colonel and Armstrong, for we have often declared (between ourself) the realization of our early childhood dreams." From Rome on July 3, the king described his trip as if a "mixed panorama and a dream. We have seen Emperors, Kings, Temples and pagodas until one gets apparently confused which end to commence and where and how it will be finished, so many varieties of people, the different nationalities the customs and scenery of the places we have visited that has (sic) made our travels so pleasant."

The route of Kalakaua's journey was to first visit San Francisco, where for ten days he visited friends and associates such as the sugar baron, Claus Spreckels, with whom the King would later have a controversial political and personal relationship. On February 8, the royal suite left on the *Oceanic* for Japan, where they arrived in the bay of Yedo on March 4.

Although His Majesty had intended to travel incognito under the title "Alii Kalakaua," the treaty relations between Hawai'i and Japan in 1881 necessitated that the Japanese government receive the monarch as a royal dignitary. Informed of Kalakaua's arrival, the Japanese treated Kalakaua with extraordinary kindness and fanfare. Not only was he the first foreign monarch to visit their island nation, but the two countries had been negotiating a new agreement by which Hawai'i would be the first nation to remove the despised and internationally humiliating rights of "extra-territoriality" in a treaty with Japan. The "Great Powers" of Europe and America had insisted on such a stipulation in their treaties, relegating Japan to second-class international status. Although the Japanese and Hawaiian representatives would complete a treaty arrangement which recognized the equality of Japan with other nations, the treaty would not be signed in deference to the reaction of the "Great Powers." Still, the openness of the Hawaiian government and king to respect Japan as a great nation was reciprocated by the lavishness of Kalakaua's reception. The Emperor

Mutsuhito invested His Majesty with the Order of Chrysanthemum, at that time the highest honor to be bestowed. In turn, Kalakaua conferred on the emperor the Grand Cross of the Order of Kamehameha I.

During his stay in Tokyo, Kalakaua arranged for a private audience with the emperor, proposing an extraordinary arrangement between Japan and Hawai'i. Recognizing the aggrandizing influence of American sugar interests in his islands and hoping to offset what seemed to many as the eventual annexation of Hawai'i by the United States, the King suggested that an alliance between the two Pacific island nations be formalized as the "Union and Federation of the Asiatic nations and sovereigns." With the protection of Japan, the Hawaiian kingdom under the rule of an Hawaiian monarch would be preserved against the "Manifest Destiny" of the American march westward into the Pacific. To formalize the union of the two nations into this "oceania empire," Kalakaua also proposed the marriage of his young niece Princess Ka'iulani to a young prince whom he had met during his travels, Yamashina Sadamaro, later known as Higashifushimi no Miya Yorihito, or Prince Komatsu.

While both proposals were later politely declined, the written response of Emperor Mutsuhito reveals the growing Pacific tensions which would fifty years later engulf the region in war:

> While Your Majesty was in my capitol, you have in course of conversation alluded to a Union and Federation of the Asiatic nations and sovereigns. I highly agree with Your Majesty's profound and far-seeing views. Your Majesty was also good enough to state that I might be the promoter and chief of this Federation. I cannot but be grateful for such expression of your love and confidence in me.

> Oriental nations including my country have long been in a state of decline and decay; and we cannot hope to be strong and powerful unless by gathering inches and trea-

suring foots gradually restore to us all attributes of a nation. To do this our Eastern Nations ought to fortify themselves within the walls of such Union and Federation, and by uniting their power to endeavor to maintain their footing against those powerful nations of Europe and America, and to establish their independence and integrity in future. To do this is a pressing necessity for the Eastern Nations, and in so doing depend their lives.

But this is a mighty work and not easily to be accomplished, and I am unable to foretell the date when we shall have seen it realized. . . . . I desire Your Majesty to understand that unworthy as I am it is impossible to bear the great responsibility which the position of the promoter and chief of such a vast undertaking imposes.

However, I ardently hope that such Union may be realized at some future day ... I desire Your Majesty will oblige with further advises relative to the question.

The Far East Asian Co-Prosperity Sphere had been born.

While Kalakaua's far-reaching political alliances had not been achieved, the arrangement for the importation of Japanese laborers was commenced. In 1885, the first laborers from Japan arrived in Honolulu, initiating over two decades of immigration as tens of thousands of Japanese men and women established themselves in the Hawaiian Islands. The legacy of Kalakaua's tour of the world would be the foundation for Hawai'i's population of Japanese-Americans who have played a prominent role in the emergence of modern, twentieth-century Hawai'i.

On March 22, 1881 the Hawaiian royal suite left Japan with indelible, fond memories of their experience. In his travel diary, Kalakaua simply wrote, "Adieu Japan — Beautiful Japan. I felt as if I would have a continual longing to see this interesting country with its king and hospitable inhabitants for a long time. Aloha nui."

In China, the King visited Shanghai and Tientsin, meeting the Viceroy Li Hung Chang before traveling on to Hong Kong, where the British colonial authorities gave him a gracious reception. From Hong Kong, the royal suite visited Siam, the Malay States, Burma, Calcutta, and Bombay before boarding a steamer to Suez in Egypt. The King and his companions then traveled in the Khedive of Egypt's private railway car to Cairo, where the ancient pyramids were visited upon small donkeys. From Alexandria the suite crossed the Mediterranean Sea, arriving in Naples, Italy, where they met King Humbert and Queen Margherita.

In Rome His Majesty had an audience with Pope Leo XIII at the Vatican. The suite then quickly traveled through France and arrived in London, England, on July 6. At a reception hosted by Queen Victoria, Kalakaua was appointed an Honorary Knight Grand Cross of the Order of St. Michael and St. George. In a letter home, Armstrong confided to a friend that "I desire to assure you that the many persons who have met His Majesty, since His arrival here, express themselves as highly pleased with His Majesty's appearance, bearing and intelligence, and I am compelled to believe that this visit is of great advantage to the Hawaiian Islands in creating a just and proper idea of the civilization of our country."

Returning to the continent, His Majesty then toured Belgium, Germany, Austria, France, Spain, and Portugal, where negotiations were initiated to increase the immigration of Portuguese laborers to Hawai'i. At a brief return to Edinburgh, Kalakaua received the Masonic rank of Knight Grand Cross of the Imperial Council of Scotland. At Liverpool the king boarded a steamer for New York.

In Washington, D.C., His Majesty met President Chester A. Arthur, who had recently assumed the office after the assassination of James Garfield. In stature, bearing and facial features, the two men bore a striking resemblance to one another. After a visit to the Hampton Normal and Agricultural School founded by

General Samuel C. Armstrong, friend of the King and younger brother of William N. Armstrong, the suite journeyed across the United States, boarding the steamer *Australia* in San Francisco, bound for Honolulu. The "royal girdle" was finally wrapped around the earth on October 29 to the tumultuous aloha of the kingdom. Honolulu streets had been elaborately decorated for the King, who was paraded with his suite through downtown to the cheers of his subjects. The celebration continued for several days with music, dancing and feasting as *mele* were sung commemorating the king's journey and his safe return.

The only fully detailed account of King Kalakaua's tour of the world to be printed is *Around the World With a King* by William N. Armstrong. Published in 1904, long after King Kalakaua had died so to permit, as the author notes, "a freedom of narration, an adherence to truth, and 'the painting of a portrait with the wrinkles,'" the account is said to be based on day-to-day notes taken over twenty years earlier. Although King Kalakaua kept a traveling diary with random commentaries and wrote several letters home to his sister and friends detailing his experiences, Armstrong's version remains the most complete description of the tour.

For readers curious about the romantic age of monarchs when the footsteps of kings and queens still heralded awe and reverence as if placed there by the gods themselves, *Around the World With a King* will be an enjoyable, nostalgic journey to a long-gone era. After visiting the opulent and lavish palaces of Asian potentates and European blue bloods, the modern reader can only wonder how far the royal houses of the world have fallen, now more familiar in the sensational headlines of supermarket tabloids.

In *Around the World With a King*, the student of Hawaiian history will have the opportunity to view one of Hawai'i's most complex and enigmatic personages, albeit through the distorted vision of Armstrong. While widely known as the "Merrie Monarch" and frequently spoken of in terms of 'Iolani Palace, Hawaiian nationalism and the revival of the *hula,* King Kalakaua still remains an allusive figure in recent Hawaiian history. So often condemned for his extravagance or praised for his nationalistic ardor, the man, the leader and visionary is obscured by the rhetoric. Part of the difficulty in understanding Kalakaua is the lack of primary sources from his own pen. The modern student views the King mostly from a second-hand perspective that more often than not has a hidden agenda.

In that regard, the reader of this reprinted edition of *Around the World With a King* should beware of the distorted view of Kalakaua presented by Armstrong. The book is infuriating in that nearly every page is seeped in the age's sentiments of racism and paternalism which flow from Armstrong's unabashed social Darwinism. The framework of the author's worldview is locked into English philosopher Herbert Spencer's notion of the "survival of the fittest" incorporated into social forces of evolution. Predicated on what is now generally viewed as the fallacious notion of "race," Armstrong's perception of the superiority of the Anglo-Saxon race to the "weaker," "crude," "superstitious mind" of a Polynesian race and king completely distorts his appraisal and true understanding of his royal traveling companion.

By his own admission, Armstrong saw his loyalty to Kalakaua as only a professional obligation associated with his position as Attorney General and Royal Commissioner of Immigration. Effusing a condescending tone of arrogance and disdain for Kalakaua, Armstrong wrote that his "relations to the King, as a Hawaiian-born subject but an American by inheritance, put me under an obligation to him like that of the apprentice in the 'Pirates of Penzance' who was bound until noon every day to an absolute loyalty to his piratical masters, but after that hour and until night was entirely free to circumvent and destroy them."

The description of Kalakaua that emerges in the pages of *Around the World With a King* is the perception of buffoonery and royal simple-mindedness that Armstrong consistently affixes to His Majesty and his native subjects. "The monarchy and people were rather more pagan than civilized," Armstrong moralizes and elsewhere notes that the "King's mind was naturally filled with the crude ideas, the superstitions, the absolutism of a Polynesian chief, though his experience with the whites had modified their exaggerated forms; and where experience was lacking, a vague fear of the white men's superior intelligence took its place."

Positioning himself as Kalakaua's "tutor," Armstrong saw this tour as an opportunity to instruct his Polynesian king in the Spencerian realities of the world. "My associates in the Cabinet . . .," he writes, "had asked me to instruct the King, during the idle hours of our journey, in the principles and practice of good government, but recommended that it be done so cautiously that our royal master would not be offended or suspect that he was placed under tuition: that is, as my colleagues suggested, he should be treated as the hunter treats a wild animal, by approaching him from the leeward, so that the royal game would not be startled by the smell of offensive instruction." His efforts to convenience His Majesty of the superiority of Anglo-Saxon institutions and values, however, were frustrating. "The tube through which we had hoped he would suck wisdom of the world," Armstrong laments, "was defective; all that rose in it filtered upward through Polynesian ideas."

The paternalism with which William N. Armstrong viewed Kalakaua was well-ingrained in his upbringing in a missionary home. Born in Lahaina, Maui, on March 10, 1835, Armstrong was the son of the Reverend Dr. and Mrs. Richard Armstrong, American Protestant missionaries who arrived in the islands in 1831. His younger brother was Samuel C. Armstrong, the founder of Hampton Institute, the famed school for African-Americans. In 1849, at the age of fourteen, William Armstrong attended the Chiefs' Children School with Charles H. Judd and young Hawaiian royalty, including David Kalakaua. Graduated from Yale in 1859, Armstrong practiced law in New York City and later in Hampton, Virginia, until he was called by King Kalakaua in 1880 to serve in his cabinet as Attorney General.

The appointment of Armstrong, who had just recently returned to the islands, as Kalakaua's traveling companion under the title Royal Commission of Immigration caught some political leaders offguard. Walter Murray Gibson, controversial newspaper editor and outspoken proponent of Hawaiian nationalism, monarchical authority and foreign immigration, had expected the appointment for himself. One week after the trip was completed, Gibson would be arrested by Attorney General Armstrong for making libelous comments against the Commission of Immigration in his newspaper. Charging in his newspaper that Armstrong had told foreign officials during his tour that Hawai'i needed only plantation field hands and not independent farmers and artisans, Gibson accused the commissioner of treason. The invigoration of the Hawaiian race and economy of the kingdom, Gibson believed, required immigrants of independent means, not only field laborers. Threatened with a lawsuit, Gibson apologized and Armstrong dropped the charges.

Armstrong's open sympathies for "Anglo-Saxon government" and his disdain for monarchy, intensified perhaps during his years in the United States, did not, however, diminish his own love for the pomp and circumstance. During the royal visit to the United States, Armstrong notes that Kalakaua "only amused the American populace and excited their curiosity. One of the papers stated that 'while he was a good fellow, his throne was only a relic of barbarism,' and others likened his court to the royal families in opera bouffe." Yet Armstrong pleasantly notes that during state functions he himself also was often bedecked in an exquisite royal uniform. A delicately worked cloth which had been embroidered in England for the royal family, "with wire of gold bullion, imitations of the beautiful leaf and flower of the taro plant together with the fine leaf of the koa, a Hawaiian tree," was tailored in San

Francisco into "a rich diplomatic uniform, the design of which was especially admired in every court visited by the King and his suite. To this was added a sword and a cocked hat."

Armstrong's self-elevation while deriding the superficiality of Hawaiian royal decorum is evident in his description of Kalakaua's meeting with the Japanese emperor. While an account of the royal encounter given in this work will appear later in Ralph Kuykendall's *The Hawaiian Kingdom,* more recent research has shown that Armstrong's version was entirely self-serving. According to Masaji Marumoto, former Associate Justice of the State of Hawai'i Supreme Court and amateur historian, the meeting between the monarchs of Japan and Hawai'i detailed in Kalakaua's travel diary was quite different from Armstrong's account. Armstrong states that the king was given the "Grand Cross of the Order of the Rising Sun" by the emperor. Then the emperor personally gave to Armstrong the "Grand Officer of the Order of the Rising Sun," "whispering some words in the vernacular," and to Judd, "an insignia of the same Order, but one degree lower."

According to Kalakaua's diary notes, however, the King had actually received the Order of Chrysanthemum and Cordon and Star of the Order from the Emperor. At that time, this was the very highest honor which could have been invested upon the king, placing him in protocol even above the premier. Kalakaua then notes that Armstrong and Judd were taken to separate apartments, where the Minister of the Imperial Household bestowed upon them the "Second Grade of Order of the Rising Sun." After an examination of Kalakaua's Order, now preserved by the Bishop Museum and through Japanese sources, Justice Marumoto has confirmed the king's account of the ceremony. Whether consciously or through lapse of memory, Armstrong's memoir had de-evaluated the special honor given to Kalakaua while inflating his own importance. One can only wonder where else in *Around the World With the King,* the "Anglo-Saxon democrat" distorted the record to tarnish the image of the Polynesian king.

Even when remarking on His Majesty's royal bearing, Armstrong could not suspend his racist judgments. *"Although a Polynesian,"* [italics added], he writes about the king, "he was capable of appearing as a well-bred man in any society or in any court." Acknowledging that Kalakaua was extremely well-read, he goes on to determine that "he had not digested his reading, and his learning was therefore somewhat dangerous, although its extent surprised visitors to his kingdom, as well as many persons whom he met during his long tour."

Armstrong's condescending attitude toward Kalakaua, his childhood classmate, reveals the complex nature of the nineteenth-century *kama'aina haole* (native-born Caucasian) relation to the indigenous people of the islands. Raised in a climate of noblesse oblige, believing that the sacrifices of their missionary parents had somehow provided them with a special interest over the "semi-civilized" natives, Armstrong's frequent reaffirmation of affection for the King reflects a destructive attitude of paternalism. Noting that Judd, the King and he had "rubbed each other's noses in the dirt thirty years before," Armstrong also reminisced how he and His Majesty, as youngsters, had dived for coins thrown by whalers at Honolulu harbor. If indeed these past experiences could be interpreted as forming the basis of friendship, then Armstrong's remonstrations against Kalakaua's "crude superstitions," political ineptitude and "simple" Polynesian "mind-set" bespeak of the deep-seated, racial separatism that inhibited him from the loyalties, affection and humility that form the basis of enduring friendships. Kalakaua's trust in Armstrong, evidenced in his promotion to Attorney General, the King's openness of spirit revealed to his companions during the tour, and the generosity shown to Armstrong upon their return (note the photograph of Armstrong bedecked in *maile* lei at a dinner given by the king), could not be truly reciprocated by those imprisoned by their own racial handicaps.

The insights provided by Armstrong into the character of Kalakaua are wholly fallacious. How can one assess someone whom one sees in a convoluted montage of paternal affection, disdain and attitude of inferiority? The assessment is by its nature superficial and, therefore, faulty. The most obvious instance of Armstrong's blindness is his evaluation of Kalakaua's royal aloofness from the concerns and sufferings of his native subjects. At one point during the end of their journey, for example, Armstrong presses Kalakaua to express what the tour of the world has taught him about the benefits of having Anglo-Saxon institutions meet the needs of the Hawaiian people. When the King seems reluctant to share with Armstrong any thoughts on the subject, the missionary son has the audacity to question Kalakaua's concern for the decline of his race. "Your people are dying out," he admonishes the king, "and will soon be extinct."

"Well, if they are," Kalakaua is quoted by Armstrong as replying, "I've read lots of times that great races died out, and new ones took their places; my people are like the rest. I think the best way is to let us be."

The response as described by Armstrong suggested a monarch who enjoys his royal banquets and uniforms while unconcerned that his people perish by the thousands. "So his conclusion," writes Armstrong, "was that he had seen nothing which his people needed but some well-bred horses and cattle." Indeed, Kalakaua had taken no "special interest in the welfare of his people" during his six-year reign. Even the purpose of the tour, as presented by the King during his Kawaiahaʻo farewell address to his people, was described by Armstrong as a sham. The King, explained Armstrong:

> ... announced to them ... that his chief object in travel was to avail himself of the experience of other nations for their benefit. This paternal solicitude greatly pleased his native subjects, who had fallen far behind their white neighbours in the march of progress, because, as one of the

King's predecessors had frankly said, they were 'shiftless, lazy, and incompetent.' The King's declaration led them to believe that he would return laden with patent and miraculous contrivances which would give them abundance without labor, and enable them to scratch themselves with tropical serenity, which was the habit of their inheritance, and they cordially approved of this royal act of self-sacrifice.

This portrait of Kalakaua needs to be juxtaposed against the private words of His Majesty written to his sister Lili'uokalani during the tour. Recognizing that the hundreds of thousands of Hawaiians who existed at the time of Captain Cook's arrival in 1778 had dwindled to just over 40,000 by 1880, His Majesty had made the motto of his reign "Hooulu Lahui" or "Increase the Race." Even as the *City of Sydney* was carrying the King on the first leg of his tour, another smallpox epidemic had broken out in Honolulu, resulting in hundreds of deaths. Once again the biologically vulnerable Hawaiians were being ravaged by foreign diseases, including whooping cough, influenza, venereal disease, and Hansen's disease. Writing home to his sister from Cairo on June 21, 1880, Kalakaua agonized over these deaths, challenging his devout Christian sister Lili'uokalani to justify her continued faith in God:

> But what is the use of prayer after 293 lives of our poor people have gone to their everlasting place. Is it to thank him for killing or is it to thank him for sending them to Him or to the other place which I never believed in the efficacy of prayer and consequently I never allowed myself to be ruled by the Churchmembers to allow a thanksgiving prayer to be offered to God for the good of the nation for in my opinion it is only a mockery. The idea of offering prayer when hundreds are dying around you. To save the

life of the people is to work and not pray. To find and stop the causes of death of our people and not cry and whine like a child and say to god "that it is good oh Lord that those hath visited us thus."

A descendant of missionaries, Armstrong assured his audience that "His Majesty admitted that the missionaries were always honest, and were the best friends of the people, and did them good by establishing schools and churches." With all of his moral superiority, Armstrong evidently had an inability to separate *hoomalimali* or flattery from truth. If Kalakaua had so honored the Protestant missionaries, he was also writing home to Lili'uokalani on August 10, 1880 that after seeing the gaiety and busyness of life in Paris, the missionary culture that predominated in Hawai'i seemed even more oppressive:

> Can it possibly be that these light hearted happy people are all going to H-ll? All enjoying nature as natures best gifts? Surely not! But what a contrast to our miserable bigoted community. All sober and down in the mouth keeping a wrong Sabbath instead of a proper Sunday, the Pure are so pure that the impure should make the Sunday a day of mockery, with such rubbish trash that we have so long been lead (sic) to believe, it is a wonder that we have not risen any higher than the common brute.

As for Kalakaua's political maneuverings to form an alliance with Japan, Armstrong interpreted the scheme as having originated in one of the "curious recesses of his Polynesian brain." Noting that Kalakaua "had a vague fear the United States might in the near future absorb his kingdom," the King's attempt to shift the balance of power in the Pacific "made the suite more watchful against escapades of the Crowned Head it was steering around the world. Had the scheme been accepted by the Emperor, it would have tended to make Hawaii a Japanese colony; a movement distasteful to all of the Great Powers."

The "vague fear" sensed by Kalakaua proved to be far from vague. In the Spencerian logic which justified the westward expansion of the United States into the Pacific, Armstrong stressed that the monarchy's extinction was a result of the "cold and inexorable law of political evolution." In the conflict between the "stronger Teutonic races against the weaker Polynesian," survival went to the "fittest." However, due to the prevalent influence of the American missionaries who were the harbingers of this American takeover of Hawai'i, the decline of the Polynesian "was peaceful and bloodless; for of all weak races which have come in contact in any land whatsoever with the stronger races, the Hawaiians have suffered the least from injustice and physical dominance. On the other hand, they have been cared for and coddled by the whites to an unwholesome extent."

With the Anglo-Saxon race and institutions firmly entrenched in the Hawaiian Islands, the eventual annexation of the islands to the United States in 1898 was a completion of an over-fifty-year process. "At the tap of the Federal drum . . .," Armstrong concluded on a breast-beating note, Hawai'i "wheeled into line and took up its march to the music of the Union without an awkward step, and is now the advanced picket line of American civilization in the Pacific."

For those who may claim that the overthrow of the monarchy was based on legitimate legal, economic or benevolent motivations, the language of *Around the World With a King* should be a reminder that racism was also a central factor in the justification for the events of the 1880's and 1890's. Armstrong's worldview was not unique among those who would eventually work for the overthrow of the monarchy and American annexation. After his world tour, he continued to support the Spencerian unfolding of "Anglo-Saxon institutions." Living in New York City, where he was Commissioner of the Supreme Court, and later Washington,

D.C., Armstrong advised Lorrin Thurston during the visits of the Hawai'i delegation seeking annexation. For a short time he returned to the islands to recuperate from a reoccurring bout of malaria and worked as an editor for the proannexationist *Pacific Commercial Advertiser.* His description of the world tour was published in 1904, the year before his death in 1905. The book remains one of the more widely read apologia for the controversial events of 1881-1898.

With all of its shortcomings and racist overtones, *Around the World With a King* serves an important purpose for the modern reader. As you journey around the world with this Hawaiian monarch, contrast the denegation of Hawaiians by the author, with the world-wide recognition and acceptance Kalakaua and his kingdom were given as an independent ruler and nation, with separate and legitimate treaties between scores of nations. Upon what legal right (in accordance with Anglo-Saxon law) had the United States absorbed this nation, transforming it into a territorial colony and then a state? Upon what legal or moral ground does the continued denial of sovereignty to the indigenous descendants of that nation rest?

Armstrong had noted that the forces of social Darwinism then shaping his world seemed to evade King Kalakaua. "The King did not understand this law of evolution," he wrote, being "alien" to the tide of Anglo-Saxon dominance. Unfortunately, the King probably understood the rising tide of American domination better than Armstrong knew, yet believed that the trend was reversible. After the triumph of his royal tour, his coronation on February 12, 1883, and the completion of his grand 'Iolani Palace, the vision of an independent Hawaiian Kingdom that preserved his native race while perpetuating the ancient rule of chiefs perhaps seemed within his grasp. This vision was not based upon the racial theories of social Darwinism, but the ancient Hawaiian value of *hanai* or adoption. In the inclusive worldview of the Hawaiian, bloodline never precluded the full, equal acceptance of someone else as a member of the 'ohana or family. The *hanai* children never felt less loved or outside the inner family circle—they were fully incorporated into the 'ohana.

Kalakaua's quest to reach out to the rest of the world, to bring to his island nation representatives of the people of Asia, the Pacific and Europe to repopulate his land, was to bring renewed life to his people and their ancient way of life. As his opponents delimited their racial parameters, misinterpreting their use of economic, political and even military force as reflecting "social evolution," Kalakaua embraced a culturally pluralistic world where races, cultures and various religions could live together in harmony and independence. The concept of cultural pluralism in a world bonded to racial superiority may indeed have been too farsighted. Yet in modern, multicultural Hawai'i the vision of this king who first circumnavigated the world has not been vanquished. While his detractors in their self-righteousness now seem smallminded and racist, Kalakaua's open-hearted inclusiveness has reawakened his nation and native subjects who today seek to prove through the restoration of their sovereignty and dignity that one hundred years of "Spencerian evolution" was neither inevitable nor inexorable.

For Kalakaua's account of his tour around the world see:

Letters from "The Royal Tourist — Kalakaua's Letters Home from Tokio to London," edited by Richard Greer, Hawaiian Journal of History, V. 5, 1971, pp. 75-109.

Masaji Marumoto, "Vignettes of Early Hawaii-Japan Relations: Highlights of King Kalakaua's Sojourn in Japan or His Trip around the World as Recorded in His Personal Diary." Hawaiian Journal of History, V. 10, 1976. pp. 52-63

AROUND THE WORLD
WITH A KING

CHAPTER I

King Kalakaua Plans a Tour — The First Sovereign to Put a
Girdle Around the World — Selects His Companions — His
Valet — Proposes to Travel Incognito — Scope of His Tour —
Delay in Publication of This Memoir — The King Addresses
His Subjects — Ceremonies Attending the Departure — The
King's Character — His Minister and Chamberlain — Kala-
kaua's Knowledge of Royal Etiquette — His Unfortunate
Predecessors — Theoretical and Practical Astronomy.

KALAKAUA I, King of the Hawaiian Islands,
said to me, his Attorney-General, early one
morning in January, 1881, while we sat under the
cocoanut palms which towered above his little Summer Palace at Waikiki, near Honolulu, and the surf
of the Pacific Ocean, foaming over the coral reef,
broke nearly at our feet, —

" Now that my troubles are over, I mean to take
a trip around the world, and you must go with me."

He had been upon the throne for six years, and,
with the true instincts of sovereigns, had availed
himself of several opportunities to engage in difficulties with some of his white subjects, who held
the brains and most of the property of the kingdom.
They had lately threatened insurrection because he
had committed several serious political errors, but

he had yielded to their demands, and on the night preceding this declaration of intention to travel he and a hundred of his white subjects had met in a grand banquet; they had together emptied the loving cup; and the white doves of peace again swept through the tropic air.

I took his remark as an idle fancy which would quickly be replaced by other similar ones. But as we rode into the city I said:

"If your Majesty makes a tour of the world, you will be the first sovereign of the earth who has ever travelled around it, and your subjects should erect a high monument of lava stones on the crown of Punch Bowl [1] with this inscription upon it:

"To the First Sovereign
Who Put a Girdle Around the Earth.
a.d. 1881."

Since the concert of the morning stars, or the appearance of man on the globe, sovereigns have done many great and many small things; but not one of them, even in these later days, has had the audacity or pluck to circumnavigate this little planet. Like certain sagacious animals which never travel far from their holes in the earth through fear of being dispossessed of them by an enemy, rulers seldom stray far from their thrones lest rivals seize and occupy them. Besides, there are the perils of land and sea. Sir John Mandeville, that great traveller, said in 1356: "Although it be possible to go round the world, yet of a thousand persons not one might happen to return to his country." The sov-

---

[1] An extinct volcano rising behind the city.

Colonel C. H. Judd, King Kalakaua's Chamberlain.

ereigns before his time anticipated his forecast, and those who came after him observed his cautions and the wisdom of the brute creation and left to a Polynesian king the honour, if there be any, of achieving this deed.

Before night I discovered that his Majesty was in a serious mood, for he convened his Cabinet, of which I was a member, declared his intention to make the journey, and requested a meeting of his Privy Council, at which the necessary funds could be provided. The Cabinet and the Council approved of the project and were willing to provide abundantly for it. He declared also that he should take with him, as companion, the author of this memoir, who would receive the commission of " Minister of State," which would place him in the same rank as the Cabinet Ministers of any sovereign, and entitle him to the respect and courtesies due that rank, while, in order to give the appearance of a useful purpose to the royal expedition, he made him also, " Royal Commissioner of Immigration," with instructions to seek over the world recruits to the depleted population of the kingdom, a depletion so steadily growing that there was imminent danger, within a few generations, of the singular case of a native monarchy without a native subject. In addition to the Minister of State he selected Colonel C. H. Judd, his Chamberlain, and one of his most trustworthy friends, as his second companion. His personal attendant, or valet, was a German known as " Robert," an educated man of prepossessing appearance and a remarkable linguist. Owing to his intemperate habits he never remained long in any situation. He had served as cook on sailing-vessels, and on landing in Hawaii had become the King's *chef*. But his unreliability had cast him out of this situation. There was a rumour that he was the Baron von O———. This was verified by the suite during the tour. In spite of his habits, the King, for reasons which I did not then know, consented to engage him as valet upon a new pledge of sobriety; but the engagement was made under the mild protest of the suite.

Before recording the incidents of this royal tour it may be said, in anticipation, that the King of Hawaii executed his mission as a circumnavigator within the ten following months, during which time he became the guest of, or was received in state ceremonies by, the Emperor of Japan; General Li Hung Chang, of China; the Governor of Hongkong, in the name of the British Queen; the King of Siam; the British Governors or Commissioners of Singapore, Penang, the Malacca Straits, and of Burmah; the Vice-Regal Court of India; the Viceroy of Egypt; the King of Italy; the Holy Father in Rome; the British Queen; the King of Belgium; the Court of Emperor William of Germany; the officials of the Austrian Empire, in the absence of the Emperor; the officials of the French Republic; the officials of the Spanish Court, whose Regent was absent; the King of Portugal; and finally, the President of the United States, from which country he returned to his own kingdom.

The memoir of the incidents of this tour were noted from day to day by the writer, his " Minister of State " and companion; but its publication has been delayed for some years, and until after his death, in order to permit a freedom of narration, an adherence to truth, and " the painting of a portrait with the wrinkles;" nor has it been found necessary to follow Macaulay's aphorism, that "the best portraits are those in which there is a slight admixture of caricature." Kings, above all men, resent any language but that of adulation, and if one would avoid censure he is wise to await the co-operation of Death, and reserve his narrative until the subject of it is in the other world, where, according to Lord Bacon, Menippus, in his travels through hell, found the kings of the earth distinguished from other men chiefly by their louder wailings and tears.

Before the King began his tour I incidentally called his attention to certain omens which might disturb his Polynesian and somewhat superstitious mind.

One of his predecessors, Kamehameha II, King of the Sandwich Islands, as they were called in the early days, and his spouse Kamamalu, in the year 1824, while the people were pagans, visited England as guests of the British monarch. Both of them died of the measles, in London, and their bodies were conveyed with royal honours to their kingdom in the British frigate "Blonde," commanded by Lord Byron, a cousin of the poet. Their sudden and nearly simultaneous deaths were reported to Theodore Hook, giving the wit the opportunity for his well-known couplet, announcing the sad event:

> "'Waiter! two sandwiches!' cried Death;
> And their wild Majesties resigned their breath."

At the moment when their successor, nearly sixty years later, proposed to travel in foreign countries, the small-pox broke out in his own capital, with much loss of life. He wisely concluded to let the monster gratify his insatiate appetite on common Sandwiches, while he removed himself, as material for a royal Sandwich, out of the kingdom.

In order to prevent a large retinue of his loyal native and white subjects from following him in his tour, at his own great expense, he announced that he would travel incognito under the title of Prince. His sister, the Princess Liliuokalani, now the ex-Queen of Hawaii, was by royal proclamation designated as Regent during his absence.

Several days before his departure he invited his native subjects to meet him in the largest church of his capital, and although he had not, during the six years of his reign, taken any special interest in the welfare of his people, he announced to them from the platform that his chief object in travel was to avail himself of the experience of other nations for their benefit. This paternal solicitude greatly pleased his native subjects, who had fallen far behind their white neighbours in the march of progress, because, as one of the King's predecessors had frankly said, they were "shiftless, lazy, and incompetent." The King's declaration led them to believe that he would return laden with patent and miraculous contrivances which would give them abundance without labour, and enable them to scratch themselves with tropical serenity, which was the habit of their inheritance, and they cordially approved of this royal act of self-sacrifice. The Protestant missionaries had brought to them the blessings of civilisation, but the seafaring countrymen of the missionaries had also brought to them its curses, and it was an act of kingly philanthropy for their sovereign to seek in foreign lands some method of relief, if there was any, from their unfortunate sufferings between the upper and nether millstones of Christian civilisation.

When the day arrived on which the steamer from Australia, bound to San Francisco, was due, the natives loyally gathered at the Palace, to fulfil those rites and ceremonies which were fitting on such an unusual event as the departure of the King from his country, and groups of singers and dancers gathered on the thick sward under the royal palms. Each dancer had a gourd filled with pebbles, and shook it, in measured time, with one hand, while with the other he described graceful motions in the air. Wreaths of sweet-scented vines and many-coloured flowers encircled or streamed from their bodies, or were entwined with their glossy black locks. No jewelled necklace or spangled dress of the European ballet rival these natural ornaments from the flower-bearing valleys. The singers, squatting in groups, dressed in the glory of the fields, told the story, in a plaintive minor key, of the greatness of the Hawaiian kings, their miraculous exploits, and their imperishable renown. Many of the words of the songs were in the ancient language and were understood only by the older people; but if translated they would have promoted intense activity in a Society for the Promotion of Moral Literature, if one had existed there. As one group of singers and dancers became exhausted, relays of new performers replaced them, in order that there might be no gap in movement or melody.

The steamer did not arrive on time, but traditional etiquette required that these ceremonies should continue unbroken until the King embarked. Many hours passed, and there was no end to the dancing or singing, and at midnight the trade winds died away and the moon arose. In the dreamy stillness of the soft air the low monotonous chanting, the measured rattling of the gourds, rose above the trees, with intervals of European music by the military band. I was on a high balcony overlooking this strange scene, with its extraordinary mixture of the airs of Polynesia and of Europe. Beyond the forest of tall cocoanut palms I heard the surf of the Pacific Ocean, with " great white avalanches of thunder," rolling up on the coral beach. This music of intermingled paganism, civilisation, and ocean ended only with the dawn, and with the dawn the steamer arrived, and the King promptly embarked. Some ancient cannon of large calibre, situated on the height above the city, discharged a royal salute of twenty-one guns, and the King and his suite stood on the deck, buried in a wilderness of flowers; for it is the agreeable custom of the country to decorate departing friends with wreaths of flowers and scented vines, and their quantity on this occasion was sufficient to have dressed the masts, yards and rigging of the steamer from stem to stern. Every native had brought a tribute of these, and their perfume filled the air. As the " City of Sydney" swung away from the dock, the national band played " Auld Lang Syne," and " Hawaii Ponoi" (po-no-ee), the national anthem; and the wailing of the natives followed her to the mouth of the harbour until their piercing cries were lost in the roar of the surf.

The tour thus auspiciously begun, the King, in the expressive words of Lord Bacon, was now ready to " suck " the experience of the world.

The Queen, who had supervised the packing of the King's luggage, had filled many packages with shoes and clothing of all kinds; among them were six hat-boxes, and a canvas bag which, I soon discovered, held the royal standard. I then suspected that the " Prince," for he began his journey incognito, was providing for the fortunes of travel, and, if he desired, could throw off his borrowed plumes and assume his crown; but his manœuvre was praise-worthy in that it had prevented the burden and expense of a retinue.

This memoir will not be understood without a preliminary description of the King, and the personal relations which existed between him and his suite. Although a Polynesian, he was capable of appearing as a well-bred man in any society or in any court. He was above the medium height and of large proportions, and had received an education in the English language in a school especially organised to instruct the young chiefs of Hawaii. Its instructors were carefully selected by the white men of the government for the purpose of giving the future rulers the best preparation for their coming responsibilities. In this royal school there were at one time four young chiefs, who afterward became kings of Hawaii, and two young women of rank, who afterward became queens. The children of the white members of the King's Cabinet were, by favour, admitted to the school, and the Chamberlain, Colonel Judd, and I, now Minister of State, were scholars in 1849. Thirty years afterward, and after three of our schoolmates had become kings and had died, and two of them had become queens, it so happened that Kalakaua ascended the throne, and with his two old school-mates began his royal tour. Of the queens, one, Queen Emma, an attractive young woman, now the Queen Dowager, had been the guest of the British Queen, and of the Empress Eugénie in Paris, where she became a favourite; while the other, Liliuokalani, the sister of the King, who became his successor on his death, and ruled so unwisely that she drove her white subjects into revolution and extinguished the Hawaiian monarchy.

Both Minister of State and Chamberlain, the only companions of the King besides his valet, were sons of American missionaries who had enlarged their usefulness by entering the Cabinet of one of the King's predecessors thirty years before, and had done important service in organising and maintaining civil government. The Chamberlain had always lived in the islands, but I had lived in the United States for many years, and had returned at the King's request and taken office in his Cabinet, as Attorney-General, a few weeks before the beginning of this tour.

The King had a retentive memory. He had read many books in the English language on religion, science, and politics; but he had not digested his reading, and his learning was therefore somewhat dangerous, although its extent surprised visitors to his kingdom, as well as many persons whom he met during his long tour. He was an excellent musician, and had collected a band of native musicians, numbering about thirty, who, under a German leader, had made a reputation for skill in rendering foreign music which reached Europe through the reports of tourists and of the officers of warships. He often referred with a smile to his first savage predecessor on the throne, who once received a serenade from the band of a British warship; and when at the close of it he was asked if he desired the repetition of any piece made it known, but not without some difficulty, that the tuning of the instruments gave him the most pleasure.

The King knew the usages and customs of European courts, for after the independence of his islands had been recognised, and treaties had been negotiated with nearly all the civilised states of the world, a diplomatic and consular corps was established at his capital; and this, with the ceremony of receiving the officers of warships and other noted visitors, had established the etiquette of civilisation in his own court. His kingdom was recognised as civilised by all nations, and he was a monarch in good and regular standing among his royal brethren. This was due to the unselfish labour of the American missionaries and their allies, who had created the framework of an institutional government and placed the administration of law in the hands of intelligent and honest white men who had the confidence of both foreign traders and residents.

But, the King being Polynesian, neither he nor his native subjects understood the nature of Anglo-Saxon government, and if they had been allowed to have their own way political conditions would have quickly fallen into those which are found in the South American republics or among even less-civilised people. The self-rule of the Anglo-Saxons is not the working out of a theory, but the evolution of long-acquired political habits and customs. The King could not understand this, nor could he be criticised for his ignorance when the majority of Anglo-Saxons cannot lucidly explain their own system of rule, but govern themselves mainly on inherited sentiments. The King's mind was naturally filled with the crude ideas, the superstitions, the absolutism of a Polynesian chief, though his experience with the whites had modified their exaggerated forms; and, where experience was lacking, a vague fear of the white men's superior intelligence took its place. So in kingly behaviour he was, and proved to be, the peer of any monarch he met on his tour. His three predecessors on the throne had fallen into what moralists call " drunkards' graves;" but the graves were an impressive mausoleum, situated in a beautiful valley, shaded by trees of everlasting green, and by no means repelling or likely to serve as a deterrent from the downward course to whose end they bore peaceful witness. The King was unlike his predecessors in this regard, and did not exhibit the great vice of Christendom oftener than his official duty demanded. It was his pagan humour to say, when he gave way to the custom of civilisation, " I am drunk, but I am also civilised."

The party was a singular one. They were schoolmates who had rubbed each other's noses in the dirt thirty years before, and were now King, Minister of State, and Lord Chamberlain, with a German baron for a valet; and though the kingdom they represented was a tiny affair, it was, for all that, one of the family of Christian nations, and they were entitled to royal ceremonies according to the usage of nations. But because our country was only a few dots or elevations in the Pacific Ocean, an insignificant affair so far as territory went, we modestly anticipated no royal receptions. If the monarchs, the brothers of my royal master, gave him a brief audience and shook his hand, it would be, we thought, after the manner of rich and powerful men who greet an obscure relation by extending two fingers of the hand, and, if generous, serve him some refuse meat in a side chamber. We were ready to be satisfied if we received the slightest greeting; and, in order to avoid any embarrassment, had our incognito dress at hand, so that we could quickly jump into it. At no time did the King make any formal announcement to the court of any country that he intended to visit it; in short, we travelled modestly, so as to avoid a snubbing.

Among our passengers on the voyage to San Francisco was a well-known Englishman, a lecturer on astronomy, returning from Australia. He discussed with the King the astral theories of the Polynesians, which were, it must be confessed, not as advanced as those held by the present generation of Europeans, but quite as valuable as those of learned men two centuries before, who believed that comets were sent by the Almighty to frighten men into obedience. The King became much interested in these semi-scientific conversations, and at the end of the voyage their effect upon him was shown after a not altogether unexpected fashion.

During the usual celebration which occurs before a vessel enters port, the Australian passengers, who had much respect for royalty, so entertained the King, with the aid of the distinguished man of science that when he reached the upper deck, long after midnight, his royal eyes were able to perceive double stars and planets without the aid of a telescope. As the sun rose above the Golden Gate of San Francisco Bay, I entered this note in these memoirs: " His Majesty has sucked his first experience of foreign civilisation."

CHAPTER II

AS the "City of Sydney" moved up the Bay of
San Francisco the next morning, her ambitious
captain urged his Majesty to permit him to hoist the
royal standard. The Chamberlain and I suggested to
the King that a modest introduction to San Francisco
would befit the entrance of the monarch of a midget
kingdom into the domain of a great republic. But he
had been received with extraordinary display on a
visit to this place six years before, and it had increased his appetite for public honours. The valet,
Robert, therefore extracted the royal standard from
its canvas covering, and it was quickly floating from
the main truck. This was soon detected by the commandant of the federal forts, and salutes of twenty-
one guns were at once discharged. The rain fell
heavily as the vessel reached her dock, so the King's
friends in the city, instead of driving him through
the streets in an open conveyance, took him in a
closed carriage to the Palace Hotel. The weather
had displayed the same disrespect for him that it did
for George IV, who landed in a severe storm at
Leith, upon which a loyal Scotchman exclaimed,
"Your Majesty, I am positively ashamed of the

Almighty for letting the rain wet your Majesty's person."

The King was a generous host at home; many residents of San Francisco had been his guests at breakfasts and dinners, with attractive settings of tropical vines, flowers, and plants, and he met, therefore, a warm welcome. Nor did it detract from their interest in him that he was a Crowned Head. He was also a " coloured man," unusually dark for a Polynesian, and several of his features suggested negro inheritance. But the generous citizens of both sexes smothered antipathies, if they had any, and, rising to the occasion, cordially declared that black was white.

General Upton, a soldier of the Civil War, said, after he had conversed with the King, that his knowledge of military manœuvres and strategy was most creditable, and, no doubt, exceeded that of most of the militia officers of the United States. The King visited the Legislative Assembly of the State at Sacramento, and at a dinner given to him in that place he heard the " thrilling eloquence " of several American orators. Among these was one who in fervid eloquence described the importance of the Hawaiian kingdom in the rising commerce of the Pacific Ocean, and predicted the final union of the inhabitants of all Oceanica and Polynesia under one rule, and, he shouted, " it will be that of King Kalakaua, the Colossus of the Pacific." The King was therefore suddenly conscious of a call to a high destiny, although he was quite uncertain as to the term " Colossus," and this consciousness was not lessened by the speech of the Governor of the State, who gave free play to his capacity for patriotic prophecy.

On the King's return to San Francisco he attended

a banquet given to him by the Consul-General of his
Imperial Majesty the Emperor of China, in the Hang
Fen Lou restaurant. It was said to be the cost-
liest dinner ever given by the Chinese in America.
Twenty tables were covered with heavy embroidered
crimson satin, with fringes of gold bullion and silver
stars; heavy silk scrolls hung from the ceiling, upon
which were inscribed words from the wise sayings
of Confucius; American, Hawaiian, and Chinese
flags were intertwined on pillars; the Consul, in a
gorgeous costume of silk, sat with the King on his
right hand. On receiving his Majesty at the door
he had ignored the delicate and artistic pump-handle
hand-shaking of Christendom, and, placing the closed
fist of one of his own hands in the palm of the other,
shook them together with the enthusiasm demanded
by the rank of the guest. The dishes served were the
pride of China: bird's-nest soup, white snow fingers,
imperial fish brains, preserved bird's eggs, shark's
fins, fish maw, tender bamboo shoots, stewed duck
with Teintsin sauce, chicken with Satow dressing,
turtle stew, melon and many other kinds of seeds,
sweetmeats, pear-wine, and many *bonnes bouches*
unknown to Parisian restaurants. Chopsticks were
laid beside the guests' plates, but forks were also
furnished, as a liberal concession to the crude habits
of Western civilisation.

The Consul toasted the King, and, as the spokesman for all Chinamen, thanked him for the just
treatment they had received in his kingdom; there
was but one place in Christendom, beyond the lines
of the British Empire, in which all Chinese immigrants could live without fear of unjust assault; it
was, he said, in the King's dominions. And when this

" pagan " King rose to reply, he stood on American soil at the time when the descendants of the Puritans at the capital of the nation were passing a law which deliberately violated their treaty with China, and just before that august tribunal, the Supreme Court of the United States, decided that the obligations of a treaty might be violated by an Act of Congress.[1]

At the close of the banquet, which was the tribute of men of the largest nation of the world to the fairness and justice in the administration of law in the kingdom of Hawaii, I said to the King, —

" You may be a pagan king, and I the Minister of a pagan king; but our first important experience in a foreign land is the gratitude, expressed in this grand banquet, to your government for its justice; and it is done on the soil of a nation that deliberately does injustice to the Chinese."

Although we were only at the beginning of our journey, I noticed that my royal master's mind was expanding. The fervid words of the orators in Sacramento, and foolish praise of visitors, opening to him a vision of himself as " the Colossus of the Pacific," he began to realise his possibilities as the coming man " that shalt be king hereafter " of the countless islands of Oceanica. He therefore commanded — for a king's request is always a command — that a uniform be made for his Minister of State. Instead of a cocked hat and pair of old boots, which his predecessors had adopted as the courtly uniform at no very distant period, there suddenly appeared, from the miscellaneous luggage, cloths on which were delicately worked, with wire of gold bullion,

[1] See 136 United States Supreme Court Reports.

imitations of the beautiful leaf and flower of the taro plant (*Calladium esculentum*) together with the fine leaf of the *koa,* a Hawaiian tree. This costly material had been embroidered in England on the orders of a former king, but had never been used. A tailor quickly made for me a rich diplomatic uniform, the design of which was especially admired in every court visited by the King and his suite. To this was added a sword and a cocked hat.

The party was now equipped for a tour, — either royal or incognito, and while an American democrat is bashful at first in the gorgeous trappings of a court official, the instinct of his race, when in pursuit of either business or pleasure, quickly adjusts him to the dress of a savage or to that of an archangel.

The King, with his great size and dignified presence, was an imposing person in his military dress, to which was added some insignia of military orders given to him by European sovereigns on the exchange of treaties. To obtain more of these was, in truth, one of the objects of his tour. The Chamberlain, with the rank of Colonel on his Majesty's staff, appeared in the uniform of that rank, and, being of the same size of the King, the two, when standing together, towering above other persons, gave to the Hawaiians the credit of producing a race of unusually large men.

The King wished that there should be some suggestion of Hawaiian costumes in his suite, but throughout his pagan possessions there had been but two extremes of fashion: one presenting the wearer clad in decorative tattoo, "only that and nothing more;" while the other bedecked the chiefs with rare and magnificent feather cloaks, made from the minute and delicately coloured feathers of tiny birds, with a gloss and richness that no art could rival. But the wearing of these cloaks over a European military or diplomatic uniform would be incongruous. How he finally preserved a suggestion of Hawaiian fashion in the dress of his suite will be related hereafter.

The day after our arrival in San Francisco, Robert, his Majesty's valet, got drunk. In spite of the alacrity with which he had accepted the position, he scorned his humble office; menial services were iron in his soul. He informed strangers and lookers-on that he was the King's private secretary, or that he held the office of " Keeper of the Royal Standard," which, he said in confidence, was one of much honour in Hawaii. Being tempted by strangers with invitations to the bar of the hotel, he became hopelessly drunk, and on one occasion walked through the corridors wearing, by mistake, the King's silk hat instead of his own. The suite insisted on his dismissal, but the King, upon the valet's earnest promise of reformation, declined to accede to the demand.

CHAPTER III

Departure for Japan — Logs on the Ocean — Washington's Birthday — Losing a Day — Slapping a King in the Face — Attempts to Instruct the King in Political Science — The Conflict of Races in Hawaii — Failure of Educational Efforts.

ON the 8th of February, 1881, the King, with his suite, embarked for Japan on the steamer "Oceanic," Captain Metcalf. The royal standard was at the main truck; the federal batteries of the port gave a royal salute of twenty-one guns; and we were quickly on the breast of the great "Tranquil Sea," so viciously untranquil in its seasons. We entered the warm winds of the Pacific anticyclone, which distribute tropical warmth over the western coast of the American continent from Alaska to Lower California, and in a vast sweep finally touch and cool the Hawaiian Islands, making them a subtropical group, relieved from excessive heat. On the third day after leaving port we passed a huge floating pine log. It had left its home in the forests of Oregon, coursed down the Columbia River, struck out into the waste of waters, and in solitude was searching for a landing somewhere in Oceanica. Many such timbers, after making their automatic voyages of three thousand miles, find their last harbour among the coral reefs of the Pacific Islands. Traces of the United States ship of war "Levant," which, it is believed, foundered in the North Pacific, without a survivor to tell its story, were found by the casting of one of her masts upon the beach of Hawaii.

Our course toward Japan was unbroken by islands; no vessel crossed our path on this lightly travelled ocean; it was a boundless solitude waiting for Asia to rise and vex it with a challenge to the commercial marine of America.

To avoid the cold head winds of the northern latitude, the steamer's course was laid to the south, so that on the sixth day out she was within six hundred miles of the Hawaiian group.

Without a pause for rest or repair, the propeller, with its monotonous rumble, drove us for many days " down to the baths of the western stars," until the 22d of February, a day noted for two events, — the anniversary of the birthday of George Washington and the loss of a day from our calendar. On crossing the 181st meridian of longitude, navigators, in order to maintain correct time, drop a day from their reckoning when moving westward, and add a day when going eastward. When the captain declared that the 22d of February would be officially dropped from the log-book in the interests of navigation, and therefore the celebration of the anniversary would be jointly lost, the passengers, members of several races, declared, and the King attested it with his royal assent, that the lost day had been picked up from the sea and should be celebrated. Thus Americans, Englishmen, Japanese, Chinese, and Hawaiians forgot their racial lines for an hour, and, as members of a universal nation, gave tribute to the man who laid the warp upon which the woof of American history has since been and is still being woven.

The King, whose islands were discovered by Captain Cook at the time Washington was dislodging the British from Rhode Island, during the Revolutionary War, and the Count d'Estaing was refusing to fight the British fleet, made a response to a toast, in which he spoke of the far-reaching labours of the great leader in building a nation which within fifty years from the time of his death reached out beyond the continent and made his own little islands an independent kingdom. A Japanese student, returning home from America, said that when Washington was surveying in the woods the sites of future commonwealths, Japan had an old civilisation; but that when the Japanese reconstructed their ancient political system they sought wisdom in the books which taught the principles of government in America, and the name of Washington was written across every page.

While these men of incongruous races were thus lauding the Father of our country on the far Pacific sea, one might imagine the old hero, seated on his Colonial porch at Mount Vernon, looking down at the Potomac at his feet, his vision of American Empire limited by the Ohio River. If, then, an angel had whispered in his ear that within but threescore years his work would reach islands in the Pacific Ocean, of which he had hardly heard, and would be, moreover, the guide for men who were reconstructing an Asiatic empire of thirty million souls of which he knew nothing, he would have called these whisperings the vagaries of a dream, and, turning in his courtly way to his wife, have said, " Madam, I am becoming childish."

The next day a westerly gale struck the vessel. As she fell off in her course, for a moment, into the trough of the sea, the King happened to step out of the saloon. He lost his hold as she lurched, and Royalty rolled into the lee scuppers. He had hardly reached his feet before a hoary-headed and insolent wave sprang over the weather taffrail and — let it be said in whispers — struck his Majesty flatly in the face; then, with the howl of a demon, jumped overboard, and in some cave of the winds where cyclones are kept on tap boasted to his riotous companions that he had slapped a king in the face.

My associates in the Cabinet, especially Mr. H. A. P. Carter, who was a man of much force of character, had asked me to instruct the King, during the idle hours of our journey, in the principles and practice of good government, but recommended that it be done so cautiously that our royal master would not be offended or suspect that he was placed under tuition; that is, as my colleagues suggested, he should be treated as the hunter treats a wild animal, by approaching him from the leeward, so that the royal game would not be startled by the smell of offensive instruction. The King and his predecessors and their subjects had voluntarily, and without trained reflection, of which they were incapable, accepted the forms of Anglo-Saxon institutions, of the nature of which they had no clear idea. The white subjects of these native monarchs also accepted the rule of the native kings so long as it did not imperil liberty or property. There remained, however, the irrepressible conflict between Hawaiian traditions and habits and Anglo-Saxon traditions and habits. So long as the native rulers could be persuaded to govern along the general lines of the latter, the conflict would hardly be apparent, though in the political evolution it was inevitable that it should finally take aggressive form and close the native dynasty. The members of the King's Cabinet were also his personal friends, and they earnestly desired that he should avoid repeating the serious political mistakes already made, and that his reign might be a long and useful one.

I therefore approached the royal mind, in our idle hours, with much caution. I commented on the wickedness of men in the wanton destruction of royal lives; with an appearance of indifference I named many of the monarchs who had been strangled, beheaded, poisoned, or dethroned because they were in somebody's way. In his own palace were original portraits of Louis Philippe and Napoleon III, presented by those sovereigns to the King's predecessors. Using these as a text, I recited the blunders which had overturned their dynasties, but I drew no morals, or what the preachers call "applications." He calmly replied, however, that the most of the monarchs who suffered were very stupid, and if he had been in their places he would have avoided their errors. Inasmuch as through his own error, committed several months previous to the beginning of this journey, his own throne rocked near to overturning, I confidentially informed my colleagues by letter that if there was a royal road to learning, our pupil had not found it, and my attempts to introduce wisdom into his spiritual system by hypodermic injections had failed. But he so closely resembled the majority of monarchs as they are described by historians, and was so simply human in his thoughts and projects, that he would be indeed an audacious person who could honestly censure him. Nor can we wonder at the blunders of kings when so many of their wisest counsellors honestly lead them astray. Ships have the advantage over kings that they are warned by fixed lighthouses and bell-buoys, while kings find in the warnings of many advisers false lights, and whistling-buoys that have drifted away from their true anchorage. As I knew that I should never be the adviser of any other monarch, I plied him with the maxims and aphorisms of statesmen; but my royal master usually fell off into a quiet nap, leaving me only the consolation of doing a duty which I supposed, however, would be without profit.

In these efforts to fertilise the royal mind the Chamberlain adroitly aided by taking the part of the chorus in the Greek drama; he made judicious responses with an appearance of indifference; repeating often some story of a king's dethronement with the comment, " Risky business; risky business ! " When our royal master flung directly in our faces the maxim of British statesmen that " the King can do no wrong," and reinforced it by a quotation from an eminent orator in Parliament, that " the King can do no wrong, even if he breaks the seventh commandment," I discovered that he did not understand the political distribution of power by which this maxim could be approved. I remarked with studied indifference that subjects never disciplined their monarchs with rods or probations, but rudely knocked them out when they committed gross mistakes. To this he replied that kings were justified in resorting to stratagems to suppress agitators; and he believed that some of his own subjects should be banished for opposing his will. My royal school was a failure, and my majestic pupil learned nothing.

CHAPTER IV

The Bay of Yedo — Fusyama — Saluted by Foreign War-
ships — The King Becomes the Guest of the Japanese
Emperor — Lands to the Music of His Own National
Anthem — The Secret of Our Reception — Lessons in
Etiquette — Japanese and New England Bells.

A T early dawn on the 4th of March we steamed
up the Bay of Yedo. To the westward we
caught a faint glimmer of the snow-clad summit of
sacred Fusyama rising in a truncated cone 13,000
feet from the level plain. Though in our little kingdom there were mountains of nearly the same height,
with several a thousand feet higher, not one of them
rose as abruptly or as symmetrically from the sea
or plain. The many small fishing-villages along the
coast, and the fleets of oddly rigged sampans, marked
a thickly settled country.

The King hesitated to display the royal standard,
for the suite advised him that if no notice was taken
of it he would have voluntarily humiliated himself.
For the same cautious reason we sent no notice of
the royal intention to visit Japan, but had requested
a fellow passenger, who was a resident of Yokohama, to secure for us lodging at one of the hotels.
But the captain wished to announce the fact that he
carried a distinguished person, and as the King's
inclination coincided with his desire, Robert, the
valet, extricated the royal standard from its canvas
bag, and it was soon flying at the main truck. We

did not expect that under the circumstances it would receive a salute.

While we leaned over the rail looking at the Bluffs, or foreign settlement of Yokohama, we saw a number of warships in the harbour; seven Russian, two British, one French, and three Japanese. It was an imposing line of sea-fighters, stretching for a mile before the city. They rode at their anchors in silence and without a sign of life. As our steamer crossed the bows of the first ironclad, a Russian, there was a sudden discharge of saluting guns from her batteries. At the same moment the Hawaiian flag was broken out on the mainmast. Swarms of sailors sprang aloft and manned the yards, that is, stood, in line along them, each man extending his arm to the shoulder of the next one. As if by magic the ship was dressed from stem to stern with the flags of all nations. The report of the first gun was followed slowly by a royal salute of twenty-one guns, and our royal standard was dipped in response. Within a minute we passed the bows of the next warship. From her mainmast also the Hawaiian flag was unfurled, her crew also manned the yards, the ship was dressed with flags as had been the Russian, and the slow discharges of her saluting guns swelled the volume of noise. The royal standard on the " Oceanic " was again dipped in response, and as we crossed the bows of all the warships in succession, the same ceremonies were repeated. The crews mounting and manning the yards, cheering as we passed; the roar of two hundred and seventy-three cannon; the smoke rising in clouds and rolling away in dense volumes toward the bay; the innumerable flags with which the warships were dressed, appearing and disappearing in the smoke, — made an extraordinary and brilliant scene, and a startling one, because unexpected. The King stood impassive, lifting his hat as we passed each vessel, while our royal standard dipped in response.

The anchor chain of our steamer had hardly ceased its rattling when a boat from the Japanese warship "Mikado" reached the gangway. An admiral, six other naval officers, and two Imperial Commissioners, from his Imperial Majesty the Emperor of Japan, all in full uniform, boarded our steamer, and asked, with due official etiquette, to be presented to the King of Hawaii. This was done by our Chamberlain. The Imperial Commissioners stated that they had been commanded by his Imperial Majesty to receive and welcome his Majesty the King of Hawaii, and invite him to be the Emperor's guest so long as he remained in the Empire. The King towered above them with his large stature, received them easily and gracefully, and replied that it would please him to become the guest of the Emperor. After a brief conversation he was asked, with his suite, to enter the boat of a warship, and be conveyed to one of the Emperor's palaces near the city of Yokohama. He remained for a few moments to receive the calls of the admirals and commanders of the British and French warships. We were not prepared for this very splendid reception; we were in the negligent clothing of travellers eagerly in search of bath-tubs, but the King stood impassive in this group of brilliantly dressed officials, making no apology for his appearance, for a king never apologises. We entered the boat of the warship; the royal standard of Hawaii was fixed in her bows, and a launch towed us to the landing. As the boat drew close to the shore we noticed great crowds on the docks, and long lines of troops in the street. When the boat touched the landing, the strains of " Hawaii Ponoi " burst from the shore. This unexpected compliment from the Emperor's military band, this music of our own country in a strange land, upset us instantly, and a snivelling monarch, with a snivelling suite, uncovered, our Japanese escort uncovering also, until the anthem ended.

Now for the first time in the history of this Empire one of the kings of Christendom was on her soil. The royal party walked a short distance between lines of troops to a public office near the landing. Many officials were presented to the King; confections and wines were served. An imperial carriage, brought from Tokio by railway, drove to the door, and the King, with his suite and the Emperor's Chamberlain, entered it. Both sides of the streets, for a mile or more, were lined with troops, and behind them were crowds of people, silent and stolid; to them it was a rare sight. Intertwined Japanese and Hawaiian flags appeared on nearly all the slight frame houses fronting on our line of march. We were slowly driven, through the thickly settled part of the city of Yokohama, to a grand house or palace on rising ground overlooking the city; built for the convenience of the Emperor's guests. It was furnished with exquisite articles of Japanese art, but European beds, chairs, sofas, and bureaus had been added for the comfort of foreign guests. A retinue of servants put us in our chambers, and we were left to ourselves. Mr. Nagasaki, the Imperial Chamberlain, was graduated at the College at Ann Arbor, Michigan, and, with a romantic faith in the future of his country, was an apostle of American ideas. The Emperor had assigned to him the duty of attending the King while he remained in the country.

The succession of surprises was now suspended for a few hours. The suddenness of this spectacular reception dazed me. We lit cigars and sat down in the King's bedchamber and looked at each other.

"Maikai no!" ("Very good!") said the King. "What do you think about it?" he asked.

"I do not think," I replied; "I am confused; there comes into my head every moment the story of the American humourist who relates how a farmer on the remote prairie returned home after a few days' absence to find his home burned by the Indians, his stock run off, and his wife and children butchered. He gazed for a moment at this desolation, and exclaimed, 'This is too redicklus!'"

But we were impatient to know the reason for this grand reception, and at luncheon the Imperial Chamberlain told us that the Imperial Consul-General in San Francisco had telegraphed that the King would visit Japan. The government consulted the diplomatic corps, especially Mr. Bingham, the American Minister at the Japanese Court, and it was advised that the existence of a treaty between Hawaii and Japan placed the Japanese government under an obligation to receive the Hawaiian King as it would receive the monarch of any country under treaty and friendly relations with Japan. We had not realised the force of this obligation when we left our islands, and besides, if it was an obligation, it might not be a strict one, or it might be ignored. But the King was prepared to "straddle" in the matter of rank, and was ready to appear in his proper character as king, or incognito as prince. And as to our national anthem, our clever consul in Japan, Mr. R. W. Irwin, a great-grandson of Benjamin Franklin, had, with the sagacity of his illustrious ancestor, ferreted out a copy of the music, owned by a lady who had been a missionary in Hawaii, and had furnished it to the imperial band-master.

The government of Japan was well aware of the importance of the Hawaiian Islands, situated at the cross-roads of the Pacific Ocean, while its treaty with the little kingdom gave the latter the arbitrary and "extra-territorial" power which the European nations held in the treaty ports of Japan. Besides, her trading ships and navy found the port of Honolulu most convenient.

The Emperor, therefore, commanded that the first visit to Japan of one of the kings of a nation of the brotherhood to which his own nation did not belong should be cordial and memorable.

Our luncheon was served in the European style. There is nothing which a French *chef* can cook which a Japanese cannot successfully imitate. The meats and vegetables were perhaps inferior to those used in Europe; for the Japanese consume little meat, and their vegetables are of a different kind from those commonly used in Europe and America.

We were now allowed to rest during the day, after the serious business of the reception by the Emperor on the morrow had been arranged. The details were with much deference submitted by the Imperial Chamberlain to the King, and he approved of them. These arrangements were novel, for there was no precedent for the reception of a foreign monarch; but the etiquette of European courts was closely followed. The Governor of the Province of Kanagawa called in the evening, but etiquette forbade general presentations until the monarchs had exchanged visits.

The delicate subject of the exchange of speeches was disposed of by the understanding that none should be formally made; we were relieved of the dreary incident of the two sovereigns pulling manuscripts out of their pockets and reading high-sounding phrases to each other. My royal master, who was, as I have said, familiar with royal etiquette, now instructed his suite regarding their attitude and behaviour. The Chamberlain needed none, for he had been long in his Majesty's service. I, the Minister, however, was an untutored American who until lately had been denied the priceless blessings of royal associations, and, unless well instructed, there was danger that I might commit an error like that of an American Minister to Austria, who at an imperial reception discovered an empty chair which he innocently occupied, though, as he was later informed, it had been reserved for the Emperor. The King directed me to stand at his right, and closely watch the conduct of the Prime Minister of Japan, with whom my rank was equal. As I was about to wear a sword for the first time, he warned me against allowing it to get between my legs.

I noticed that the valet, Robert, had strongly impressed the lower Japanese attendants with the dignity of his office of " Standard-Bearer," and, instead of occupying servants' quarters, was placed in a richly furnished room, with an attendant.

By the order of the Governor of Kanagawa there was an exceedingly grand display of fireworks during the evening. Just as the darkness closed on the last of the fiery devices, the deep rich tones of the bell of a Buddhist temple rose from a distance, and seemed to fill the air with a solemn sweetness. I recalled with no pleasant feeling how the orthodox bell-makers of New England, in my early days, mixed the harshness of the old theology with the bell-metal, so that the bell-tongue struck " salvation " on the saving side of its rim, and then swung angrily through its arc till it struck " damnation " on the opposite side. Here the air was filled with a sweet melody that suggested final rest, — if one manages, that is, to struggle through the five hundred monstrous reincarnations which the faithful enter before they reach the eternal repose upon the lotus-flower.

CHAPTER V

THE following morning we dressed for the imperial reception. When I put on my gorgeous trappings for the first time, with sword and cocked hat, I was as much absorbed in it as the Chinese pirate who at his execution was kindly supplied by a British officer with a pair of English boots, which so engaged his attention that he showed a culpable indifference to his own hanging.

At ten o'clock the imperial carriage with its mounted escort was at the door, and we entered it with the Emperor's Chamberlain, followed by another with the Imperial Commissioners. We took the imperial railway car at the station and arrived in Tokio in an hour. There a large number of officials received us, and led us to a room decorated with flowers, where confections and wine were served. There was the same quiet in the room, though it was filled with officials in uniform, as if the Emperor himself were present: the same respectful, and what many, who fail to understand the Japanese nature and custom, would regard as abject, service. One of the Imperial Princes now appeared, and, after his presentation to the King, declared that by order of the Emperor he was to attend his Majesty during his stay in the Empire. The King, with the Imperial Prince, now entered one of the Emperor's open carriages, while the Chamberlain and I entered another. As the carriages moved into the street they were surrounded by a large body of lancers. The railway station was decorated with Hawaiian and Japanese flags, and along the route of travel toward the Emperor's palace, a distance of four miles, these countless flags, intertwined, decorated the houses. The troops lined both sides of the streets, and behind them, as in Yokohama, the people were massed, silent, sober, and deeply interested. An ancient custom, recently forbidden by the government, required the people to prostrate themselves on the approach of the Mikado. The new order of things directed the people simply to bow respectfully. Many of them seemed to be quite uncertain as to their duty in the presence of a foreign king. All, however, bowed low, some even to the ground.

Tokio is a city of castles and moats, formerly the military encampment of the Shoguns and their great retainers. The carriages passed over many bridges spanning these moats, until, after a journey of four miles, the bugle announced our arrival at Akasaka, the palace of the Emperor. The etiquette of European courts requires a monarch to receive a visiting monarch at the threshold of his palace. The Emperor left his audience-hall and awaited the King in a room close to the entrance of the palace. The King stepped out of the carriage, and with the Imperial Prince entered this room, in the centre of which the Emperor stood alone. The suite, with officers of the imperial household, followed, and remained a few feet distant from the monarchs. They shook hands — an unusual proceeding on the part of the Emperor — and, through an interpreter, who stood in a bowing attitude behind the Emperor, conversed for several minutes. The Emperor then looked toward his own Chamberlain, and I, as the next in rank, was presented to him, and the presentation of the King's Chamberlain followed. The Emperor then turned, and with the King by his side walked briskly through several richly furnished halls to the audience-room. The Emperor walks alone when before his people; the Empress is never at his side; the belief in his divine origin permits no person in the Empire to appear to be his equal, and the Empress follows him. But for the first time in his own reign, and in those of his predecessors, he walked by the side of his kingly guest.

In the audience-chamber the Empress (called by the nation Kogo-Sama — "Empress of Spring") sat near a table covered with richly embroidered silk. She was magnificently dressed in Japanese costume, though she urges the ladies of her court to adopt European styles, and does so herself in informal ceremonies. Her face was enamelled, and her lips and eyebrows were stained with cosmetics. The Emperor, "Son of the Heavenly Light-Giver," presented the King to her. She did not rise, but returned the King's salutation with the least movement of her head and eyes. The Emperor raised his eyes, and the Imperial Chamberlain presented me, and then our Chamberlain, to her Imperial Majesty. She recognised us with the same slight

movement of the head. The Emperor and the King
then sat down, while the large body of courtiers, in
full uniforms, and we of the King's suite, stood at
a short distance. There was no attendance by the
ladies of the Court, but I noticed some cautious
peeps from behind the screens. I had observed
a pretty Japanese girl, in a Parisian dress and a
Gainsborough hat, standing by the side of the Empress. The lips of the Empress moved, and her
voice was hardly above a whisper. The young lady
bowed low, so as to catch the sound. Then, turning to the King, with the clear, charming accent of
a well-bred Englishwoman, she said:

"Your Majesty, her Imperial Majesty welcomes
you to this country. She hopes that you have had
a pleasant voyage."

The King replied that the voyage was a long but
a pleasant one. He made no reference to his struggle
in the lee scuppers of the "Oceanic." The young
girl bowed to the Empress and interpreted the reply.
The lips of the Empress again moved, and the girl
translated the words in charming English to the
King. The Empress hoped that he would enjoy his
visit in Japan. The King replied that he should.
The pretty interpreter, the daughter of Count Inouye, the Minister of Foreign Affairs, had recently
returned from England, where she had been for some
years at school.

Lacquer trays, with confections, were now placed
on the table, but were not touched; it is the custom
to send these articles to the residence of the guest
after his departure. The Emperor and the King
now rose and stood beside each other. The Emperor was slightly above the average height of his

race; his complexion was dark, and his face an open
one; his forehead was unusually high; his eyes
black and penetrating; nor did he look like one
who would put himself entirely in the hands of his
Ministers; his dress was a European military uniform, and the breast of his coat was decorated with
Orders. The King, with a complexion unusually
dark for a Hawaiian, towered above him, graceful,
imperturbable. The contrast was striking; but the
inscrutable face and eye of the Emperor disclosed
the stronger character. The gossips of the court, as
we soon learned, admired the large size and excellent manners of the King. Now the Emperor's subjects believed that he was the son of Ama-Terasu,
the sun-goddess, with a lineage running back for
twenty centuries. In former days, they believed, he
was a sacred dragon, and their historians warned
the people to behave, "lest their troubles ruffle the
Mikado's scales." I ventured seriously and respectfully to ask one of the members of the Court, who
had been educated in Europe, if the higher classes
accepted this belief in the Emperor's divine origin.
He replied, — "Certainly, why not? Your people
believe that Adam and Eve were made out of dust;
you run the human race back into a mud-hole. We
believe that a ruler of people has a more creditable
origin than that."

After an interview of twenty minutes the King
retired with the Emperor at his side. In the last
room of the suite they shook hands again, and we
entered the imperial carriage. It carried us, surrounded with a squadron of lancers, for four miles,
to the palace of the Enriokwan, which had been
assigned to the royal visitor. This was one of the

ancient castles of the daimyos, surrounded by a wide moat, and reached by a bridge. Two years before this time it had been occupied by General Grant and his suite. In the large court-yard a battalion of troops was stationed as a guard of honour. The building contained numerous chambers, furnished with the richest Japanese and European furniture. On the table of the dressing-room we noticed, as we passed through it, the trays of confections and sweets which had been placed before us in the audience-chamber; these had been carried by swift messengers and reached the palace before we arrived. There were now in this spacious building only three guests, — the King and his two companions; but a score of servants stood in the parlours and at the doors of the bedchambers. In a distant part were rooms occupied by the officials who were assigned by the Emperor to attend the King. It was assumed that we had European "habits," and spirits and champagne were tendered to us promptly; the Emperor, fortunately, did not place his royal guest under the restrictions which his government placed upon the American instructors who were employed in the Japanese schools, one of which, in a written contract, provided " that the said teacher shall not get drunk."

After we had admired the rich and delicate furniture which adorned this romantic palace, we entered the King's bedchamber. Here we found the valet, Robert, lying on one of the sofas in a tipsy sleep.

The suite had discovered in the morning that the King had resolved to give a distinctly Hawaiian colouring to the appearance of his party. He had also, with a view to contingencies, secretly placed in one of his trunks a rich feather cloak, one worn by some of his predecessors. He directed the valet to wear this cloak, but under no circumstances to appear to be a member of the royal party. This additional service delighted Robert, who now, according to a confidential statement made to his Japanese attendant, was " Keeper of the Royal Standard," " Groom of the Feather Cloak," and " Valet in Ordinary." While in the imperial car, on the way to Tokio, the King's suite had suddenly seen Robert, sitting in state in the luggage car, dressed in a silk hat, white gloves, and with the gorgeous royal cloak hanging over his shoulders, the tableau being completed by a group of Japanese attendants who were standing before him, lost in admiration. According to Hawaiian custom this cloak could be worn only by kings or by chiefs of the highest rank. Several of the high officials noticed its brilliant colours and respectfully asked the King about its quality and significance. He replied that it was part of the insignia of the highest office in his kingdom. They at once began to apologise for omitting to pay sufficient respect to the wearer of this rich emblem, and inquired whether they should not forthwith bring the wearer into the imperial car and place him near his Majesty. The King, finding himself in a scrape out of which we, the suite, could not help him, replied that the Hawaiian chiefs might order a servant to wear it for convenience' sake; but this explanation puzzled the Japanese, for, on this principle, a monarch might order his lackey to wear his crown for the sake of convenience. The Japanese asked no further questions, but greatly admired the cloak. After reaching the station in Tokio the valet was taken, with the luggage, to the palace assigned to us, where he found abundance of wines and spirits, which he consumed until we arrived and found him asleep in the King's bedchamber, with the silk hat far down over his head and the gorgeous cloak askew on his shoulders. He was at once deposed from his office of " Groom of the Feather Cloak," but the King refused to discharge him, because he believed he would be useful in Europe.

We were now left to ourselves for a short time. After taking off our heavy uniforms we wandered through the chambers of the palace, filled with delicate and exquisite furniture and priceless vases of Satsuma ware, but were soon called to prepare for a reception of the Emperor. It is the rule of European etiquette that a monarch's visit must be returned within an hour, and a bugler had arrived with word that the Emperor was approaching our palace. We resumed our official dress and entered one of the drawing-rooms, where the King stood, near its door, with his Minister of State, while the Chamberlain received the Emperor at the door of the imperial carriage. The King met him as he entered the drawing-room, and they took seats with the interpreter behind them, his body bent in a suppliant posture. The courtiers and the King's suite stood in a group a few steps distant, while their Majesties contrived some conversation. After a short interview the Emperor arose, and with the King walked to his carriage; the battalion presented arms, the bugle sounded, and the imperial carriage crossed the bridge over the moat amid the clattering of the lancers' sabres. The Imperial Princes then called; several of them spoke the English language fluently and had lived in Europe. After these came a score of officials, and then came Judge Bingham, the American Minister, who gave us excellent counsel in all things; kindly assuming to advise us, for our kingdom in truth lay within "the sphere of American influence," where, from an international point of view, it slept for protection like a black-and-tan terrier between the paws of a powerful mastiff.

The King was asked if he would receive men of note and consideration in the Empire at luncheon and dinner each day, so that they might be honoured with his acquaintance. These luncheons and dinners were in fact State banquets, continued from day to day during our visit of ten days, and were attended by scores of prominent men. An Imperial Prince presided over them, as the ever-present representative of the Emperor. Their service, both in dishes and in table furniture, was entirely European, and would have been creditable to any European court.

After the strange events of the day, when quiet and strange silence fell upon the moated castle, I asked myself if I were not indeed in a dream, for these events seemed to be as unsubstantial as a vision. I had, as a youthful traveller struggling in the common crowd, seen the Queen of Great Britain open the Holbrook Viaduct; the procession of the Emperor and Empress of the French on their way to the Tuileries, to the opening of the Legislative Corps; the entrance into Berlin, through the Brandenburg Gate, of the victorious army of Prussia after its victory over France; the burial of an

American philanthropist in Westminster Abbey; and the largest exhibitions of civic splendour in the United States. But here I was suddenly cast into, and become a part of, a pageant of Oriental splendour which far exceeded these others in its romantic aspects and gorgeous display. The Polynesian is only a child at best, and I suspected that my royal master did not regard these events other than as a child would regard a glittering toy. But, aside from these superb spectacular effects, the truly impressive feature of it was that I should be suddenly placed in intimate relations with the men who were making the most brilliant political romance of the century; the reconstructors of an ancient and large empire without the use of a bastille and guillotine; men who were more daring than Columbus in driving without compass or star into the stubborn waves of an unknown political sea; men, too, who were honestly believed to be " pagans " by the people of Christendom, and in the contemptuous sense of that word. We were face to face with vast experiments which concerned the fortunes and destiny of over thirty millions of people. I blessed myself, therefore, for being in this respect a fortunate creature of circumstance.

CHAPTER VI

The Shrines of Shiba — Curious Worship — The King's Aphorism — The Japanese Press Discusses the King — Curiosity about His White Attendants — Count Inouye, Minister of Foreign Affairs — Invitation to Prolong the Royal Visit — An Important Diplomatic Event — Proposed Abrogation of an Unjust Treaty between Japan and Hawaii — Delight of the Emperor and His Government — Drafting a New Treaty — The Great European Powers Disturbed Thereby.

EARLY the next morning three imperial carriages took us to one of the Buddhist temples and the Shrines of Shiba. One form of worship arrested our attention. Around a large image or idol was a wire screen with meshes an inch in diameter. The worshipper wrote his prayer on paper and then chewed it into a paste, which with his fingers he moulded into a wad. This he cast with force at the image, and if it passed through the meshes and stuck upon the face or body of the image the prayer was granted. The tranquil idol, spotted on his forehead, cheeks, breast, and arms with these salivary prayers, as if he were tattooed, seemed to look through his round, motionless eyes at his worshipful marksmen with some disgust, as if he had received the most humiliating assignment, in the distribution of duties, by the divine conference of gods. Even this grotesque worship was no more absurd than some of the forms of worship common in Christendom.

Before another image was a large monkey, which, when he picked up the coin we threw down, bowed and touched the ground reverently with his forehead, and then passed it to his master, who cast it into the offertory box before the image. We stood near an image with a weary expression. He was gradually being rubbed down to nothing; for his worshippers, passing him in line, vigorously rubbed their hands on his defenceless head, in the belief that this act relieved some kinds of disease. These incessant rubbings had worn away a part of his forehead and greatly impaired his sightliness if not his usefulness; nor did there appear to be any shops where worn-out deities could be restored. No doubt his cures for disease were as valuable as the " patent medicines " of Europe and America.

The Japanese appear to excel all people in the preparation of suitable and imposing places for the repose of their dead monarchs, as in the Shrines of Shiba, where the groves of lofty and solemn cryptomerias, gigantic and dark-plumed sentinels, stand with immutable dignity over the royal tombs.

As the imperial carriage in which we rode passed under the branches of these watchmen of the dead, a flock of crows flew up, and with much cawing settled in their branches. The King, who was half-asleep from the reaction and strain of the previous day's extraordinary excitement, listened, and then uttered to the Imperial Prince by his side this aphorism: " The noblest aspiration of man is to hear birds sing." The Prince was no doubt surprised at this crisp summary of man's nature and aspirations, but, like a true courtier, he bowed and replied: "Your Majesty, it is true." The King's head began to nod again in peaceful nap, and the crows gave him a screeching encore.

The daily papers of Tokio published translations of articles in the foreign encyclopædias and geographies on the Hawaiian group of islands, and translations from the press were daily presented to us by one of the officers who attended the King. His bearing and appearance were commended, but the skin colouring of the party puzzled the Japanese writers. It was said that we were Hawaiians, which was of course true so far as place of birth went; but here, the press said, was a dark, almost black, King; a Minister of State who was of the light Anglo-Saxon type; and a swarthy Chamberlain. "It must be," wrote one editor, "a curious race which produces such different types of colour." When the members of the Japanese court learned that the suite were men of American descent, though born in Hawaii, they looked upon it as singular that the King should travel without any native member of his court. They suspected that the white men had already become dominant in his kingdom, and that he was only a figure-head. It typified to them the coming supremacy of Anglo-Saxons in the Pacific regions.

Count Inouye called with a message from the Emperor, requesting the King to change his purpose of leaving the Empire within three days, as he had informed the Emperor he intended to do; the Emperor wished to give him a banquet, and, as he was the first King of Christendom who had entered the Empire, he desired to mark his visit with a grand ball in the palace, which would, it was intimated, be the most notable given since the new order of things was established; there would also be a grand review of the imperial troops, special theatrical exhibitions, and other entertainments. The King assented to his request, for he was gaining much knowledge, but unfortunately it was through the distorting medium of Polynesian ideas and vagaries.

In this interview there took place the one serious diplomatic event of our tour, — one which was most creditable to the King and worthy of an humble place in history.

The humiliating position of the Japanese under their existing treaties with foreign nations was mentioned during this interview. These treaties largely excluded Japanese sovereignty from a number of its own seaports, known as the "treaty ports;" they permitted foreign consuls, some of them being incompetent and ignorant, to be the supreme judges of matters involving the rights of the Japanese. It was admitted by all that these treaties were in violation of international law; but as they had been executed by the Japanese government when it was powerless, and under what Secretary Seward called "gentle pressure," the nations now refused to modify or abrogate them, in spite of the earnest requests of the Japanese government and the demands of the people. The case was illustrative of the use of brute force by the powers of Christendom. The treaty between Japan and the Hawaiian Islands was similar to other treaties, but it was of no practical value, because there was little commerce between the two countries. The King's government had been requested, as other governments had been, to abrogate these objectionable treaties; but the request

had not been granted. I had been asked by my
colleagues to discuss the subject with the Minister
of Foreign Affairs of Japan, if we should visit the
Empire.

I now asked Count Inouye to remain while the
King, and I, as Royal Commissioner, could briefly
consult in private. We soon returned, and I, speaking for the King's Cabinet, said to the Minister that
the King would at once consent to the abrogation
of the harsh and unjust clause of our treaty with
Japan, subject to the approval of his entire Cabinet,
though we were satisfied that it would abide by our
act. Speaking for the King, I said that he hastened
to do a just and friendly act, since he had been so
cordially received by the Emperor. The Minister
was deligthed. He declared that the day on which
our treaty was modified would be a red-letter day
in Japanese history, and this prompt consent to abrogation would give the Emperor and the people of
Japan unbounded pleasure. It was then agreed between ourselves that this act should remain an open
State secret until the Hawaiian Cabinet had approved
of it; for the publication of it officially would greatly
disturb the ambassadors and ministers of the European Powers, who would see in it an entering wedge
which would, by example, force open the humiliating
clamp of iron wherein the Powers had held the Empire
for twenty years. As soon as the Japanese Minister
left, I sought the American Minister, Mr. Bingham,
and related the results of this interview. He approved of what we had done and smiled at its
audacity. An instrument abrogating the unjust
clause in the treaty was immediately drawn up. I
addressed a letter, with the King's cordial consent

and the approval of the Chamberlain, who was an
excellent adviser, to the Minister of Foreign Affairs,
in which was written:

" The Hawaiian government is willing to incorporate
in a treaty a full and complete recognition of the integrity of the Japanese Empire, and it will relinquish all
claims of whatsoever nature which may arise out of
what is known as the extra-territorial rights in the
existing treaty."

This was the first diplomatic business in which
I had been engaged, and I looked at it as a boy looks
at his first successful composition. The use of such
condescending language to a nation which could flip
the Hawaiian people into the sea by a turn of its
hand seemed to be absurd, but our little kingdom,
so far as maintaining this obnoxious treaty was concerned, had behind it the power of Europe. Aside
from being a party to an act of justice, I rather
enjoyed the fun of throwing fire into the dried grass
of the international prairie, — a fire which would
soon force the uneasy diplomats who represented the
Great Powers to scurry about to extinguish it. This
tour was therefore not without its uses. I have no
doubt, when the diplomats discovered this deed after
we left, they exclaimed in private, " Oh, bother the
little Hawaiian beggar for getting between our
legs!" [1]

[1] The instrument abrogating this treaty was not executed, owing to
the strenuous remonstrances of the European governments. Seventeen
years after this negotiation the humiliating clause was removed from
all the treaties, and the complete integrity of the Japanese Empire was
recognised by all nations.

When the Emperor and the men of the Empire were confidentially told of this transaction, they were greatly pleased, and resolved to make the King's visit most memorable if lavish hospitality could do it.

CHAPTER VII

Entertainments in Our Palace — The King Receives the
Representatives of Foreign Nations — Dr. Benjamin Frank-
lin's Japanese Descendants — The King Carefully Guarded
— The Position of the Hawaiian Kingdom in the Pacific —
Its Growth — The Japanese Character — The Sudden Rise
of the People and Their Reformations — Review of Japanese
Troops — An Earthquake — The Skeleton in Our Military
Closet — The Hawaiian Army and Navy — A Japanese
Drama — The King Presents a Drop-Curtain to the
Theatre — The Hawaiian Minister Visits Count Inouye
— His Residence — Strange Adventures of Two Japanese
Statesmen.

ON the day following this transaction our evening banquet was unusually fine. At its close
twenty noted singers and dancers entertained us in
one of the drawing-rooms. Following them was
a seemingly grotesque dance, in the costumes in
fashion two centuries before this time. The performers at certain intervals turned somersaults,
producing effects which were undeniably amusing
and picturesque.

The next day the King received the ambassadors
and ministers of foreign nations at the Japanese
court. These, the British, French, German, Austrian,
Russian, Chinese, with their attachés, made a brilliant
company, as they appeared in court attire. The King
announced that he should appoint Mr. R. W. Irwin,
the Hawaiian Consul, and the clever great-grandson
of Dr. Benjamin Franklin, to be the Hawaiian Minister at the Japanese court. Mr. Irwin had married

a Japanese lady, by whom he had a number of children. The old Doctor never dreamed of his descendant in the third generation living in an Oriental empire of which he had not heard, and of his own blood mingling with a curious and strange race which had leaped in a moment from paganism into European "civilisation." The predictions of "Poor Richard," in his "Almanack," never included such an extravagant horoscope as this.

Whenever we drove in the imperial carriage to the public parks, temples, and gardens, extraordinary care was taken of the Emperor's guest. By adroit management he was not allowed to appear as a common person; he did not enter any of the shops or inns; and whenever the carriage stopped, a body of police surrounded it at once, so as to prevent any assault by a Japanese crank.

Many of the prominent men, the leaders in political affairs, did not understand why the kingdom of Hawaii had been promptly admitted as an independent sovereignty into the family of nations, almost at the moment its people came out of barbarism, while Japan, with its high civilisation, had been excluded.

Speaking for the King, I said to them that the prominent geographical position of our islands, lying at what would in time be the cross-ways of commerce in the Pacific, attracted the attention of traders, and especially American whalemen, early in the century; their relative propinquity to the United States brought them within the indefinite sphere of American influence; the British had once captured but had quickly restored the Islands; and that the commercial nations, jealous of one another's acquisitions in the Pacific, had been a practical guaranty of their independence. But the humiliating and conflicting device of " consular jurisdiction " in defiance of international right, as it then existed in Japan, would have been quickly introduced if there had not been established, at an early day, a remarkable and effective administration of justice, through Anglo-Saxon laws, by native rulers who were mainly ignorant of the nature of the laws which they adopted and enforced. This was the direct work of the American missionaries, who had received permission to remain in the country and instruct the people, and in whose intelligence and honesty the kings, chiefs, and people acquired such confidence that the administration of the laws, which were essentially Anglo-Saxon in spirit and letter, was voluntarily placed in their hands. This was so satisfactory that the subjects of the great commercial nations who resided in the little kingdom rarely disapproved the Hawaiian administration of law, and there was therefore no reason for introducing the offensive extra-territorial power of consuls and diplomats.

I did not say — for it would have displeased my royal master to say it — that the natives of Hawaii were, until recently, without a written language, without the arts, and hardly above the state of savages, but were a singularly docile people, readily yielding to the influence of honest and intelligent men. They could not be compared to the Japanese, who had an ancient and in many ways a remarkably high civilisation, and who would not quickly abandon their own political system and inherited ideas on the advice of foreigners.

A noted Japanese statesman said to me privately,

in reply to my explanation, " Then the natives of your kingdom are under foreign rule." I replied, " Substantially they are, but the Polynesian monarchy will be preserved by the Anglo-Saxons so long as it does not violate their sentiments of justice and order. We who are born in the kingdom are loyal to the throne."

Among the foreign residents of Japan we found that the majority of them, who are merchants and traders, declared that the Japanese are unstable, not truthful, mere imitators, and incapable of maintaining what is called a " civilised form of government."

There are defects in the Japanese character which the thoughtful Japanese candidly admit. But they declare that if the history of their own nation be justly compared with that of other nations, aside from mere material progress, the standard of their own civilisation, defective as it is, will not greatly suffer in the comparison. It was said not sixty years ago, by that wise Englishman, Sir Samuel Romilly, that " the code of the English was the worst code of all nations, and worthy of cannibals;" and McCarthy writes, in the " History of Our Own Times," that " not until Victoria's reign was there a legislative enactment which fairly acknowledged the difference between an English wife and a purchased slave." If this be true of English civilisation, which has developed for a thousand years under the burning light of the Holy Cross, what comment can the Anglo-Saxon make upon the civilisation of a nation upon which the light of the Cross has never shone, — a civilisation which advanced only under the dim moral lights of Buddhism, Confucianism, and Shintoism.

Whatever the virtues or vices of the Japanese are,

it is one of the marvels of history that this people, numbering over thirty millions, has, in the twinkling of an eye, measuring time by slow historical growth, shaken off an ancient feudal system, destroyed the autocracy of the powerful daimyos, and reached the open highway of political regeneration, with far less turmoil, bloodshed, and revolution than has marked the progress of Occidental political institutions.

In honour of his royal guest the Emperor ordered a review of the Japanese troops, of all kinds, which were stationed in Tokio. Of these about ten thousand were in parade. The King and suite, in an imperial carriage, arrived at the barracks and alighted before the Emperor's tent, which was lined with silk, but otherwise was not adorned. The Emperor, at the opening of his tent, received the King. While the monarchs stood before it, the entire Diplomatic Corps in full uniforms were presented to them. Horses with rich trappings of gold cloth were now brought forward, and the monarchs mounted. The Emperor rode well, while *bettos,* or running attendants, one on each side of the animal, kept close to his head. The King was a superb horseman, for he was trained in his early days to the use of the lariat in the capture of wild cattle. The cavalry horses in this part of the empire were stallions; the mares were kept in the western provinces. The animals were small, stocky, and active.

The Cabinet Ministers, the General Staff, the King's suite, and the Diplomatic Corps made a considerable cavalcade behind the monarchs. At this time foreign military men undervalued the power of the Japanese for military organisation, though a few of them, who were acute observers, suspected that it would prove to be singularly strong. In our cavalcade were the Japanese officers who subsequently chased but hardly fought the Chinese in the war of 1894. At the close of the review the monarchs entered the tent alone for a few minutes, and then parted.

At the State luncheon in our palace the next day an earthquake shook the building. The table rocked as if it were tipsy. Mother Earth was on a " spree," reeling and shivering as if her bowels were filled with alcohol instead of fire. She has these unseemly bouts in this land to the number of five hundred a year, and occasionally she gets upon a fearful " tear," ripping up the fine clothing of forests and meadows on her back, defiant of the text that " earth was made for man." The Japanese guests showed no excitement; they laid down neither knife nor fork; not one of them looked around or made comment. Here they displayed the delicate refinement of the people, who in social life ignore disagreeable events, even to an extreme. No allusion whatever was made to this seismic orgy until the King asked if earthquakes were dreaded. The venerable and noble Prince Date replied that though they were common they were dreaded, because at times they were destructive, and, like tamed beasts, could not be trusted. A facetious Japanese, who had been educated in England, remarked, when I noticed the equanimity and silence with which the riotous earthquake was received by his countrymen, that it was mainly due to the fact that there were no profane words in their language; but whenever the people learned to use the English language with freedom its superb equipments in forcible oaths would provoke them to make suitable comments on such an event.

A small and unwelcome military skeleton now appeared in our royal closet and began gently to rattle at our feasts. The army of Hawaii, its size, formation, and use, interested the Japanese court. The large and commanding figure of the Chamberlain, with his brilliant Colonel's uniform, made him conspicuous, and provoked many questions about the army. Now, on a " war footing " it numbered about seventy-five men, who were merely volunteers, and were, it was said by an irreverent white subject, lavishly fed on bananas in order to stimulate their courage. Their duties were to guard the Palace, parade on holidays, and " present arms " to the court and distinguished visitors. In the event of trouble it was generally believed that they had no fervent desire " to kiss the hot lips of the enemy's guns " or achieve any heroic act whatsoever. We had hoped that the subject of our military establishment would be ignored in our intercourse with foreign courts, for a correct statement regarding it might abate the King's dignity.

At the " squirrel point " in this banquet, — when the guests began to crack the nuts, — an inquisitive Japanese statesman turned to the Chamberlain and inquired, " Colonel, how large is your army? " Thereupon the little skeleton rattled so that we of the royal party distinctly heard it, and the Colonel hesitated. His Majesty was silent, and I waited to see how the Colonel would escape a truthful reply. It was customary, in the Hawaiian celebrations, for the King's poet laureate to represent the army as larger than that of Milton's devils in array to fight the angels; an army so large that its rear lay wrapped in night while breaking day roused its broad front; but on this foreign soil there were no loyal and sympathetic Hawaiian subjects to applaud such an estimate.

The Chamberlain took refuge in brevity, — "The army is not large; it consists of volunteers," — and became silent. The question was not repeated at this time, but during the tour it frequently and sorely confronted us, and as often as it did the little skeleton grimly rattled and the King and suite were depressed in spirit.

The information regarding our navy was proudly given. For home use a tugboat with a howitzer mounted on its bows was quite enough to sweep our inland seas. As a nation, however, our independence was carefully protected by the jealousy of the European and American nations, so that for all practical purposes their navies were our navy, especially that of the United States. Whenever, therefore, the matter of our navy was suggested at grand banquets, the King usually designated me to answer, which I did by boldly stating that we commanded the largest navy in the world, following the statement with explanations that justified it. We said to the Japanese, "Your navy is our navy, because you are interested in maintaining our independence." At the same time, as an American, I felt that the star of American empire was rapidly moving toward Hawaii, and no other nation was likely to attempt to hitch a line to it to draw it away from its course.

By command of the Emperor one of the tragic dramas was presented in the theatre. It depicted an historical event which involved many sanguinary deeds. The actors declaimed in falsetto voices; the orchestra, between the acts, uttered sounds which to our ears seemed to be the invariable and monotonous repetition of the vowel "uu-uu." The audience consisted of the higher class of the people and were specially invited. The transition of fashion in dress from the old Japanese to the European forms was apparent. Ladies in kimonos and those in Parisian clothing were side by side. Paths of boards on a level with the heads of the audience were laid from the stage toward the doors; and the actors at times strode down these alleys declaiming in the midst of their hearers. The streets adjoining the theatre were illuminated in honour of the King, who at the close followed the example of General Grant and presented to the theatre a large drop-curtain covered with figures and inscriptions in memory of the event.

The next day I returned the official call made on me by Count Inouye, the Minister of Foreign Affairs. On reaching the entrance to his residence a servant removed my shoes and led me over a fine matting to an exquisitely furnished room. On a lacquer table was placed a *hibachi* filled with white sand, and on this a small charcoal fire was burning, at which we warmed our fingers. The Anglo-Saxon warms his toes, but the Japanese, for some hygienic or other reason, warms his body through his fingers. Snow was gently falling at the time, but the people, like most Europeans, are accustomed to a low temperature which would make Americans uncomfortable. Since the time of this visit the Minister has become justly distinguished as a far-seeing, prudent, and wise statesman. He related to me some of the incidents of his early life. He and Ito, now the Marquis, were members of the Satsuma clan, and

Ito (1881).

were sent by their chief to England in order to ascertain the causes of English power. Boarding an English vessel at Shanghai, and unable to speak the English language, they failed to make the captain understand that they were passengers, and were at once placed in the forecastle and served during the voyage as common sailors. On reaching London they were unable to communicate with their bankers for several days for lack of an interpreter, and therefore begged their way on the docks.

The Minister again told me of the pleasure which our willingness to abrogate the Japanese-Hawaiian treaty had given his government. As I returned to our palace of the Enriokwan in the imperial carriage, I chuckled over the fact that our little insignificant kingdom was throwing some sand into the ponderous machinery of international law. It was the release of a mouse in a ball-room.

CHAPTER VIII

The King Proposes a Matrimonial Alliance Between the
Royal Families of Japan and Hawaii — The Plan Fails —
The King Visits the Christian Church in Yokohama —
Japanese Views Regarding Christian Missions — Their
Political Danger.

THERE now occurred an unexpected and romantic incident which gave the King's suite some
anxiety and annoyance. The King, without informing us of his scheme, suddenly and rather mysteri-
ously left our palace in company with the Emperor's
Chamberlain. It was a neglect of his own suite
which was entirely contrary to etiquette. Its secrecy
puzzled us, as he usually placed the fullest confidence
in us. On his return he did not disclose to us that
he had made a secret visit to the Emperor, and that
he had asked that it should be treated as a confidential affair. The Emperor, however, for "reasons of
State," had told his Foreign Minister about it, and
the Emperor's Chamberlain, in order that the King's
Cabinet might understand the affair, confidentially
intimated to the suite the nature of it. But it was
not until we returned to Hawaii that the details of
it were disclosed.

In the curious recesses of his Polynesian brain the
King had contrived a scheme of matrimonial alliance between the thrones of Japan and Hawaii.
He had a vague fear that the United States might
in the near future absorb his kingdom. He therefore
proposed a marriage between one of the imperial

princes of Japan and the Princess Kaiulani, his niece, and heir to the throne, which would naturally enlist the Japanese government against any annexation schemes of the United States. Knowing that his suite would vigorously oppose his plan as utterly impracticable, he chose to take the affair into his own hands. The Emperor received his suggestion with excellent humour and politeness, but declared that it required much reflection and would be a startling departure from Japanese traditions. Soon after we reached home the Imperial Chamberlain of the Emperor appeared in Hawaii on a secret mission, bearing a letter from the Emperor respectfully declining the proposition for a matrimonial alliance. Aside from social reasons, the Emperor, with his advisers, would not aid in any scheme which impaired the "sphere of American influence over Hawaii." This incident did not in the least disturb our pleasant relations with the Japanese court, but it made the suite more watchful against escapades of the Crowned Head it was steering around the world. Had the scheme been accepted by the Emperor, it would have tended to make Hawaii a Japanese colony; a movement distasteful to all of the Great Powers.

The Japanese Christians of Yokohama earnestly petitioned the King to receive from them a copy of the New Testament in the Japanese language. We received an intimation that the Japanese government would not be offended in the least by a public reception of this gift by the Emperor's guest. The King, with his suite, accordingly went privately to Yokohama, and in the Protestant church, partially built with aid from Hawaiian Christians, received it, and, standing in the pulpit, declared that Protestant missionaries had rendered most valuable services in his kingdom. This public testimony to the value of Christianity made by a monarch, the guest of a nation which coldly tolerated it, was not without advantage to the promotion of evangelical missions in the Empire.

The establishment of Christian missions in Japan was often discussed in our interviews with Japanese statesmen. The missionaries were not students of political science, and they failed to see the inseparable union, in all nations, of political and religious habits and ideas. In the present state of human society, governments, which essentially represent the people's habits, traditions, and beliefs, and do not create them, must rule through those settled beliefs and usages. A disturbance, therefore, of religious beliefs invariably disturbs the political situation. Any religious doctrine which impairs the prevailing creed of a nation impairs the political power of the nation's rulers and tends inevitably toward peaceful or forcible revolution. The missionary is therefore an unconscious political revolutionist, however vigorously he may deny it. The stability of the Emperor's throne in Japan, in the opinion of its statesmen, largely depended upon the abiding faith in the Emperor's divine origin and infallibility. The teaching of the doctrine by the missionaries that no human being or sovereign had a divine origin, though not intended for any political, but purely for a religious purpose, tended to impair the political power of the Emperor and made the missionary a dangerous person in the community. The Japanese leaders well knew the power of Christianity for good in the

Western civilisation, but they feared that in the transition state of Japan its general prevalence might unsettle the political condition and retard the reconstruction of the Empire. They believed in the toleration of all religions, because the great nations tolerated them; but they feared the political disturbance which might follow toleration. They desired, during the transition period of Japanese civilisation, to use the popular belief in the Emperor's infallibility as a means of preserving order; as a scaffolding for holding the people together until the new order of things had hardened. The bitter and absurd conflicts of the creeds of Christendom, represented by the many denominations in the Empire, astounded the thinking Japanese. "Unless," said one of their noted men to us, "Christianity can be brought to us with a common creed, converts from the lower classes may be secured; the thinking men will stand aloof."

I deemed myself thrice fortunate that I, a common citizen of America and Hawaii, had been, by some curious circumstances, suddenly cast upon the plane of high political office, and that the rank which I now held enabled me to have intercourse upon a common footing with the men who were the reconstructors of this Oriental empire. They revealed to me no "State secrets," but from time to time frankly related some of the strange and marvellous incidents of the political evolution in which they were involved. The singular and, to a student of political science, the fascinating feature of their constructive work, of taking over thirty millions of people to a novel system of government, was their unprecedented desire to utilise the wisdom and experience of foreign States. This was a dangerous experiment, — one which the statesmen of Europe and America have invariably refused to make. The Japanese leaders were now in the days of the " O Jishiu," — a great political earthquake generated by events beyond their control, and even as we sat and conversed with them we felt its rocking.

CHAPTER IX

WE lunched at noon — and it was an elaborate banquet — in the palace of the Imperial Prince Arisugawa-no-Miya. Among his guests were the Imperial Princes Higashi Fushima, Fushima-no-Miya, and Kila-Sturakawa-no-Miya. Four of the Imperial Princesses were present, in rich native costumes. Their presence was quite contrary to the customs, which forbid the presence of women at banquets. But fashions were now in the transition period, and these Princesses wished to see a foreign king. The luncheon was served in the European style. Prince Arisugawa was educated in one of the English military schools, and translated our conversations.

In the slight delicate movements of these ladies one found a suggestion of the rare grace of the Japanese women. Their faces were enamelled or painted, and the whole effect was that of a banquet of wax figures, but at least graceful and exquisitely dressed, with charming manners. The " flashes of silence " were necessarily constant, in the absence of a common language. There was the sweetest dignity in their silence; an absence of the high-strung nerves which would have embarrassed a European lady. They were self-possessed, for they were Princesses; but even self-possession is usually disturbed during protracted silence, unless it be that of a beast or a god.

When we entered the drawing-room we discovered a large mass of flowers on a tray placed on a lacquer table in the centre of the room. Across the surface of the flowers was prettily interwoven the Hawaiian word " Aloha," which signifies " Welcome." When we returned to our palace this tray, with its mass of flowers, stood in the centre of our drawing-room. The palace of this Imperial Prince was on high ground overlooking the city; one of the ancient castles, surrounded with a moat; the garden was a specimen of the finest Japanese horticultural art.

My royal master had discovered by this time that the Japanese admired his command of the English language, and he also found that the use of big words rather increased their admiration; even those who were familiar with English speech could not always understand him when he resorted to large and uncommon words. It is a singular trait of the Hawaiians to avoid the use of English when sober, but when drunk to use it with much volubility. The King's immediate predecessor on the throne, Lunalilo, when in liquor, would often refuse to converse with his native relatives in the native language, but addressed them in English, and directed an interpreter to translate his speech; and, on the other hand, required a translation into English of their conversation in Hawaiian. The King's remarkable memory furnished him with a considerable vocabulary of uncommon words; alcohol seemed to open that part of his brain where they were stored, especially when, like the moon, he was at the third quarter and coming to the " full." On one occasion the use of the words " hippodramatic performance " secured to him the prestige of a learned man. In order to celebrate himself and the antiquity of his race, he declared at a banquet that his people had occupied his country for over two thousand years; but when asked by a guest regarding the antiquity of their literature he peremptorily abandoned the subject, as it was a humiliating fact that within sixty years his people could neither read nor write, and they were indebted to the missionaries for an alphabet. As a rule, however, his conduct and conversation displayed modesty and kingly dignity.

On the day of our arrival in Tokio he said he would like to attend a dinner at which only Japanese dishes were served. Later in the day, therefore, we were taken, after the luncheon with the Imperial Princes, to the Noblemen's Club, where we were told that a banquet would be served which, in the variety of its dishes and the entertainments during its service, would exceed in cost any banquet given since the Mikado became Emperor. On reaching the door our shoes were removed by servants, and we were led over the finest matting to side rooms. In these our clothing was removed, and the attendants clad us in Japanese costume. The King's was

of a quality such as would be worn by the Emperor;
its cost was some hundreds of dollars. The Chamberlain and I were also arrayed in costly silk kimonos.

Before entering the banquet-chamber tea was
served in a large room richly furnished. A female
servant — noted, it was said, for her skill — rinsed
a delicate porcelain teacup in hot water and wiped
it dry. She then, with a small ladle, dipped a
thimbleful of pulverised tea from a lacquer bowl
into the cup. Over this, with another ladle, she
poured hot water, and with a small instrument re-
sembling a camel's-hair brush, removed the grounds
with a quick and dexterous movement. The cup
was then handed to a guest.

In the large banqueting-room the arrangements
resembled those of the Grecians and Romans around
the triclinium. The guests were seated cross-legged
on the floor, around three sides of the room, in the
order of their respective ranks. One of the Imperial
Princes presided.

Forks were placed by the side of the chopsticks of
the King and suite, for in Asiatic lands meats are
well cut up before serving, and knives are unneces-
sary. On the open or fourth side of the room there
was a slightly raised platform for the use of singers
and dancers. Geisha girls, noted for their skill in
dancing as well as for their beauty, entered the room
with dishes, and each of them, after placing the dish
before some guest, knelt and touched the floor with
her forehead. The dishes were not removed, but
accumulated as the banquet continued. Saki, the
light liquor distilled from rice, was served hot in
small glasses.

The platform was occupied by the dancers, singers,

and actors, the "stars" of the Empire, many of whom had risen above the practice of their art and were noted instructors. The singers are usually blind men, whose loss of sight, it is believed, aids them in the concentration of their musical faculties. We did not appreciate the music of the *samisan*, with its meagre effects and monotonous airs. But our hosts did, and the pretty geisha girls, noted as they were for skill in dancing, listened in raptures. It was said that to hear the four most celebrated blind singers of the Empire in combination was an event in their lives.

The dancing we appreciated, for it resembled that of the Hawaiians, but was more graceful. It was in a sense allegorical. It was all in changing lines, sober, and never extravagant, rhythmical movements which delicately present succeeding pictures of ideas; softly fluttering garments, gracefully gliding feet; while those who represented flowers in the dance seemed to wave like slender plants moved by the breeze. A gentleman seated next to me interpreted the dancers as if he were reading a libretto. Without his explanation I should have entirely failed to see its marvellous beauty and dramatic sense.

When one's limbs are not flexible, the cross-legged position at a three-hours banquet is a torture. Cushions are placed behind the guests upon which they may recline, and change their position slightly, but to me it was a pillory. As the same custom prevails in Hawaii, the King and the Chamberlain fell to it naturally enough.

At a certain stage of a banquet rice is served, and no wine is taken after it. On this occasion, however, out of respect to a king of Christendom, where a

State banquet would be regarded with contempt unless there was an increasing amount of wine and spirits offered to the end, champagne was served; but with the exception of this we were at a banquet such as would have been served five hundred years ago.

The manners of the guests, of the geisha girls, of the singers and of the dramatists, seemed to pervade the air of the chamber with what some one has called "the universal silent social compact of the Japanese to make existence as agreeable as possible."

After a banquet the Japanese do not linger, stupefied with food and liquor, but promptly go home.

The grounds about the club-house were brilliantly illuminated, and there was an exhibition of rare fireworks. We removed our kimonos, resumed our own dress, at the door received our shoes, and returned to our palace, where in our apartments we found the costly Japanese dresses which we had just put aside; these we kept as souvenirs of this rare entertainment.

Between the official reception and banquets we visited the Naval Academy, where the cadets gave the King a parade and drill; the military barracks, where, according to the written law, minor offenders are released from imprisonment on the visit of a royal chief; the beautiful gardens attached to the houses of some of the old nobles; the museums; the factories in which is produced the beautiful *cloisonné* enamel; and the studios of the painters.

At one o'clock of the 14th, the King and suite, in full uniform, rode again in the imperial carriage, surrounded by a troop of lancers, to the palace of Akasuka, to dine with the Emperor. The ceremony of the reception was a repetition of that of our first introduction. After a few moments of subdued conversation the Emperor arose and took from a lacquer box in the hands of the Minister of Ceremonies the star and broad scarlet cordon of the " Grand Cross of the Order of the Rising Sun." These he placed with his own hands upon the King. He then took from the Minister another lacquer box holding the star of the " Grand Officer of the Order of the Rising Sun," and presented it to me, whispering some words in the vernacular; and to the Chamberlain he also handed another box, containing the insignia of the same Order, but one degree lower. We retired for a moment to an adjoining room, and these were fastened and adjusted to our uniforms; the parchments containing our certificates of membership in the Order being sent to our palace. The King now nominally invested the Emperor with the " Grand Cross of the Order of Kamehameha " and the Imperial Princes and the Ministers with the Order in a lesser degree; these were forwarded from Paris, where such insignia are usually made, under careful regulations. The members of the " Order of the Rising Sun " are entitled to certain special distinctions in the empire: the privileges of an annual interview with the Emperor; to attend receptions in his palace, and, at death, to a military funeral.

Before moving from the reception-chamber to the dining-hall, the Minister of Foreign Affairs informed me privately that he had just received a telegraphic message which announced the assassination of the Tsar of Russia, Alexander II. If the Emperor and King were informed of this, etiquette might require them to withdraw and postpone the dinner. The

Minister and I therefore agreed that the news should be suppressed until the close of the banquet. The royal grief upon the sudden loss of a Crowned Brother was delayed two hours. We entered the dining-hall, and the Emperor took a seat at the middle of the long table, with the King on his right hand. Directly opposite to them an Imperial Prince was placed, upon whose right hand I sat, while the Chamberlain was placed on his left. The guests, numbering fifty, were arranged according to their rank toward the ends of the table. The table furniture was of heavy gold plate, valued, it was said, at $200,000. The royal dragon appeared on each piece. Fifteen large ornamental pieces, with most graceful outlines, were placed along the central axis of the table. Great vases filled with flowers were arranged around the room, producing a most attractive effect.

The military band stood on the lawn. As we took our seats it played "Hawaii Poni" and the Japanese national anthem. A servant stood behind each monarch, and the dishes were served by placing them at the same instant before them, so that there could be no suggestion of preference in rank. The *menu* was printed on silk in both Japanese and English. There was no hint of Japanese diet; it was a European dinner in all of its details. Nor were any of the guests dressed in their native costumes; all were in European military and diplomatic costumes. Conversation was carried on almost in whispers, so as not to infringe the rule of etiquette which forbids loud talk before royalty. The Emperor was suffering from a cold, and fifteen physicians braced him up for the banquet.

If the dinner had not been dreary it would have lacked the marked distinction of royal dinners throughout the world. The quiet and almost abject interpreter stood behind the monarchs, and whenever the royal minds moved toward each other, he served as a connecting link. The music of the band, and the brilliancy of the entertainment, in this court, as in other courts, relieved the monotony. A poetic ethnologist sitting in my place might have taken inspiration for verse in the contrasts between the monarchs in their origin, in their strains of blood, in the mysteries of their inherited ideas, in the contrasts between the subjects of one of them, — who had a high civilisation before Columbus touched the land on the margin of the Caribbean Sea; and the subjects of the other, — who only within a hundred years had permitted themselves to be discovered by Captain Cook. Perhaps these monarchs had a common strain, for it is possible that from the enormous coast line of Japan, in prehistoric times, the people of Japan were carried by current and tempest to the Ladrone and Caroline Islands, thence to the Marshall Group, to Samoa, Tonga, to New Zealand, and northwardly to the Hawaiian Islands, a grand sweep of ten thousand miles toward the American continent. The meeting of these monarchs perhaps signified the union of relatives whose ancestors had separated five thousand years before. It was apparent that the Polynesian was physically much superior to the Japanese, but the latter was intellectually incomparably superior to the former. Once during the banquet did our irrepressible little skeleton threaten to force itself into notice. For the Emperor asked the King, " How large is your Majesty's army? " But the King replied vaguely, " I do not keep my army on a war footing." So we still managed to conceal our weight in the estimate of the balance of power among nations.

As the banquet closed, the national hymns were again played by the band; the monarchs side by side, followed by the guests, retired to the reception-room, where the Empress sat, with the sweet little lady-in-waiting standing by her side. Coffee and cigars were served. The Minister of Foreign Affairs now approached the monarchs and informed them of the assassination of the Tsar of Russia, although during the banquet the fact had become an open secret to the guests. The King arose at once, and with his suite took leave of the Empress. The Emperor conducted the King to the imperial carriage, and, guarded by a troop of lancers, we returned to our palace.

The Japanese court went into mourning at once, and the Imperial Chamberlain announced that the invitations to a grand ball at the Emperor's palace, in honour of the King, were recalled. If the Russian nihilist had considerately postponed the execution of his act for three days, we should have attended a brilliant, unique, and notable event.

The King received a letter from the Russian Minister announcing the death of the Tsar, and our Chamberlain, according to usage, called on the Minister, leaving his own official card, as monarchs have no cards. The King, as required by etiquette, went into retirement and grief over the loss of his Royal Russian Brother for the rest of the day, but as a matter of fact most of the time was spent in admonishing Robert, the valet, because, while drunk, he had seated himself on the royal silk hat and crushed it. The King recalled our conversations on the voyage across the Pacific, regarding the violent deaths of sovereigns, upon which I gravely used the phrase of American frontiersmen, that the Tsar's misfortune was another case of a man's " dying with his boots on." To which he replied naïvely, " Yes, a soldier should die with his boots on."

He then said that he often became weary of the Crown of his own little kingdom. I suggested that he should follow the example of the Saxon king who abdicated his throne and entered a monastery, where he was assigned to the labour of milking the cows. If he would follow this example, with the same results, he might, I pointed out to him, become the author of a book titled " From the Crown to the Cow-Yard."

Although the death of the Tsar ended all grand entertainments, the etiquette of the court required that the Emperor should dine with the King in our own palace. He did so on the next day, and the ceremony of the previous day was strictly observed. On this occasion the monarchs met for the last time. At the close of the banquet a few moments were spent in conversation through the interpreter; expressions of good-will and high consideration were exchanged, and they bade each other good-bye, cordially shaking hands. The national anthems were played, the Emperor entered his carriage, and, surrounded by a body of lancers, drove over the bridge which spanned the moat.

When we retired to our chambers we found there a number of rare and valuable presents from the Emperor. To the King were given magnificent *cloisonné* vases, rich silks, exquisite lacquer boxes, bronzes, and embroideries; to each of the suite were given silks and lacquer boxes. The suite suggested that in return the royal feather cloak should be presented to the Emperor, but the King refused to part with this ancient heirloom; he secretly meditated its use again when an occasion should arise. As our Hawaiian countrymen were hardly out of the " Stone Age," there was no work of fine art of their manufacture which compared with that of the Japanese. After the King's subjects became " civilised," it was a common practice for ardent friends to display their esteem by exchanging trousers. I suggested this loving and simple practice to the King, but he scornfully replied that it was beneath the dignity of monarchs.

CHAPTER X

Departure for Yokohama, Kobe, and Nagasaki — The Emperor
  Sends Imperial Commissioners with His Guest — Japanese
  Evolution — Kobe, and the Old Capital of Kioto — Mis-
  takes About the King's Identity — Visit to Osaka — At-
  tempt to Dine Incognito at Japanese Inn — The Disguise
  Penetrated — Visit to an Old Missionary in Kobe — The
  Inland Sea — Salutes — The King's Reflections — Favours
  Buddhism — At Nagasaki — Japanese Navigation — Pro-
  miscuous Bathing — Imperial Commissioners Leave at the
  Boundary of the Empire — Chinese and Japanese Morality
  — The Steamer Coaled by Women and Children.

AFTER a visit [1] of ten days, filled with splendid
and extraordinary imperial hospitality, we left
Tokio with the same grand ceremony with which
we entered it. On reaching Yokohama, the Imperial
Princes and many members of the court bade the King
good-bye at the gangway of the steamer. The warships dipped their flags; but the yards of the Russian
ships were "crossed" in mourning for the dead
Tsar; and salutes were not fired.

We embarked for Kobe and Nagasaki in one of
the steamers of the Mishi-Bishi Company. But the
hospitality of the Emperor had not yet ended. Three
Imperial Commissioners attended us. It was their
office to remain with the Emperor's guest until he

[1] The result of this visit was an emigration of Japanese labourers to
the Hawaiian Islands, where they are employed in the sugar plantations. At the present time (1903) they exceed in numbers all other
races in the islands, being many thousands in excess of the native
inhabitants and Anglo-Saxons, and their native-born descendants will
in the future largely furnish the backbone of the territorial community.

reached the boundaries of the Empire. One of them was an old nobleman of high rank, with a kind and genial face, whose history was full of startling incidents.

As we moved quietly toward the great Inland Sea of Japan I reflected on the strange and unexpected events of the last ten days. Our abode had been in the altitudes, the upper air of Oriental royal life, but we had now descended by a parachute to the common ways and stood on the deck of a trading-steamer. One act in the comedy of "The Royal Traveller" had closed. What would be the scenes and incidents of the next? As we smoked our cigars in a quiet conference we could see how circumstances had shaped for us this splendid reception in Japan, but we could not conceive any reason why any other people should recognise, beyond the merest civilities, the existence of such a small nation as Hawaii. My own pleasure in this generous reception was that it had brought me face to face with the reconstructors of a great empire. Christendom calls these men pagans, but by the worldly standard they measure well as statesmen. There is before them a more difficult task than that of the founders of the American Constitution. For these founders took the existing wise and wholesome laws, political habits and usages of the people, and with little innovation shaped them into a great Constitution. They simply grafted better stock on the healthy roots of self-government, already deeply fixed in the soil. But the Japanese statesmen, Saigo, Ito, Inouye, Okubo, and Katsu, with the aid of the Emperor, are placing a modern and parliamentary structure of government upon a narrow, and ancient, foundation of absolute feudalism.

They will be ranked among the leaders of men if within one hundred years their plans are successful. To-day they are only at the dawning of their new civilisation. Griffith, one of their ablest and most impartial historians, gives them this high praise: "The noblest trait in the character of the Japanese is his willingness to change for the better when he discovers his wrong or inferiority."

The King and the suite were now members of the conspicuous military Order of the Rising Sun, and upon the King's asking the nature of our obligations as such members, I, as his law officer, instructed him that if the Emperor of Japan demanded his active assistance in the event of war he might be obliged to order out our Hawaiian fleet of double war-canoes to protect the Japanese fleet; but that the question was one which should be submitted to a conference of nations.

On landing at Kobe the royal party went by train to the ancient capital and city of Kioto. The Governor of the city received us and led us through the ancient palace of the Mikado. The grounds were excellent examples of Japanese skill in gardening; the palace and the buildings connected with it were richly furnished, but simple in construction, for it was one of the rules of Shintoism, the State religion, that the Mikado should lead a simple life.

We occupied three carriages in driving about the city, but they were no longer imperial. As we were not in uniform, and no special effort was made to distinguish the King from his suite, the many thousands of people who filled the streets, but opened a passage-way for us, were unable to pick out the King. Some of them pointed to the Chamberlain as the King, some of them looked at me. At one place our carriages were separated for a few moments and drove through different streets. For a few moments I received the adoration of the people, many of them bowing to the ground, to the amusement of the Imperial Commissioner by my side, who said the mistake would cause much discussion among the people for many years, as to the complexion of the King: some would insist that he was a white man, and others that he was a dark man. The sensation of being received as a monarch is not a disagreeable one; but it is quickly succeeded by the feeling that you are, even innocently, imposing on the crowd. It is not convenient to rise in the carriage and say, " The man you are looking after is around the corner."

After some presentations of local authorities to the King, in the Governor's residence, the royal party returned by train to the city of Osaka, where there was another reception in the residence of the Governor of that province, and a visit to the Mint followed. While in the street we were suddenly asked to leave the carriages and mount jinrikishas.

The King, while in Tokio, said he would like to visit a common inn of the country, but etiquette forbade the guest of the Emperor from entering one in Tokio. In the distant city of Osaka, however, it was arranged that he should, incognito, visit and dine in one of them. After riding some distance and walking through a narrow street we entered a common inn on the bank of a river, and quietly went to the dining-room as if we were foreign tourists of note. Royal etiquette was now carefully put aside, and the King was placed on the floor at an inferior seat. The dinner was, however, an elaborate one, and the geisha girls were extremely pretty and graceful. After serving the dishes, with the usual bowing to the floor which is customary before the higher classes, there was dancing and music. The dancing resembled that of the Hawaiians, but was not so " abandoned." Believing that our identity was well concealed, one of the Japanese officials asked a geisha, " Do you know who these people are? " She replied promptly " that one of them was the King of the Hawaiian Islands." We had been betrayed. After dining for several hours we hurried to the train, for it was then nine o'clock in the evening; and we arrived at Kobe at midnight. The King called at once upon Mrs. Gulick, a venerable missionary residing in Kobe, who was for many years a missionary in the Hawaiian kingdom. The house was filled with Japanese Christians who wished to see the King of a Christian nation.

He was then received by the Governor and the Consular Corps at midnight, and shortly after resumed the voyage to Nagasaki. The trip through the Inland Sea seemed to be through a lake with an ever-receding boundary. The hundreds of islands, many of them pyramidal in form, were so thickly grouped as to cut off the sight of a channel before us, and, with the mountains on either hand, formed a vast amphitheatre, a lake enclosed by mountains. The steamer moved directly toward what seemed an impassable barrier of hills, but a slight turn revealed a sheet of water, and beyond this another apparent barrier. While steaming the next morning over the unruffled water, we passed a British cruiser; our royal standard was raised, and the cruiser hoisted the Hawaiian flag and fired a salute of twenty-one guns. The report of the guns struck the surrounding hills, and the echo gave the effect of a double salute.

The King now gave to the Imperial Commissioners some of his reflections. The Buddha temples had greatly pleased him. Their bizarre architecture and gaudy ornaments were more attractive to him than the severe, cold, church buildings which the Puritanism of New England had erected in his kingdom. He said such temples would adorn the beautiful valleys of his islands, and suggested to me correspondence with my colleagues in the government on the subject of introducing Buddhism to his people. He consulted the Imperial Commissioners about the probability of securing priests; but they did not encourage him. He told me that he believed in reincarnation, though I do not think he understood it clearly. But I respectfully replied that to carry on reincarnation on a working scale in his kingdom would require large numbers of tigers, snakes, hippopotami, wildcats, monkeys, and other dreadful creatures, into which the souls of the believers could enter and be reincarnated; that each soul, according to the true doctrine, passed through five hundred reincarnations before it received a ticket for a reserved seat on the everlasting lotus-flower, and it would take many beasts to give every soul a chance; so that if he really desired to introduce Buddhism to his people he should, on the tour, buy up the contents of bankrupt or superfluous menageries which were offered for sale, take them home, and turn the animals loose in his kingdom, in order that they might co-operate with him in the establishment of Buddhism in Hawaii. Thereafter the

King said confidentially to the Chamberlain that the Minister had trifled with a matter which deeply interested him, but he would pursue the subject on reaching home. I knew that his desire was a temporary fancy which would pass off with new sights, and that he would probably be in favour of formally introducing Confucianism when we reached China; for in fact the Chinese male Confucianists then exceeded in numbers all the male Christians in his kingdom.

From several remarks made by my royal master I suspected that the common belief of the Japanese in the divine origin of the Emperor had strongly affected him, and he was planning the culture of a similar belief among his own people regarding himself. The Chamberlain and I saw symptoms of his scheme in his declaration one day that the kings of Hawaii descended from the *akuas* (gods), but that the missionaries had denied it. To establish or revive this belief among his superstitious subjects would be a ringbolt to which he could fasten his throne. On his return home he attempted this as a means of strengthening the loyalty of his people to himself, which was never over-strenuous.

Entering the landlocked harbour of Nagasaki, the royal standard was again raised, and six warships gave a royal salute. The Russian admiral put at the King's disposition his steam launch, and he was received by the Governor of the province. Among his callers was the Yankee captain of a Japanese steamer, who had been in that service for twelve years. He illustrated the ancient and even modern art of navigation in the empire by a story of a Japanese steamer commanded by a German captain, who, after leaving port, set the course of the vessel to the north and then went to his cabin. Waking up during the night, he noticed that " the stars were not right." He looked at the compass and saw that his vessel was heading South. He rushed out, and, demanding an explanation, was gravely told that the Japanese officers, being in doubt about the course he had directed, had at once consulted the cook, who declared that the foreign captain was in error, whereupon they had promptly reversed the ship's course. From time immemorial the cook has been the chief person on a Japanese junk. Kinglake, recounting his travels in Greece, says he found the cook of a Grecian trading-vessel the most important person on board; he did not hesitate to overrule the captain.

In Nagasaki we noticed the promiscuous bathing of the sexes in public; it had been forbidden in Tokio and Yokohama as a concession to European sentiment. I asked one of the Imperial Commissioners why a sensitive people had permitted such a practice. He replied that it was a time-honoured custom; and that on the other hand many Japanese who had been in Europe were equally shocked at the ballet, which they looked upon as positively vulgar and indecent. This was also the opinion of a Chinese Minister at the Court of St. James, who wrote to his government that he had great aversion to the dresses with low necks which the British Queen " commanded " should be worn by ladies on State occasions. The Japanese vernacular press also, I noticed, severely condemned the nude, in art and sculpture, of Christendom; which leads me to think that if Pilate on the judgment-seat of morality should ask, " What is modesty? " — the moralist of

Christendom would fall into contradictions and confusion for answer.

The "Tokio-maru," to which we were now transferred in order to reach Shanghai, was coaled by the passing of baskets from the coal-heaps to the vessel's bunkers, by the little brown women and tiny brown children who stood in lines and earned about six cents a day. We steamed out of the harbour with the noise and smoke of more royal salutes.

At the distance of a marine league from the shore the boundaries of the empire were reached; the engines were stopped, and the Japanese Imperial Commissioners, having finished their mission of escorting the King to the boundaries, took leave of him and returned to Nagasaki and Tokio. Our royal standard dipped three times in honour of the Emperor's representatives; and they carried the King's last words of thanks to the Emperor for his unbounded hospitality.

CHAPTER XI

The Yellow Sea — The King Wishes to See the Emperor of
China — Decided to be Impracticable — Shanghai — Re-
ceived by the Taotai — An American Negro in China — A
Large Steamer Placed at the King's Service — The Boy
and the " Cannibal King " — Departure for Tientsin —
Danger from Pirates — The Peiho River and the Taku
Forts — " Blood is Thicker than Water " — Received at
Tientsin by the Taotai and Viceroy Li Hung Chang's
Secretary — Difficulties About Visiting Pekin — The King
Only a Foreign Devil — Calling on the Viceroy — Li Asks
Questions and Smokes — The Viceroy Returns the King's
Call and Asks More Questions — His Opinion About the
Japanese — People Gather to See the " Black Foreign
Devil " — Dinner with the Viceroy — The Viceroy's Son —
Chinese Democracy — Presents from the Viceroy.

WE now steamed over the Yellow Sea. While
in Tokio the King had intimated to one of
the Imperial Commissioners that he intended to visit
the Emperor of China, then a lad. With diplomatic
reserve his purpose was not discouraged, but the
suite were told that it would create complications.
Our reception in Japan had modified his modesty;
nor did he realise the strained relations between the
Chinese and foreign governments. He finally told
his suite of his intention, but they strongly opposed it.

We arrived at Shanghai at noon. No notice of
the King's purpose to visit China had been officially
given; if it had it would have created consternation
in the Yamen at Pekin. No royal salutes were fired
as we entered the Woosung River; we were now

among a people indifferent and perhaps unfriendly to us. We dropped suddenly from the pinnacle of royal hospitality to its base, and the royal standard lay dejectedly in its canvas bag. The American Consul-General, however, called on the King, who had taken lodgings in the " Astor House." He unwisely urged him to visit Pekin and be the first of foreign kings to enter the Forbidden City.

No diplomatic corps resides in Shanghai, but the *taotai* or mayor of the place was notified by the American Consul of the arrival of the King. The following day he appeared in a sedan chair, with a large retinue preceding and following him; while runners, with the beating of gongs and loud cries, notified the spectators to make the way clear. We observed at once the fine physiques, clear eyes, and intelligent faces of the men of the higher classes, but there was the inscrutable physiognomy which Europeans cannot penetrate. He said that he desired to honour the King of a foreign country, and asked if the King would condescend to dine with him. The invitation was accepted, but the dinner was postponed until after our return from Tientsin.

The manager of the China Merchants Steamship Company, which owned a fleet of thirty-six large steamers and looked for trade in the Pacific, had already sent several vessels to the Hawaiian group. In order to make favour with the King he placed at his Majesty's disposal a large steamer, the " Pautah," for the trip to Tientsin. The manager was a fine American negro who had shown much ability when employed by the American Legation in Pekin; he was not only well educated, but spoke several languages, including Chinese; his father was a negro preacher in Washington, D. C. He had married a handsome English girl in Shanghai, who was an artist; but his marriage to a white person had much incensed the Americans living in Shanghai, though it was cordially approved by the English, Germans, and French residents. He caused some cabins of the " Pautah " to be refurnished and made provision for a sumptuous table. Though the steamer was on the regular line of travel between Shanghai and Tientsin, he refused to permit any persons to take passage in her, reserving this great vessel for the exclusive use of the King and suite; she became, therefore, for this trip, the private yacht of the royal party. The cost was great, but the shrewd Chinese no doubt expected favours in their future trade with Hawaii.

On the morning of our landing in Shanghai, an American lad who lived in the Astor House showed great curiosity to see a " live king." He dressed himself neatly and waited near the door of the King's chamber. An American living in the city, who knew the lad, warned him against getting within the King's reach, for he said, " He is the King of the Cannibal Islands, and is uncommonly fond of roasted little boys." The little fellow disappeared instantly, but returned in a few moments covered with mud. The gentleman who had warned him asked his reason for rolling in the dirt. He replied, " The King would not eat a dirty boy."

We smiled at our luck in becoming the sole occupants of a fine steamer for the next ten days. We embarked without salutes or ceremonies of any kind. The captain was a Yankee skipper, with three American officers, while the crew were well-trained Chinese.

The numerous stewards stood about the saloon, with
no duty but to wait upon the King's party; the table
of an Atlantic liner was not better supplied. Around
the sides of the main saloon were fastened racks
filled with muskets and cutlasses, and amidships were
several cannon, for there is danger, although remote,
of piratical attacks on the Yellow Sea. It was possible that a Chinese Captain Kidd might bear down
upon us, and if he captured us, the King and suite
might be directed in forcible pidgin-English to " walk
the plank." The King did not like the warlike look
of the steamer, and asked the skipper whether he
would fight or run if pirates should make an attack.
The answer was characteristic: " Fight, by gum!
Mr. King. I'd like to get a show at those yaller
dogs!"

At the close of the day the steamer reached the
mouth of the Peiho River. Extended fortifications
stretched along the left bank, while on the right
were the low batteries which crippled the British
naval forces in 1860, upon which occasion the American commodore, Tatnall, allowed his boat's crew to
man the British guns, and declared the future international policy of America and England: " Blood
is thicker than water!"

Crossing the bar, we steamed up the river to
Tientsin. The royal standard was hoisted and was
recognised by the Consular Corps. The docks were
soon covered with people, who stood silent and stolid.
The King's arrival was announced to the *taotai*, who,
with a large retinue, paid a formal visit to the King,
who received him in the " compound " or premises
of the steamship company. The *taotai* said that the
Viceroy, General Li Hung Chang, had ordered a

search to be made for suitable apartments for his Majesty, but they could not be readily secured. He asked if the King's country was a part of America, and if he had come around Cape Horn. He retired with much ceremony. After he left, a mandarin, Li-Sun, the secretary of the Viceroy, called. He spoke English, informing us that he had been graduated at Hamilton College, Clinton, N. Y., many years ago, and that he had a son who was a student at Yale. He had known relatives of the King's Chamberlain, who lived in the town where the college was situated. We told him that we preferred to remain on the steamer, where we had excellent accommodations. He dined with us. While a member of the Consular Corps engaged the King's attention, the Secretary asked me if the King intended to visit Pekin. I told him that the King wished to meet General Li Hung Chang and would visit Pekin if it was practicable. Li-Sun replied that the Viceroy would appreciate the visit, but a trip to Pekin would require much preliminary study; many communications would have to be exchanged, and the Yamen would carefully consider the matter; he thought it would be at least five weeks before it could be definitely settled. He declined, however, to represent the views of the Imperial Government. After he left I told the King that it was quite clear to me that he was not wanted at Pekin; in the eyes of the Dowager Empress and her consort he was only a fanqui (foreign devil). Foreign ambassadors were received by her only through fear of the sword; if he persisted, he would catch a genuine "Tartar," who was quite as fierce as the bogie Tartars in the story-books; instead of making an ever-glorious journey to the Forbidden City, he would find the Celestial Family " not at home," and a sign on the gate-post, " Beware of the dog; " besides, as he had no army or navy behind him, he might be seized, put in a bamboo cage, and paraded through China. The King finally abandoned his intention of going to Pekin.

Mandarin Li-Sun returned with a message from the Viceroy that he would send his own sedan chairs to the steamer in the morning, and they would bring the King and suite to the Yamen, which was the Viceroy's palace.

During the day several members of the Consular Corps called on the King, and we visited a part of the city; a number of Chinese merchants called and tendered banquets to his Majesty.

The Viceroy's sedan chairs arrived in the morning, with Secretary Li-Sun, and we, in uniform, entered them; each was borne by four men. The bamboo carrying-poles bent as if they would break under the heavy weights of the King and the Chamberlain; the wiry and lean coolie bearers were soon in a profuse perspiration. The route lay through several miles of narrow streets, whose walls were so close to each other that the extended hands of one seated in a chair could almost touch both sides at the same time. The people, at the sound of the Viceroy's gong and the cry of the Governor's guard, packed themselves close to the walls, and gazed silently and stolidly into the dark face of the King.

At the gates of the Yamen a troop of soldiers awkwardly presented arms, and an explosion of three large fire-crackers — the regular salute — was made. Alighting in the court-yard, we advanced a few steps

to meet the Viceroy, who stood alone, in a brilliant
dress, while behind him was a retinue of his officials.
He shook hands with himself cordially, according
to Chinese custom, and then, in deference to the immemorial pump-handle welcome of the Europeans,
shook hands with the King and with the suite. He
led the way, between lines of bowing officials, through
several large rooms, to a reception-chamber, where
we sat around a large circular table. The room was
ornamented with beautiful vases; and on the walls
were silk curtains upon which were inscribed moral
precepts. One of them, translated for me by Mandarin Li-Sun, was quite like the motto over Lord
Coke's chambers in London, in the last century,
" Prudens qui patiens," — which his negro servant
broadly translated, " The prudent man never hurries
when he tries to catch a monkey."

The Viceroy at once began to ask questions : " How
many islands are there in your kingdom? " — " How
old are you? " — " Do you have a Parliament? " —
" How many people are there in your kingdom? "
By his side stood his pipe-bearers. The bowl rested
on the floor, and a servant holding a live coal knelt
at the bowl, watching the Viceroy's face; the other
bearer stood by the side of the Viceroy, who at
intervals, without moving his head, raised and opened
his hand, into which the vigilant bearer instantly
placed the stem of the pipe, and the kneeling servant
applied the fire. He took several whiffs of smoke,
opened his hand, and the bearer removed the pipe-
stem, while the lighter recharged the bowl with fresh
tobacco. The Viceroy, who had information about
the Hawaiian kingdom which Li-Sun had given him,
continued :

Li Hung Chang (1881).

"You have many Chinese in your country, and you treat them well." — "Are you the son of your predecessor?"

"No," said the King, "I come from another old dynasty."

"What did you do when you were a boy?" asked the Viceroy.

The King hesitated for a moment, reflected, and replied at a venture:

"I went into the army when I was sixteen years of age."

This provoked instantly the ever-vexing question, "How large is your army?"

"I have few regular troops," replied his Majesty; "I rely on volunteers."

"Are the gentlemen in your suite Hawaiians?" continued the catechiser.

"Both are Hawaiians," replied the King.

"I see," said the Viceroy, "that he [pointing to Colonel Judd] is dark; but he [pointing to me] is white. Why are they different? Do you have white natives among your subjects?"

"The parents of both were Americans," was the reply.

"You have missionaries; do you like them?" was the next question.

"Yes, they are good people," said the King.

His Majesty was rather confused with the rapidity of the questions. Secretary Li-Sun was the interpreter.

The Viceroy rose and led the King to another room, where there was a table loaded with sweetmeats. Champagne was served. The Viceroy said he would return the King's visit the next day, and then walked with him to the court-yard and stood near the sedan chair while the King entered it. He remained there bowing until we had reached the gates and another salute of three explosions had been given. Mandarin Li-Sun arrived soon after, and his conversation gave us much interesting information about the Chinese, the life of the Viceroy, and the international relations of China with the Great Powers.

The scope of this memoir excludes a general discussion of the Chinese problems which are vexing the European Powers. My own opinions would be those of a globe-trotter. Those things which make up the character and tendencies of a nation or a community, and shape its career, are not open, but concealed, and only patient industry or rare insight can detect them.

The next morning our temporary yacht, the " Pautah," was decorated with flags, and the Viceroy's barge brought him down the river at ten o'clock. After some ceremonies on deck he entered the saloon with the King, and after tea was served he renewed his cross-examination. The suite aided the King, and the Viceroy would frequently turn to them and spear them with sharp queries. The King remarked that the Emperor of Japan had shown him great hospitality. The Viceroy replied that the Japanese could not be depended upon. He said he regretted he had no palace to which he could invite the King, but would give him a banquet the next evening in the compound of the steamship company. He then rose and walked slowly to the gangway with his Majesty; they appeared to be of the same height.

During the next day crowds of people pressed to the edge of the dock, peering into the doors and windows of our steamer. Some of them were motionless for hours, for they saw in the Viceroy's guest not only a " foreign devil," but a black foreign devil. The children were brought to the dock in their fathers' arms that they too might see the awe-inspiring sight.

Late in the day we walked across the street to the compound. The Viceroy had already arrived in his brilliant dress, and we appeared in full uniform. The Viceroy received the King at the door and led him to the reception-room, where the prominent men of the city, both Chinese and foreigners, were presented to the Viceroy and King. Tea was served, and we entered the dining-room. The Viceroy placed the King on his right hand, and myself on his left, and next to me his son, a young man who was studying the English language and spoke it with hesitation. When this young gentleman discovered that I was an American, he asked me many questions about the relation of the States to the Federal government, for he could not understand the dual system; he thought it confusing and dangerous. The dishes and food were entirely Chinese, but they were served at tables, and forks were furnished to the foreigners. The fine ware had been brought from the Viceroy's residence. The room was decorated with silk curtains and embroideries, upon which were worked moral texts from the Chinese classics, quite like the pious aphorisms which appeared on the walls of New England homes in early days, but which are removed as prosperity increases, because they are annoying and impracticable.

The democratic life of the Chinese was seen in the freedom allowed to the crowd to enter the compound and look at the guests through the window while they

ate. The people stood on one another's shoulders and
backs; some of them raised themselves with bamboo
sticks, so that the windows were filled to their upper
frame-work with stolid faces pressing against the
glass. The Viceroy occasionally asked questions, but
Li-Sun was seated at a distance from him and could
not interpret with ease. He asked me questions
through his son: " Why is not your office of Minister
filled by a native? " — " Are the natives incapable? "
— " Do you fear the United States? " — " How
much good have the missionaries done? " — " Do
you know General Grant? — he is a great man."

While I sat by the side of this celebrated ruler I
felt some aversion to him, for it was he who, after
the Taeping rebellion, had beheaded 80,000 Chinese
prisoners in Canton. After all, he was no worse
than Napoleon, who said to Metternich at the sign-
ing of the Peace at Tilsit, " What are a million of
lives to me if they come in my way? "

One could only admire the fine, strong faces of the
Chinese merchants and mandarins at the banquet,
and yet De Quincey, in his scholarly ignorance of
them sixty years ago, wrote: " It must be said that
the Chinese are in their childhood." De Quincey
did not foresee the time when the citizens of the
Great Republic would tremble at the industrial energy
and economy of these children. The Secretary,
Li-Sun, told me that the Viceroy realised the need
of political reconstruction in China, but he could not
move far in advance of the people he governed without losing his prestige. He realised Burke's aphorism
that " he who leads must in a great measure follow."

At the close of the banquet the Viceroy, the King,
and the guests returned to the reception-room, and

MENU.

DINNER GIVEN IN HONOUR OF
H. M. KING KALAKAUA
OF HAWAII
BY THE VICE ROY LI
AT TIENTSIN
ON THE 1ST OF APRIL, 1881.

Bird's nest soup.		燕
Fish, stewed and fried.	菜	炸魚巴
Shark's fins	魚	燴魚羊
Meat balls.		翅地炸
Mutton Cutlets.	圓	肉排白
Fried Pork.		骨棗凉
Quail paté.	甸	盖鴒車
Cold Chicken		布拌燒
Ham and mushroom Pudding	肉	雞厘烚
Roast Turkey		路火燒
Boiled Ham.		雞火火
Roast Mutton.		腿羊五
Chocolate sponge cake.	糕	肉眼大
Jelly, white & red.	厘	蛋色牛
Plum pudding &c.	甸	這提
Ladies finger cakes.		布子脚
		餅

Menu of Dinner given in honour of King Kalakaua,
by Li Hung Chang.

the King and the Viceroy parted. It was our final
interview with this man, whose fate it was, not to
rule the great wave of Chinese humanity, but to
float on it, be swayed by it, and be landed in the future
on some unknown shore, as all great statesmen are
landed by the wave of popular will.

When we boarded the " Pautah," the King found
valuable presents of tea and silk which the Viceroy
had sent to him.

CHAPTER XII

EARLY next morning we steamed down the Peiho. At the mouth of the river the forts displayed Chinese flags for a mile on the ramparts, and gave the royal salute of twenty-one guns. On the third day we landed in Shanghai, where we were received and entertained by Mr. J. J. Kiswick, the head of the large British mercantile house of Jardine, Matheson & Co. We attended a banquet given by the *taotai;* it was like those given by the Viceroy, and by the Chinese Consul in San Francisco. At its close there was another example of the working-out of the dining problem in Chinese civilisation, as it has also been solved in Japan. Within a few moments after reaching the reception-room after the dinner, servants, without request, appeared with our coats and hats and offered them to us. The Chinese believe that repose should follow a feast; animals, after feeding, need sleep and not action. They avoid the inebriate loquacity of the European dinner. The guest is not left to choose the time of his leaving, which he might delay, but angels of mercy, in the shape of servants, enter with hats, coats, and umbrellas, and release the host from post-prandial stupidity.

The next day we left in the " Thibet " for Hongkong. The King had " sucked " some instructive knowledge in China; he could regard with some equanimity his failure to see the Forbidden City. If the ambassadors of the great European Powers were not permitted to approach the Imperial Chinese Throne without striking the ground with their heads nine times before that awful Presence, Majesty itself would certainly refuse to humiliate itself. My royal master had without due consideration approached the sacred city, looked over its walls at the imperial door, and had put his hand on the door-bell. But before he pulled it he discovered the notice, posted near the Celestial gate, of which I had warned him: " Beware of the dog." He took his hand from the bell and retired without urging an entrance. From that time forward he was pleased whenever the European Powers pulled the Celestial noses of the Chinese Imperial Family.

Among the passengers were several Englishmen and Americans who with much Anglo-Saxon conceit related many of the singular characteristics of the Chinese people as evidences of their heathenism and present childhood: the whipping of their idols if prayers were not answered; their offering, at the tombs of their ancestors, wooden pigs and ducks instead of the real articles; stealing back at night the food offered during the day; their belief that evil spirits infest the world, but invariably travel on straight lines, so that garden paths are made crooked in order to deceive them, and the roofs of houses are made so irregularly that the demons lose their way when moving over them and withdraw. These self-satisfied Occidentals, however, forgot that there were many millions of people in their own country who devoutly believed in the " manifestations " conducted by "mediums," which are quite as grotesque and superstitious; these mediums, like the priests of the Chinese joss-houses, revealing the secrets of the supernatural world only on a cash basis.

Nor are the Chinese superstitions, in their most extravagant forms, more grotesque than the very recent belief of Christendom, and by no means wholly abandoned yet, that the many hundreds of millions of Asiatics are condemned to eternal torment for not accepting a religion of which they have never heard. The tourist in the Orient, as well as the merchant and trader, forgets that the Occidental civilisation of the nineteenth century is, as Emerson says, "yet in its swaddling-clothes," and if taken as a whole, instead of in its parts, is so badly composed that the wisest philanthropists would not advise the Chinese to take it as it really is, but would recommend them to pick out only its virtues. If the wisdom of Providence has leisurely taken nineteen hundred years from the erection of the Cross to bring European civilisation up to its present imperfect conditions, in which brute force represented by armies and battle-ships is largely the evidence of a nation's progress, China may justly claim that her own civilisation should not be subjected to any violent changes, but only be placed in the course of a gradual evolution which is normal and healthy.

The missionary in China is confronted by the same difficulties that exist in Japan. His teachings, sound and admirable in themselves, tend to overturn a political principle accepted throughout Christendom, that no foreigner shall preach in any State a doctrine which tends to impair the supreme political power. The doctrine of the missionaries in China does not

directly attack that power, but it does attack the idea
of ancestral worship, upon which political power
stands. The missionary, as I have already said, is
inevitably a political reformer. He is impatient. He
wishes to see Christianity rise in the Far East as the
tree rises in the trick of the Hindoo juggler, who
spreads his mat, places a flower-pot on it, plants in it
a seed, and holds his wand over it till it sprouts,
throws out leaves, rises to a tree, extends its branches,
and casts its fruit to the ground, all within the space
of an hour. It is this haste of Christendom to see
" results " which prevents it from adjusting its
methods to the existing conditions; that is, from
adopting the " scientific," which is the divine method
of making progress; of building up, instead of de-
stroying what exists. No one has yet discovered in
the Chinese mind an insuperable barrier against progress. No class of men has yet studied that mind for
the purpose of reaching it. The humble locksmith
opens a vault, the key of which is lost, not by trying
it with common keys, but by studying its combinations and taking impressions of its intricate devices.

When the missionary, with a psychological lantern,
explores without preconceived ideas the mysteries of
the Chinese mind, he will devise a way to lodge in it
the best truth; above all, he will, as one of the ablest
of missionaries has said, not destroy what is good in
the Chinese religion, but preserve it and add to it.
He will not destroy ancestral worship, but gradually
enlighten and improve it, so that in the fulness of
time it will eventually assimilate itself to the true
worship, whatever that may be.

CHAPTER XIII

THE " Thibet " anchored in the evening in the harbour of Hongkong, but it was after sunset, and thus past the saluting-hour. Owing to the considerable commerce between this place and the Hawaiian kingdom, the King was represented here by a Consul-General, a British merchant of high standing. He promptly boarded the steamer for the purpose of taking the King to his fine residence, as an invitation to stay with him had been telegraphed to Shanghai and accepted. But the twelve-oared barge of Sir John Pope Hennessey, the Colonial Governor, suddenly appeared at the gangway, and Dr. Eitel, his private secretary, brought an invitation from the Governor, asking the King, in the name of the British Queen, to be his guest. The King was forced to break his promise to his own Consul. He was, however, on British soil, and his Consul was an Englishman. He broke his promise on the ground that in social affairs the Queen's wishes take precedence. The Consul and the private secretary wrangled over the matter on the deck of the steamer. My own Solomonic way of settling the matter by dividing the King into two parts, one of which should go to the Queen's representative, and the other to the Consul, was rejected, and we entered the royal barge, rowed by twelve oarsmen in the Queen's livery. At the landing we entered sedan chairs, borne by coolies, also in the Queen's livery, in which we were taken to the Government House, which has a superb situation on a hill overlooking the city. Here the Governor received the King at the door, and led him to his audience-room, where he, with the suite, were presented to Lady Hennessey. It was a royal reception, and restored the continuity of the Royal Progress, which had been broken by the conduct or indifference of the little yellow five-clawed Dragon at Pekin.

After the King retired, the Governor, who was a clever and brilliant man, listened to the story of our adventures in Tientsin. He was surprised that the suite allowed the King to attempt an interview with the Brother of the Moon, but when he was reminded of the fact that few can check a Royal Horse that takes the bit in his mouth, he gave us his sympathy, and believed that our interview with General Li Hung Chang had compensated for the loss of the sight of the Forbidden City.

While we were taking coffee the next morning, the forts, with seven warships, fired the usual salute of twenty-one guns. From the balcony of the Government House, high above the city, we looked down on a dense mass of smoke, rolling away to the mainland, pierced with the flashing of the guns; the Hawaiian flag at the mainmast of every warship;

the merchantmen also, who like to show their bunting, hoisting the King's colours. It was a pretty sight, very noisy and warlike.

The Government paper contained an announcement, which is presented with the Chinese and English words side by side.

We learned that a tramp steamer would shortly leave for Siam by direct route. By taking her we would avoid doubling on our tracks in a voyage to Singapore and return. We resolved to take advantage of this chance, although the steamer was not a passenger-carrier and did not attract us. When we informed Sir John Hennessey of our intention he said that he proposed to give two State banquets in honour of the King, at which His Majesty would meet the chief British and foreign naval commanders, the British officers commanding the garrison, the Consular Corps, and prominent citizens. To facilitate our necessarily early departure he promised to give them at once and in quick succession.

With those who promptly called upon the King was the American Consul, Colonel John S. Mosby, the Confederate guerilla, who a few years before, in the Civil War, had harassed the Federal forces around Washington and greatly disturbed the peace of President Lincoln. He had taken at a bound the "bloody chasm" between North and South, and by the kindly act of President Grant he had received this Federal office, and was now as loyal to the Flag as any Union veteran.

Mr. Chetar, a rich merchant, gave a luncheon party, or tiffin, in honour of the King, at Kowloon, on the mainland opposite to the city. Men of all nationalities were there, — the men drawn to this

GOVERNMENT NOTIFICATION.—No. 131.

His Majesty the King of Hawaii arrived in Hongkong on Tuesday evening, the 12th instant, and was welcomed to the Colony by the Governor, in the name of Her Majesty Queen VICTORIA. His Majesty, the King KALAKAUA, was accompanied by His Excellency W. N. ARMSTRONG, Minister of State, and Colonel JUDD, Chamberlain.

By His Excellency's Command,

FREDERICK STEWART,
Acting Colonial Secretary.

Colonial Secretary's Office,
Hongkong, 16th April, 1881.

憲報第一百三十一號

署銜改使司史為議國大君主加拉鳩嗹華臨

大英后帝威克多理阿名迎接登岸為此特示俾眾週知

威儀國大君主加拉鳩嗹華隨帶

宰臣暗送前來於本月十二

日即德護送拜即紙捲晚祗用敬用

香滿總督即敬用

為憲驗諮事照得現有

二千八百八十一年

四月十六日 示

Extract from Hong Kong Newspaper.

great free port by commerce, as fish are attracted to a net by a torchlight: English free traders, American protectionists, large-framed and clever-looking Chinamen, Portuguese from Macao, Parsees from Bombay, Frenchmen in exile from the Parisian Jerusalem, and Japanese getting into Western ways.

In the first toast, after tiffin, " To the Queen!" we saw the impassioned loyalty of the British colonists to their Queen, the centripetal power which makes the British Crown, with its setting of colonial diamonds, the central figure of the world. The Governor then gave a toast to the King. He declared that the British power protected rather than injured or absorbed well-regulated States; there had been trifling incidents in the relations of her Majesty's kingdom with the Sandwich Islands, in past years, such as the killing of Captain Cook by his Majesty's predecessor, on one of his islands, and a British captain had once captured the group and deposed the king in the name of the British Queen; but he had quickly restored it, and the British government was the first to propose that the Great Powers should recognise and protect the independence of that kingdom, for it was for the interests of commerce that it should be free from any foreign control.

The King replied by thanking the Governor, who, in the name of the Queen, had tendered to him such gracious hospitality. He said that he did not make speeches, but that there was with him a Minister who had been commissioned to speak for him. Upon this his Minister said that the King and his suite recalled a day in the year 1842, when a British sloop-of-war, the " Carysfort," seized the Hawaiian Islands, and annexed them to the British possessions.

For three months the king and his suite had been British subjects, but were extremely disloyal. At the end of that period the British admiral voluntarily restored the islands to the native sovereign. The British had originally interfered with the islands by directing Captain Cook to "discover" them; but he had exceeded his instructions, for after he had discovered them he permitted the natives to worship himself as a long-lost god, by means of which he had secured pigs, chickens, and vegetables. But disputes had arisen, and the native King, in order to test his divinity, had stricken him with a club, and the experiment was fatal. This was therefore a unique case of a monarch without breeches committing a breach of international law; it was a serious question and had never been decided by the publicists. Captain Cook had personified a god, and had obtained pigs and chickens by doing so. By the law of England it was a criminal offence for one person to personify another for gain, but in the vast literature of the law, from the Roman Pandects down, there was not a single instance of a case where a man had been charged with falsely personifying a god, as Captain Cook had done. The British government, in spite of the death of the great navigator, had been generous, and refused to make war on the early kings of Hawaii; the relations of the two countries had been friendly. In 1810 the celebrated King Kamehameha employed a British sailor, named Campbell, to aid him in shipbuilding. The sailor told the King about George III, his own sovereign. The King asked if George III ever went to war. Campbell replied that he did. "Tell him," said the King, "as soon as you reach home, that if he gets

into any more wars I will go over and help him."
Now, two years after this kind and kingly offer was
made, George III went to war with the American
nation. But not a single historian, either English
or American, has alluded to this neglect of an offer
which might have enabled the British to destroy
the American navy. The King was now about to
visit some of the British colonies, and he hoped to
meet some of the statesmen who had made British
rule in distant lands wise and safe.

After this luncheon the party returned to Hongkong, where, in the Government House, the King
received the calls of a number of Chinese merchants
who traded with the people of his islands. Many
thousands of coolies had emigrated from this place,
to serve as labourers on the sugar plantations, and
although they were of the lowest class in China a
number of them had acquired wealth in Hawaii and
had not been treated unjustly. These merchants
told the King that their countrymen in his kingdom
were entirely loyal to his government.

During our brief visit we saw the attractive features of the place. It is located, however, behind a
mountain, so that it is cut off from the cooling
winds.

At the two grand State banquets which swiftly
followed each other, the dishes, the service, and the
wines were such as are found on an English table
in London; but coolies patiently pulled the punkas
which stirred the lifeless air in which, with the heavy
food, one becomes drowsy. There were present
admirals, generals, noted citizens, and fine-looking
Chinamen, who did not show the "childhood"
which De Quincey declared was their condition.

This port was the feeding-ground of the commercial ducks of the trading nations; migrating here for profit, as the northern birds fly to the tropics for food. Not one of these guests, excepting the Chinese, had a " home " here, but although these men came and left, and were succeeded by others of their kind, there remained enduring and solid the British power, which maintained law and order and made it the largest free port of the world excepting London.

I must preserve in this memoir an incident of the last banquet. I pray that the King's ghost will not vex me for relating it. The numerous receptions and late hours had deprived the King of sleep. His eyelids drooped, and soon after we were seated I noticed his hand idly held his fork, and his anointed head slightly nodded. The banquet, like all royal banquets, was without wit or hilarity; a monotonous decorum pervaded the chamber. The Governor's wife was seated on the King's right, and I was seated next to her. I feared a nasal explosion if the King's doze should deepen, and devised several ways of preventing it. It was a case of emergency. I whispered to the Governor's wife what my fears were, and asked her to aid in preventing a loss of royal dignity. She hesitated to break through the divinity which hedges kings, but she saw that a crisis was near. Moving her fan with dexterity, she hit the royal shoulder as if accidentally, and the King opened his eyes. I said, in the native language: —

" Your Majesty, naps are dangerous."

He replied: " It is very hot; how can I get away? "

He glanced up and down the long table to see if his doze had been noticed. But the air was hot, and the food heavy. Within a few moments he quickly dropped his fork again and closed his eyes. The royal dignity was drifting on a lee shore and would soon be on the rocks, and a Crowned Head would be struggling in the breakers. The clever wife of the Governor whispered to me, " Will any special piece of music waken him up? "

I replied, "Only our national anthem; if that does not do it, we are lost."

She quietly called the major-domo, and in a minute the military band in the balcony filled the air with the music of " Hawaii Ponoi." The King woke up. I advised him, afterward, to decorate the lady who had thrown out a life-line which saved the royal dignity from shipwreck.

It is the inexorable rule of courts that guests do not leave a reception-room or table until royalty has withdrawn. I imagined the King falling into a deep slumber in his chair, and the banquet ended; the guests waiting for him to rise; the whisper " His Majesty sleeps; " the final weariness of the guests until they too, bound to their chairs by a remorseless rule, fall asleep also; an admiral slipping from his chair, a diplomat in a wild nightmare, the walking of a somnambulist on the edge of the furniture, and the company in general with lax figures hanging on chairs and table, waiting for the cock's crowing to rouse the sleeping monarch and release them. " Hawaii Ponoi " had " saved our face," as the Chinese say, and we were out of our peril, by the tact of a woman.

From the high balcony of the Government House

we looked down upon the harbour flecked with ships, junks, sampans, and steamers, war and mercantile, great fortresses protecting this commerce, and within the city an Asiatic population of two hundred thousand, of whom hardly three thousand were Englishmen; yet it is the third in importance of British ports. Standing over it, one realised the important relation of this place, with its solid British sovereignty, to the great unknown empire that is divided from it by only a narrow sea. It is more than a great free port. It is the visible and perpetual object-lesson to all China of the advantage of law and order.

It stands for even more than an example of good government. It is the warm sun of Western civilisation in the Far East, the heat of which will slowly melt the edges of this great Asiatic glacier. The European has not studied the Chinaman and knows little about him. He constructs him out of his own interior consciousness, and deals with that fiction as the real man, as Englishmen and Frenchmen have for three hundred years taken each to be, — not what they really are, but what each has imagined the other to be. Whatever the Chinese are, they will be reformed or reconstructed from within, and not from without, as the Japanese have reformed themselves. The influence of Christendom, sorely needing vast reformation itself, will have no more power over the masses of Chinese than a stream of water from a three-inch pipe would have in increasing the volume of the ocean. The Chinese, of their own accord and in due time, will take true Christianity in their own way, through their own people; least of all will they take it from a nation whose members loudly chant "From Greenland's icy mountains" in their churches, and then, by law, exclude a Christian Chinaman from entering its domains. To the fervent missionary, preaching the vast benefits of Christianity to his own nation, the thinking Chinaman replies: "When your own nation follows the teachings of Christ and does us justice, then come to us!"

CHAPTER XIV

We Sail on the "Killarney" for Siam — The Irish Captain and the German Valet — Cochin-China — The Captain Disturbs the King with Stories of Piracy — Enter Gulf of Siam — Received at Mouth of Menan River by Siamese Officials — Reach Bangkok in the Royal Yacht — The Royal Barge—Our Reception — Siamese Attendants — "The Wine of the Coral Reef."

AFTER four days spent in royal receptions, tiffins, and garden parties, irrespective of barracks and docks, the King, with parades and numerous salutes, embarked on the "Killarney" for Siam.

When the Governor bade him good-bye at the gangway he said to me that the bearing and conduct of the King could not be excelled by any sovereign; and he only voiced the sentiments of the cosmopolitan city of Hongkong. The voluntary expression of gratitude by the Chinese merchants to the King for the justice and the impartial administration of the law in his kingdom was an event of which any king might be proud.

The captain of the "Killarney" was an Irishman, who was astounded when his agent told him that he would have a Crowned Head for a passenger; as astonished as the Yankee skipper whose sloop one morning ran into a Methodist meeting-house, which a flood in the Connecticut River had detached from its foundations and swept into the river and out into the ocean. He cleaned up his cabins, took on board fresh provisions, and received at the gangway, hat in hand, this royal derelict which he had accidentally struck in these remote seas. His cargo was mainly of Chinese provisions in numerous tubs, and if freight had been paid on their odour his voyage would have been a profitable one beyond estimate.

For some days Robert, the valet, had most properly discharged his duties and seemed to be reconciled to his lowly lot. But the Governor's private secretary, a German of great learning, had known his relatives in Prussia and verified his claim to be the Baron von O————. Before we embarked Robert had indulged overmuch. While the King and suite were standing on the after deck of the steamer, watching the smoke from the saluting guns of the shipping and forts as it floated away in dense clouds, we heard contention below. As the captain was his own purser, steward, and executive officer, he had assigned a berth to Robert which displeased him, for the accommodations were small. Thereupon Robert had made some comments on the captain's Irish origin, and the captain in return had used some picturesque language in regard to the " damned Dutchman." This controversy interrupted our meditations over the fading splendours of our farewell to Hongkong; instead, therefore, of filling our breaking hearts with noble sentiments, which the occasion richly deserved, we turned to this sudden and domestic disturbance below. The Chamberlain, who was the supervisor of our domestic affairs, at once went below and interceded with the belligerents. The captain was easily pacified, but Robert was disposed to assert his patrician privileges. Whereupon the Chamberlain declared that he had shipped as valet, and as we were on the high seas he was liable to be placed in irons and kept in the hold for disobedience. Robert had also a grievance against the Chamberlain. It was his business to look after the luggage of the party, and in doing so he employed persons at various times to aid him. In the early part of the voyage the Chamberlain had supplied him with funds to compensate such men; but he had not done so for some time, because the valet had expended the cash in treating himself with spirits. Robert, therefore, had failed on several occasions to tip the baggage-tenders, and had been addressed by some of them in profane pidgin-English: "You no top-side man — go hellee!" (The word "top-side" is the equivalent of "distinguished" or "celebrated.")

We now cruised along the coast of Cochin-China, a place from which came formerly a large and most ungainly fowl, and in later years became a sink-hole into which the French nation poured vast treasures in the creation of a colony. We passed Saigon, where the spectacular French colony exhibits a Roman Catholic Cathedral, a garrison of soldiers whose occupation is to tread upon the toes of the Chinese, and a trading-post where Parisian perfumes are on sale to a people who prefer the smell of their own malodorous sauces and aromatic joss-sticks.

The Irish captain entertained his royal passenger with accounts of his former voyages in these waters, on several of which, some years previously, he had engaged in combat with Malay pirates. He recited the story of some devilish acts committed on the captain of a vessel in the waters we were ploughing. His reminiscences greatly pleased the King until he remarked: "If the pirates knew your Majesty was on board this ship, they'd like to take you and get a pretty ransom for letting you go." The King was disturbed. He recalled the " Pautah " and her armaments, and privately charged his suite with a failure to anticipate this danger, and permitting him to be exposed to capture. We were on a vessel with only a Chinese crew, which could make no resistance to any attack, and, though there was remote danger of it, it might be made. The King did not look upon himself as a knight seeking adventures, but a royal bee sucking only the sweets of honours and experience in the meadows of the earth; and now he found himself on an unarmed vessel in waters more or less infested with freebooters. His imagination exaggerated the danger, and he declared that a king should travel only in warships. He had the timidity of a man who is led by his flatterers to believe that his life is more precious than any common lives and that unusual efforts for its preservation should be taken. I suggested to him that if we should pass any warship, signals of distress might be hoisted, and its commander be asked, under the privileges of the comity of nations, to take him on board and bear him to Siam. The suite held a private interview with the romancing captain; after which he greatly modified his tragic stories of the sea. He now assured the King that he could show his heels to any pirate craft that hove in sight; and moreover a pirate crew could smell his cargo at a distance of two miles, and it was not stuff which a pirate wanted. He said that the British gunboats, like terriers chasing rats, followed up the pirates so closely that few dared to attack vessels in these waters.

On the fourth day after leaving Hongkong, we entered the Gulf of Siam and anchored at the bar of the Menan River. Our kingdom had no treaty with that of Siam, and therefore no diplomatic representative there, so we expected no courtesy from its government. We suspected that its government did not know of the existence of Hawaii, or, if it did, it placed it in the schedule of " remote and unknown lands " of which even an intelligent Siamese might be justly ignorant. We had the address of a hotel-keeper, and through him his Majesty hoped to get a distant glance at the white elephants, of which we had heard, and then leave for Singapore. We engaged a steam tug, which was cruising on the bar, to take our party to Bangkok, twenty miles above. As we neared the customs office, a steam yacht rapidly approached, above which was flying the royal standard of Siam. She rounded under the tug's quarter, and the inquiry was made: " Is the King of the Sandwich Islands on board? " When an affirmative reply was given, the yacht came alongside, and five officials in full uniform came on board and asked to be presented to the King. After the presentation, one of them, who spoke English, said they had been commanded by the King of Siam to receive his Majesty and ask him to become his guest. The royal assent was of course given, and we were transferred to the royal yacht. The Siamese Consul in Hong-kong had written to his government that the King of Hawaii was the guest of the British Queen in that place and intended to leave shortly in the " Killarney " for Siam. It was therefore decided by the Siamese court that the King, whoever he was, was entitled to the full measure of Siamese hospitality. The yacht was an English model, richly furnished, with the yellow colour most prominent. Upon the

open deck, under an awning, a European luncheon
was served. As we passed up the river, with forests
of tall cocoanut palms on either hand, we cried out,
"This is Hawaii," with the fervour of the sailor
who, after a long voyage, exclaimed, "Home at last,"
when he saw a solitary grog-house on the beach, for
we were inveterate drinkers of the water of the
young cocoanut, and we hoped that the royal hospitality would cheerfully discharge showers of nuts
on us.

As we passed the forts a royal salute was fired,
and we had hardly dropped anchor in the river which
divides the city when the royal barge moved out from
the landing toward the yacht. It was long and narrow, with upturned prow and stern. Twenty-four
oarsmen manned it, and they kept time to the shrill
"Hoot! Hoot!" of the steersman, by dipping their
paddles and raising them high in the air. Its stern-
sheets were covered with a canopy ornamented with
yellow silk and gold embroidery, and the royal
standard of Siam floated above it. We entered it,
and at the landing carpets were laid from the edge
of the water to a street near by, where a battalion
of troops was drawn up, with naked feet, and in
rather musty uniforms. We entered the royal carriages, which were driven by coachmen dressed in
red and gold cloths lined with yellow, and covered
with unbrushed silk hats; their legs and feet were
naked. An escort of cavalry, mounted on small
horses which resented discipline, surrounded the
carriages. We entered the court-yard of the palace
of one of the Princes, which had been assigned to
us. It was a large building with numerous rooms,
the ceilings of which were high. The furniture was

rich, but a mixture of English, Chinese, Japanese, and Siamese styles, besides articles made from rare native woods. Around the palace was a large garden, well kept, with abundance of native plants and flowers. From the windows of our apartments we saw the forest of Buddhist temples, which numbered over five hundred, where the people carry on with indomitable indolence the chief industry of the place, the worship of Buddha. The chewing of the betel-nut, with the monotonous and everlasting repetition of the word " Buddha," is a devotion suited to these lazy people, who raise their heads above the waters of sin, according to the Faith, by this interminable repetition of " Buddha ! "

As soon as we entered the palace, several Princes, in which the kingdom is fertile, called; and we noticed that the etiquette was mainly European with some native modifications. Several of the Princes spoke the English language; some of them had travelled in Europe, but the inferiority of the race in comparison with the Chinese and Japanese was very evident. An officer of the King's household arranged an interview between the Kings on the following day, as we were tired and it was late.

Retiring to our apartments, we found that eight body-servants had been assigned to the King, and five to each of the suite. These were young men of good families, who were honoured with such appointment; but they were entirely ignorant of foreign ways and spoke only their own native language. An officer who spoke English, however, supervised them and acted as interpreter.

I found myself helpless in their hands. Their conception of duty to the Minister of a foreign State was to anticipate and supply every want, but they had grotesque notions of the nature of his wants. When I washed my face they surrounded me; one held a towel, another thrust soap at me, another brought a comb and brush before they were needed, another held my coat, still another my trousers if I desired to change them; all of them were bowing, standing in my way, and smoking cigarettes. I sat down to enter notes in my journal; one of them held the ink-bottle, another handed me a pen, another held the blotter, and another pushed note-paper toward me with one hand and held envelopes in the other. My directions and pantomimes were not understood. I opened my trunk; immediately one took out my diplomatic uniform, another my sword, another my cocked hat, and they stood in line holding them before me and unable to see that I wished to hang them up. I could not get rid of them; they hounded me most respectfully. When I retired late in the evening, the squad of five were fast asleep on the sofas and chairs in my chamber, while my clothing, boots, and hats had been carefully placed on the bed itself. In the arms of one who gently slept was a tray upon which was a bottle of champagne and one of whiskey.

We all thirsted for the water of the cocoanut. I drew a rude picture of the cocoanut palm on a piece of paper, making the fruit most prominent, and pointed to it. After smoking cigarettes and discussing the object of the drawing, one of them suddenly grasped the idea. At once they all rushed away. Within half an hour there was a huge pile of cocoanuts in the palace yard, enormous and young, with delicate, pulpy meat and the most delicious water. I informed the King, and for the first time on our tour we drank the " wine of the coral reef " as we drank it in the King's little summer palace near his own capital, on " the green sward which endeth in the ocean's blue." The valet managed to get our numerous attendants to leave the chamber, and the King sang in a minor key a native Hawaiian *mele* (song) about the water, which in the old days was sacred to the chiefs and the priests. In this Siamese Babylon we, voluntary exiles, sang a pathetic song of the far tropical Jerusalem, its forests of cocoa palms, and its fruit shells bursting with the waters of life.

CHAPTER XV

THE next morning one of the Princes took us
to one of the pagodas. The priests, with
shaven heads, but with scant clothing, being stripped
for prayer, chanted " Buddha! Buddha! " The huge
image of the god, with the unchangeable smile of
centuries, patiently sat on the lotus-flowers and listened, and seemed to say, as we passed him, " For
a thousand years they have talked me to death; I
am weary; this is not Nirvana." Though this faith
is barnacled with superstitions, it is still a scaffolding which at least holds the worshippers above the
earth, and, like all of the great religions, is so
weighty with lofty moral precepts that if these were
realised in the lives of their worshippers even Christendom would not make haste to offer its supreme
code of life.

Many thousands of the Siamese are born, live, and die in the frail houses which stand on light rafts near the banks of the Menan River, which divides the city. The effect of this life, and its modifications of the anatomy, the hands and feet of these aquatic residents, has not been studied by the biologists. If, according to Darwin, the environment moulds and shapes the physical faculties of all creatures, these should finally become web-footed, as Captain Younghusband says the legs of certain Tartar tribes are lengthened by their perpetual riding in the saddle. We did not, however, observe any serious modifications of the feet, or rudimentary fins on their backs, from which it may be inferred that we were not competent biologists, or that Darwin and his followers are fabulous writers.

At four o'clock the next day, in the State carriages with the nude-legged drivers, and escorted by a company of cavalry, we drove to the royal palace, which was in a park of about ten acres. A regiment of infantry lined up in the court-yard. From the carriage steps to the palace entrance the way was carpeted in red. On both sides of the entrance, members of the royal household were massed in rich, and some of them in rather grotesque, uniforms. Close to the door were ten venerable men with bare legs, but richly dressed above, each holding an ancient battle-axe. Passing the entrance, the King of Siam, Souditch Chow-fa-Chulan Korn, stepped forward and greeted the King of Hawaii in the English language. Receiving the suite, the Siamese King, walking abreast of his Hawaiian Majesty, passed through a number of rooms to his audience-chamber, a large room richly furnished

with European carpets, sofas, and chairs. Upon
its walls were portraits of Siamese sovereigns, and
many busts of foreign sovereigns were on pedestals.
The Siamese King hesitated to use the English language, and talked mainly through an interpreter.
He inquired earnestly how the King of Hawaii
spoke English with fluency; no person of his court,
he said, and many of them had lived in England,
spoke with like fluency. "Did all of the King's
subjects also speak English?" he asked. Our King
repeated his reply to like inquiries made in other
countries: that he had learned the English language
in his youth, and that a large proportion of his subjects could speak it also, for it was taught in the
public schools.

The Siamese King had a pleasant face and bright,
black, intelligent eyes; his manners were simple;
he was educated in European literature, and, as an
amateur, made experiments in chemistry. He had
also studied the political science of Europe, but he
said in a regretful tone that he found it most difficult to change the inveterate customs and ideas of
his subjects. They were contented to remain without progress, and had no desire to make money beyond their daily needs. He asked the Hawaiian
King if his people liked to work, and if they had
many industries. Now, these monarchs ruled over
equally thriftless and lazy people; but the Hawaiian
King hesitated to tell the truth about his own people.
He admitted that they did not manufacture anything,
but they were known to be good sailors. The Siamese King asked if his people built large pagodas,
such as he had seen in the city. As the limit of
Hawaiian sacred architecture had been the erection

of *heiaus,* or simple platforms of stone surrounded by rude fences, structures hardly beyond the capacity of a beaver, the King replied that foreigners had introduced new styles of church architecture. The Siamese King asked what was the old religion of his subjects.   Here again the Hawaiian King hesitated to say that the religion of his subjects had been wiped out, as it would be an admission that it was a useless affair.   So he replied that his government encouraged the worship of all religions, and he did not restrict his people in their choice of worship. The Siamese King said that this was very good.

While the monarchs were seated and conversing, the courtiers with the King's suite stood in most respectful silence.   Suddenly two cats, with piercing wails, went at each other on the roof of a building which adjoined the palace.   In this Buddhistic realm they no doubt held the reincarnated souls of dead Siamese warriors, who had taken this hour to settle an ancient feud.   The dignity of the royal reception was disturbed for several minutes and until the cats finished their duel.

The young Siamese King knew the geographical arrangement of islands in the Pacific Ocean.   He had been informed, he said, of the future importance of the kingdom of Hawaii.   He asked the King if he had trouble with foreigners.   We afterward learned that the two white men in the King's suite, instead of natives, suggested to him a disagreeable dominance of the white race.   He was surprised at the large stature of his Hawaiian Majesty and asked to what race he belonged.   When he was told that there was Malay blood in the Hawaiians, he replied, "The Siamese are partly Malay; we are related."

He asked his Royal Brother to remain in the country, to visit the interior; there would be an elephant-hunt if he desired it. He had never been visited by a brother sovereign, and he said he had commanded his officials to gratify the wishes of his great guest. These offers of hospitality were declined, owing to the brevity of our stay, but an invitation to a royal banquet was accepted. As we left the court-yard we looked upon the gloomy and ancient buildings which stood around it. What was the unwritten history of intrigues, tragedies, assassinations, for hundreds of years, which these walls could tell if they were phonographs!

We called immediately on the second King. There were formerly five official kings, who in theory were ready to supply any failure in the succession, but they were persistently "getting between one another's legs" and devising schemes for killing one another. There were now only two kings; it was the business of the second King to assist nature in bringing the life of the ruling King to an end. The present dual system in Siam was satisfactory, and had not been disturbed by any atrocious ambition on the part of the second King.

The second King was a quiet, fine-looking man, who gave himself up to the study of astronomy and recent political history. He asked for a history of Hawaii. He had been reading Professor Wallace's "Malay Archipelago." He said that all of the Polynesians belonged to the Malayans, and some of them were very good people. The Siamese were, he said, unequal to either the Chinese or Europeans in the making of good articles; they could not use iron.

We now called on the uncle of the Siamese King,

and then returned to our pleasant quarters, where we at once ordered more " wine of the coral reef."

In the evening we were taken in the royal barge, with its stately and rhythmical uplifting of long paddles, down the Menan river to the residence of the Minister of Foreign Affairs. The banquet was served entirely in European style.

The Minister was a man of remarkable intelligence, with a mind open to Western ideas; but the Siamese guests lacked the quick perceptions of the Japanese and Chinese.

Before entering the dining-chamber servants brought in trays filled with bracelets of jessamine, and these were placed around the arms of the guests. Scented bouquets were also placed in their hands. This custom has prevailed among the Hawaiians from immemorial time, but although we had now travelled many thousands of miles, it was not until we approached the Malay peninsula that we found it in use elsewhere. In regions where flowers are perpetual it naturally prevails. In the colder latitudes it would be an intermittent practice.

From the balcony of the Minister's residence we looked over the city on the river, a floating city, as far as we could see. Beyond the river were the one-storied buildings extending far inland, with innumerable temple spires rising beyond them. One of the guests in a whisper pointed to the place where the late Queen of Siam, the favourite wife of the King, had, with her child, been drowned the previous year, near the shore, by the upsetting of her barge by collision. No common person, of the many thousands who stood on the river bank, dared to touch the sacred person of her Majesty, though she was struggling in the water but a boat's length from the shore. The divinity which hedges royalty was not a life-preserver, and both she and her child were lost. The next day we visited the spot where their bodies were cremated. Upon it was erected a lofty pagoda of precious sandal-wood. Within it had been placed the bodies, and the incense from it, as it burned, filled the city with its fragrance. The cost of the ceremony of cremation, with that of the large quantity of sandal-wood, is said to have been above half a million dollars.

We were given the rare privilege, which had also been given to General Grant, to see the interior of the royal chapel, and the chambers in which the Siamese King fasted and prayed before his coronation. In this superbly ornamented building stood a lofty image of Buddha with jewelled eyes, and on a frame before it were artificial flowers in festoons and studded with diamonds; but they were dusty, for custom permitted them to be cleaned but once a year. Near this royal pagoda were six others, in one of which was an allegorical painting of the King's life from his childhood. In all of them were the great statues of Buddha, with large and dark lidless eyes perpetually staring into vacancy. When we entered these temples the Princes knelt, clasped their hands, and bowed three times.

We returned to our palace to receive the return call of the Siamese King. Following him came the second King, who appeared in a palanquin over which there was an enormous umbrella of red cloth with gold embroidery. He alighted about fifty feet from the entrance to our residence. Etiquette forbade his conveyance to stop where the first King had alighted. He therefore footed it the rest of the way. After he had retired, the Cabinet Ministers called, and after them the Consular Corps, of which General Haldeman, the American Consul, was a conspicuous member. He rendered the King and suite some valuable services during their short stay.

The second King asked, during his visit, when he heard that I was an American, whether the people of America read much about the Siamese. I replied that all of the children were taught in the public schools the geography of his country. I did not state that which I believe is true, that the people of America believe that the principal product of Siam is white elephants and Siamese Twins, while the religious portion of the community regard the inhabitants as " perishing heathen." On the other hand, the second King admitted that the Siamese believed the Americans to be wandering tribes and outcasts; a people who did not chew the betel-nut must be without pleasures.

The royal elephants were then brought to the door; they were not white, but grey, and were covered with splendid trappings. We mounted them by ladders, the King riding on a magnificent animal exclusively used by the King of Siam. Our Chamberlain, with his great weight, broke the ladder as he was mounting, and dangled in the air, with a firm grip on the seat, until another ladder was brought, while the elephant grunted at the mishap of a " tenderfoot."

In the evening a play was presented in a small theatre of one of the Princes; to this only persons of the court were admitted. Twelve girls, six of them representing males, danced and sang to Siamese music. They belonged to the harem of the Prince

Invitation to dine with the King of Siam.

and were noted for their beauty and shape; they were not seen in public. The play was mainly in pantomime; closely fitting dresses covered with spangles showed their graceful figures, and the posturing was the very poetry of motion. At times they sang while in the convolutions of the dance, but their mouths were ugly cavities which the chewing of the betel-nut had blackened. Suddenly we heard a familiar piece, one of the old hymns of Christendom. In a " pagan " theatre twelve graceful followers of Buddha stepped the measures of a Siamese dance, while they sang words which they did not understand:

> " Keep your lamps all trimmed and burning,
> For the midnight bride is coming."

A Siamese Prince who had lived in England said that the music-teacher of these girls had heard this hymn sung in India by converts of the missionaries, and had taught it to these women of the harem.

The steamer " Bangkok," on which we had taken passage for Singapore, was detained a day, by order of the Siamese King, so that we might attend a banquet in his palace.

We again entered the court-yard, the sides of which were lined with troops; over them was the weird light of innumerable torches. We walked over the carpeted pavements to the entrance, the Princes accompanying us, and following was a body of candlestick-bearers with naked legs and fantastic dresses tinged with yellow. The Siamese King received us and led us to the audience-chamber, and the band played the Hawaiian national anthem, the music of which our King had written out the previous day, and had played on a piano to the band-master. The Siamese King, in a soft, pleasant voice, then said he desired to honour the King from the Pacific islands, and placed on him the insignia of the " Grand Cross of the Order of Siam; " he then turned to me and to the Chamberlain and gave to each of us the insignia of Knight Commander of the same Order. Our King, in return, conferred on the Siamese King the Order of Kamehameha, and on the Princes the same Order, of a lesser degree, the insignia of which would be sent from Paris.

The heavy silver of the banqueting-table was in-wrought with trees and plants of gold; special glasses mounted with jewels stood before the Kings; the dishes and the service of them, as well as the wines, were European. The Hawaiian King asked for typical Siamese music from the military band, and detected in it a resemblance to the music of his own people.

One of the Princes, by whose side I sat, plied me with questions about Hawaii: " Is your King in the hands of foreigners? " — " Why does he not bring his own people with him, instead of white men? " — " Does he do what you tell him to do? " I suspected that the court gossip assumed that the King was under some foreign protectorate. Softly the little skeleton in our closet rattled as the King of Siam asked his guest, " How large is your army? " The reply spread a fog over the subject, which was deftly changed.

Near the close of the banquet the durien was served. It is the most delicious fruit of the tropics, but, when opened, yields a most offensive odour; as the delicate roses spring from the rottenest manure.

Returning to the audience-chamber, wreaths of jessamine were placed about our necks; those about the King's being arranged by the hands of the Siamese King. Some valuable presents were given to us. We visited the jewel-room, full of rare stones. When the Kings were again seated, the plaintive music of the native voices rose from an invisible choir concealed by screens at the end of the great chamber. These Asiatic nightingales were female members of the royal household, who sang in a minor key the joyless songs which pervade Asia and Oceanica; the expression of races without mental or moral freedom. One rarely hears comic songs among the races which are superstitious.

The monarchs bade each other good-bye. The Siamese King said that his royal guest was most fortunate in ruling a good people who were quiet while he was absent; he wished, above all things, to visit Europe and America, but he was unable to leave his people. If he had ventured to talk frankly he would have said he could not go abroad lest some rival would board his ship of State and seize the helm.

In the morning, photographs of the King and suite were taken by request of the Siamese King. The party, with the usual ceremony, was then driven to the landing; the royal barge, with the stately movements of its twenty-four oars, brought them to the steamer " Bangkok," and the Princes left us at the gangway. Buddhist priests, on behalf of the Siamese owner of the steamer, passed a white string around her and hung wreaths of flowers in the saloon; kneeling, they clasped their hands in prayer, repeating the name of Buddha many times; then they ate an enormous meal of rice and curry and waddled to their boat. The forts gave their salutes; the five hundred pagodas and the forests of cocoanut palms sank out of sight, and we pointed for Singapore.

In Siam the Chinese are the stronger race; they have already absorbed the business interests of Bangkok and comprise more than a third of the population. Nor are they disturbed, for they are not politicians and engage in no public affairs. They gradually abandon ancestral worship, adhere to some of the forms of their religious beliefs, and are contented to become permanent settlers in the country because they are prosperous.

Christendom is a riddle to the Siamese statesman. He does not understand the missionary. He cannot reconcile the teachings of the Gospel with the conduct of the people from whom he came. The missionary preached a religion which he declared had created the great and powerful nations of Christendom, while the traders and travellers who chiefly represented those nations in these Far Eastern lands displayed vices which shocked the people. But he who attempts to explain to them the consistency of great virtues and great vices which appear in individuals, communities, and nations to work together with harmony, undertakes that which even the subtle mind of the Asiatic cannot comprehend. One of these intelligent Siamese, connected with the Foreign Office, said to me: " Is it true that the civilisation of Europe is due to Christianity?" I replied that this was a difficult question to answer, but that such was the claim of the leaders of the churches. " Then," he inquired, " if Christianity is the cause of European progress, is it also the cause of the fleets and armies with which they are ready to destroy one another?"

We were the sole occupants of the saloon cabins of the steamer. From our upper deck we looked down on indolent Siamese chewing the betel-nut with the satisfaction of goats; on Chinese sitting on clean mats; and on Mohammedans, who squatted about in a listless way, until sunset, when they at once became vigorous and picturesque in their attitudes of prayer and prostration.

The royal hospitality of Siam had filled the steamer's lockers with mangosteens, duriens, and young cocoanuts, on which we mainly fed till we reached the latitude of $1°$ $17''$ north of the equator.

CHAPTER XVI

WE rounded the southeastern point of the Malay
peninsula, drew close to the shore, passed
many islands covered with dense vegetation, and
anchored off Singapore, another prominent free port
of Great Britain. Fort Canning and some Russian
warships fired a royal salute; and an aide of Sir
Frederick Weld, the colonial Governor, with the
King's Consul, boarded our steamer with an invitation from the Governor asking the King to become
his guest. But the weather was hot, and the King
preferred the freedom and informality of hotel life.
The invitation to reside in the Government House
was "graciously" declined. The poet who dreamed
that he "dwelt in marble halls" was never a king,
or the minister of a king. It is said in every court
that "the king does as he pleases," but the fact is
that he is like a chained animal, which has large freedom within the limits of his chain. The Grand Lama

of Thibet has absolute power and does as he pleases within limits, but his life of sacred splendour is a chain which keeps him in a narrow circle of perpetual ceremonies, and binds him to many monotonous and irksome sittings upon a golden throne. Though his legs become weary and his back aches, he cannot relieve his fatigue by a game of leap-frog. Stronger than the will of a sovereign is the etiquette which traditions and customs make for him. Those who know the inner history of courts know the efforts of princes and kings themselves to escape at times from their monotonous environments.

We therefore, in this place, took lodgings in a hotel, where we were entirely free from the strain of ceremonies and attendants. This disposition, however, may have been due to our fresh and wild natures, which had not been sufficiently subdued by contact with civilisation.

The Governor's carriage, however, took us in the afternoon to the Government House, where troops in white uniforms and white helmets lined the courtyard. The Governor received the King at the entrance and led us up a very wide stairway, on the steps of which guards were standing with muskets, and into the drawing-room, which was decorated with flowers. There we met the Governor's wife and daughter. The Governor had many years before visited the King's islands and studied their volcanic formation. With fine humour he related an incident of his experience in the Hawaiian Parliament which happened while he listened to a debate. The King's immediate predecessor, Lunalilo, was known, until he reached the throne, as "Prince Bill," and he was a member of the House of Nobles. Though he was a pure native he spoke the English language with ease, and invariably used it when tipsy, as I have before said. He disliked the reigning King, and in this debate he shook his finger at the palace, shouting: "Uneasy is the 'bloody' head that wears a crown!"

The heat in the large reception-room was intense, for the air about the seaport was saturated with moisture. The perspiration, owing to our heavy uniforms, streamed down within our clothing, and the only relief was in shortening the visit. We returned to the hotel, and within an hour the Governor, in a State carriage, returned our visit.

In the evening we drove through the city, which is situated on an island, which, through the wise policy of Sir Stamford Raffles, the British had bought without conquest. Here were a few British and German traders; a large population of Chinese, who were the leading traders, many of them men of great wealth, and not distressingly devoted to ancestral worship; here were Klings from southern India, Malays, Japanese, Arabs, Papuans, Mohammedans, Hindoos, and Parsees; Chinese joss-houses, Buddhist temples, and Christian churches. But over all these people of many races, over the vast commerce flowing into and out of this free port, stood the British power, silent and omnipotent, itself the colossal missionary in the Orient, enforcing law and order with its armaments, and holding the millions of implacable haters of one another's religions from one another's throats. Singapore is not a missionary station, but it is in fact the most stupendous of missionary enterprises, though it appears to have no god but Trade. Here the ideas of Occidental civilisation slowly spread throughout the many races and tribes which meet in commerce at these cross-ways of Asia, of which this port is the central point.

In the morning the Governor took us in his drag over one of the fine roads of the island, which is formed of many small hills, between which are dense jungles infested with tigers. It is said that over three hundred persons are killed by these beasts every year in this island. We alighted at the waterworks. While looking over the jungle from the embankment, the Governor pointed to a spot near by and naïvely said, "By the way, there is a beast of a tiger in that jungle, but he does n't attack white men." This discrimination in colour caught the King's ear. I noticed that he was uneasy, and he soon suggested that we should return. On the homeward drive he closely watched the jungle. With pirates on the sea, and tigers on land, he was "sucking" much experience of the world.

The State banquet in the evening, with its many guests, its military band, the white uniforms of the Sikh guards, the dead air stirred by the punkas, was a fair scene of British life in the tropics. The men looked tired, and the women had lost their colour. Every one longed for vacation days in England and the close of colonial life. But at this banquet, and in all others which we attended until we reached Europe, we found the British living on an unwholesome diet, because their stubborn habits and appetites refused a change to the diet which ages of experience had taught the natives of the tropics is wholesome and healthful. The scholars discuss the question: "Can the European thrive in the tropics?" In these discussions I have not yet seen any consideration given to the fact that it turns largely on the character of food and drink. The European, especially the Englishman, insists on eating, near the equator, the meats which are suitable to the cool temperature of England; as if the Eskimo should ask for whale's blubber right under the sun. The British, as a rule, retire from foreign service in the tropics with impaired health, and charge it to the climate. But wherever we visited I inquired of the physicians the cause of this debility, and the reply without variation was, the refusal of the Europeans to adopt the simple diet of the natives, — a diet of fruit, vegetables, and fish, which does not overload the stomach and excludes the use of alcohol. The European in the tropics, an exile, isolated in a measure, finds his enjoyment in the heavy diet of his fatherland, and declares that life is not worth living if he is fed on the fruits and vegetables which the wealthy classes of the tropics find most suitable. Our own country, Hawaii, is an experimental ground in the life of the Anglo-Saxon in the tropics. The missionaries, forced by necessity into a frugal life, lived on the diet of the natives and were never debilitated by the climate. The majority of them retained the energy of their New England inheritance without the least impairment due to climate. But their descendants, under financial prosperity, reversed the ways of plain living followed by their fathers, and the evidence of deterioration is becoming apparent.

The Governor toasted the King at this banquet. He said that he had seen many of the Polynesian races, and their good nature and chivalry were conspicuous among the Maoris of New Zealand, whose language was similar to that of the Hawaiians. He

The Maharajah of Johore (1881).

related that during a civil war the powder of one of
the native forces gave out, and under a flag of truce
the battle was suddenly suspended while a request
was sent to the enemy for an immediate loan of
powder, with the promise to pay for it whenever the
fight was ended; and with a chivalrous regard for
this misfortune the request was at once granted.

His Highness Sri Abu Bakar, the Maharajah of
Johore, a kingdom under the British protectorate,
invited the King to visit him, and we left in his
steam yacht, the " Pantie," for his domain, distant
fourteen miles from Singapore, and divided from it
by the Straits of Salat-Jabras. Breakfast was served
on the upper deck of the yacht, under a broad awning. In this equatorial region the cocoanut palms
have their most luxurious growth; forests of these,
close to the margin of the sea, stretched for many
miles, with villages of native huts grouped on the
shore. A royal salute was fired as we touched the
stone landing, from which the ground rose in broad
terraces to the summit of a hill on which the
grand palace of the Maharajah stood. The Sultan's
brothers, Turkus Abdul Medjid and Abdulla, received us, and led us over the pier, upon which a
lofty and graceful bamboo structure had been raised
and covered with flowers and flags. The long flight
of wide stone steps rising gradually to the *istana,*
or palace, was lined with carpets; on either side
native troops were ranged in line. In front of our
party marched a body of Malays in brilliant native
costumes, bearing long spears and swords, and wearing red fezzes on their heads. In front of all, striding
alone, was the bearer of an enormous sword sheathed
in a gold-mounted scabbard; and directly behind

us another bore an immense red umbrella of state, trimmed heavily with gold lace. At the grand entrance to the *dewan* or reception-room the Maharajah received us, taking the King's hand cordially; the Sikh guards presented arms; the courtiers bowed; and the Kings stepped on a daïs, where they sat and talked. The King's suite was presented to the Maharajah; and the principal Malay chiefs, the high government officers, were then presented to the King. Outside of the palace, on the wide lawns, crowds of natives, in their gay sarongs, chewing betel-nut, sat on their heels, watching for a sight of the foreign King of their own colour.

From the *dewan* we were led to the palace itself, which was a new and magnificent building with a frontage of three hundred feet. Adjoining the reception-room was a large ball-room. The ceilings of both were lofty; and the architecture of the whole was a contrivance to avoid the use of glass, but with shades to exclude the hot air. The furniture of these imposing rooms was chiefly French, English, and Japanese, but without that delicate arrangement which a more highly civilised people than the Malayans usually make.

From the reception-room led broad, high, and airy corridors which opened into many suites of apartments. Mine were three large rooms, twenty feet above the ground. In the corner of the sleeping-chamber there was a gilded spiral stairway leading to a large bath-room underneath it, with tiled floors, in the centre of which stood an enormous marble bath-tub; each apartment had a similar bath-room beneath it. The water, pure as crystal, did not flow through faucets, but gushed through marble troughs, bubbling and dashing in the great marble basins, in which one could almost swim.

Malay servants, in yellow livery and picturesque hats, stood at the door of each apartment; the clapping of the hands brought them to us, but our communications were mainly in pantomime. Here, as everywhere in the Orient, if the servant does not understand you, he is confident that you wish brandy and soda, or champagne, and promptly brings it.

The King was now visiting the monarch of a kindred race, and he once more tried to get an " effect " through the Feather Cloak. He did not consult the suite, but again warned his titled valet against the sin of intemperance and directed him to carry the cloak with dignity and sobriety. As we stepped from the Maharajah's yacht the valet appeared in evening dress, white gloves, a white helmet, and the gorgeous cloak over his shoulders. The display was effective, but the Maharajah's officers at once assumed that he was a person of high rank and placed him in the royal procession. The King had forgotten this probable complication and directed the valet to follow in the rear. He fell back some distance, but the Malay attendants, believing still that he held some superior position, made up a procession of minor officials, and the valet stalked in the centre of them up to the grand reception-room; in the mean time the luggage with which he was charged remained on the yacht.

The bright and unique cloak caught the eye of the Maharajah; he asked to have it brought to him. After admiring it, he inquired about the rank of persons entitled to wear it in the King's country. The King replied, " Only the highest chiefs." The Maharajah then asked the rank of the white man who now wore it. The King was again in trouble, but, after hesitating a moment, replied that on certain State occasions a servant carried it for his chief. The Maharajah asked the King if his people did not make beautiful articles, and were they as skilled as the Japanese. The King modestly said that his subjects were an agricultural people, who had made little progress in the arts.

At tiffin the Maharajah, placing the King on his right and myself on his left, asked about the origin of the Polynesians; he had heard that they were originally Malays, and if so there should be words common to both languages. We thereupon entered into comparisons, which were striking, such as Malayan, *api,* for fire; in Hawaiian, *ahi:* Malayan, *muta,* for eye; in Hawaiian, *muka:* Malayan, *alima,* for five; in Hawaiian, *lima:* in Malayan, *dua,* for two; in Hawaiian, *alua.* The similarity of many words suggests a common origin for the two peoples; but the ethnologists hold that this is not conclusive, — that it may be only an indication of mutual commerce in past ages.

These ethnological " strawberry marks " placed the rulers on good terms with each other, and they were not unwilling to assume that this meeting was one of " long-lost brothers."

During the afternoon we were driven about the superb grounds of the palace, through groves of the many-rooted banyan-trees, the holy waringham, long rows of the brilliant *Victoria regia,* past innumerable palms and ferns, and through a profusion of orchids.

In the evening the Maharajah's yacht returned from Singapore with about seventy guests invited to a State banquet, — consuls, British colonial officers, merchants, and naval commanders.

The Maharajah wore a small fez cap, on the front of which was a crescent in diamonds, and an enormous diamond star in its dip; he also wore a collar of diamonds, and diamond bracelets, while his breast was covered with jewelled Orders; even the buttons of his coat were large diamonds, and the handle and scabbard of his sword were jewelled with precious stones. My own humble diplomatic sword was a poor relation beside his magnificent weapon.

The table service was heavy gold-plated ware. Arabic characters were engraved on each piece; their cost was surely enormous.

Although there was a large variety of European wines, and the Europeans drank freely, the Maharajah, who was a Mohammedan, did not taste them. When he drank to the health of his royal guest he merely touched the glass with his lips. Our King said to him, " You do not drink wine? " He replied, " No, our faith forbids; it is bad to drink; the Europeans do not live long in our climate when they drink too much." Then he added, " You must eat our curry; we Malays are fond of it." It was brought in golden bowls filled with rice, followed by more golden bowls with varieties of meats and vegetables, and thirty different condiments served in lacquer dishes.

The Maharajah, at the close of the banquet, rose. He spoke the English language with hesitation, and occasionally used an interpreter. Turning to the King, he took his hand and said he would propose his health; he was glad to welcome a King from a land very distant, but one who ruled over the same kind of people as those ruled by himself; he was sorry that he did not speak the English language as well as the King of Hawaii; and he hoped that his royal guest would reach his home in safety and not forget the little kingdom of Johore. The royal Hawaiian replied that he had now discovered that his own people were Asiatics, and he hoped the Asiatic nations would become powerful and stand by one another.

We were then led to the wide marble balcony of the palace, which overlooked the gardens, and the dark forests of the mainland. Over all shone a bright moonlight. A band of Malay voices concealed in the dark foliage sang their plaintive songs; behind us was the vast marble palace with its great corridors filled with light. The Sikh sentries in white turbans paced the avenues, with their polished gun-barrels flashing in the moonlight through the dense foliage. The scene was that which rose before the poet, before alluded to, who had visions of his residence in halls of marble.

The two sovereigns, after repeating some of the legends of what they believed were their common inheritance, became sleepy, and retired to sleep in these marble halls, but not to dream about them. The guests disappeared in the splendid chambers. Guards with drawn swords moved to and fro before the monarchs' chambers, — Malay angels guarding the royal sleepers.

At daybreak the King called his suite to the grand balcony in front of his apartments. Dressed only in pajamas, we rested on soft rugs after bathing in the immense marble fountains. Malay servants, who much resembled our own people, served coffee and mangosteens. As the sun rose, the air was fresh, soft, and tranquil; birds of rich plumage flitted through the dense foliage of the banyan-trees; and beyond the straits were the vast forests of the feathery-headed cocoanut palms. This grand palace, of all we visited in the Orient, was the most conspicuous in its combinations of art and nature, for it stood alone upon high ground, with wide views of water, forests, and gardens.

The Maharajah joined us at tiffin, and after the ceremony of parting in the audience-hall he led the King, through lines of native troops, to the pier, which was still dressed in vines and flowers. He bade his royal guests good-bye, and his yacht carried us over to the main island of Singapore. The Maharajah's drag took us from the landing across the island, over fine roads and past many jungles, upon which the King kept a close eye lest some epicurean tiger, with a depraved taste for dark meat, should bound out of the woods and swallow the Hawaiian dynasty.

On reaching Singapore we called at the Government House and took leave of the Governor.

While we were thus crossing the island in the drag, Robert had been directed to return with the Feather Cloak in the yacht. Left for a time out of his master's sight, he had resolved to magnify his office. On the yacht were several Europeans, who told us that he had greatly impressed the lower Malay officials and servants by occasionally lifting up the cloak and bowing to it, as if it were a sacred emblem. A special guard on the yacht was detailed to protect this precious treasure. Moreover he informed several of the European guests who were on the yacht that he was the Baron von

O———. He despised the Mohammedan precepts regarding abstinence, and by the time he reached the city he forgot the cloak and returned to the hotel without it. When the King discovered the loss he directed search to be made, and it was found on the yacht, strictly guarded by two Malay officers of the Maharajah's household. Robert was again deposed from his high office.

We now embarked on the steamship " Mecca " for Calcutta and way ports. Sir Frederick Weld, with his staff, and many of the Consular Corps, attended the King to the wharf, and he left with the usual royal salutes from warships and forts. The Maharajah of Johore had kindly supplied the steamer with an abundance of tropical fruits, and by his orders the cabins were decorated with wreaths of flowers.

CHAPTER XVII

STEAMING toward Malacca, Mount Ophir, which the legends say was the source of King Solomon's riches, loomed up on the right, its flanks covered, as we approached it, with the glory of an Eastern sky.

The British Resident in Malacca boarded the steamer, and during her brief stay took us to the old cathedral, built by the Portuguese in 1520, taken from them by the Dutch, and again taken from the Dutch by the English, but now abandoned. In a large school building was a mixture of Malay, Chinese, Indian, and European children; all of them learning to read and write the English language; this virile seed of civilisation which the British Power is scattering widely in the Orient. It is the knowledge of this language which, more than any religious propaganda, acts like poison on the superstitions of the races.

At Penang the Lieutenant-Governor, Colonel McNair, received us, drove us to the Government House for tiffin, and, on returning through the avenues of palms and *Victoria regias*, called at the residence of a wealthy Chinaman, whose house, of great size, was so arranged without glass, that, with the turning of lightly made shutters, admirably adjusted, the walls seemed to disappear, and it became a huge birdcage through which the air passed without hindrance. It was fitted with rich furniture, and filled with odours of precious woods.

Into this settlement the Chinese in vast numbers have drifted. They make themselves the masters of trade, and their ties of ancestral worship, which once bound them closely to China, gradually rot with age. They are evidently the coming race of this part of Asia. They need no national flag or gunboats for protection, for above them is British law and order, and the fighting tribes keep the peace. Even the British merchant cannot compete with them, but finds his profit in the carrying-trade and in wholesale commerce. There is no more piracy on the high seas; British warships patrol them, and with blood and iron, if need be, carry the gospel of order wherever a vessel can float. It is said that if a savage pulls a Briton's nose a gunboat appears the next day and avenges the insult.

After a delay of six hours our course was laid for Maulmain. Among the forward passengers was a nautch-dancer with her company. She sent a note to the King by one of the stewards, asking for the honour of dancing before him. A part of this note reads: —

" With due respect and submission I have the honour most respectfully to state that it is my good fortune, and by the mutual Providence of the Almighty, your arrival took place here. I therefore most respectfully do offer myself as a candidate to show my dance, under your Honour."

"EMAMSU JAHU,
"*Dancer Lady.*"

Her attendants arranged a floor by covering the main hatch with embroidered carpets; lanterns were hung in the rigging, and a screen of flags was drawn behind the hatch. The "dancer lady" stepped forward, dressed in a trailing underskirt, over which was a jacket of spangled cloth, with scarfs crossing her breast and silver bells encircling her bare feet. Raising her arms, she moved only her elbows and fingers; stepping forward, she began to posture with the jingling of the bells and her body undulated as in the Hawaiian dances. Her orchestra of four bare-legged Hindus beat a drum with the forefinger and tapped a one-stringed violin. She then prostrated herself before the "Sultan," as she called the King, and concluded with that rite which is common to all nations, of "passing around the hat."

Looking from the saloon deck down upon the forward passengers, one saw the rigid observance of caste among the Hindus; the forms of a stagnant civilisation. One people of one caste ate nothing which was cooked on the steamer, and refused the excellent water provided for the passengers. Rice cakes for another caste, prepared on shore, are carefully kept from profane touch, and water is brought in jars, so that it may not be polluted. One captain said that even the Hindu monkeys observed caste and drank only from certain vessels. Monkeys, he said, were useful labourers; he had seen them gathering cocoanuts from lofty trees inaccessible to man; the master held the end of a long cord, the other end of which was fastened about the monkey's waist; when he reached the bunches of nuts he was guided in his selection by the pulls of the string.

As we steamed into the harbour of Maulmain, for a brief stay, we noticed sawmills on the river bank, and elephants moving the lumber. Here was an opportunity to verify the stories of our childhood's geographies; did the elephant do intelligent work? We asked the captain to send no notice of the King's presence to the British magistrate, so that our brief time might be given to the study of animal intelligence. We quietly landed on the river bank and went to the sawmills, where in a most unregal fashion we sat on a pile of lumber and watched the elephants in the lumber-yard. Upon a working elephant is a saddle occupied by his keeper and driver, who handles a short iron prod. The traces of the harness are heavy chains; with them the elephant draws a log to the platform of the mill; he then turns, places his tusks under one end of it, and raises it to the platform; turning to the other end, he lifts it to its place, using his trunk to prevent its slipping. If the log is not in a correct position, he apparently notes the error, stoops down, places his head or tusks against it, and moves it into its proper place. After the log is sawn, he takes up the slabs with his tusks, and, holding them down with his trunk as if it were a finger, carries them to a rubbish-heap. The sawn lumber or boards he places side by side until he has a load; under it he places his tusks and takes it to a pile, where he deposits it, and squares it into place.

He apparently runs his eye over it, and if it is not straight he adjusts it. This execution of his task apparently shows extraordinary intelligence. But he is always under the direction of his driver, who sits behind his ears and freely uses his prod. The action of the driver may therefore be the real source of the animal's intelligence.

In another instance, however, we noticed that the elephant seemed to employ reason. One of them, while waiting for a job, was irritated by flies on his belly and legs. Reaching out with his trunk, he collected a number of small pebbles. These he threw with dexterity at the flies. Again, taking a long stick, he placed the end of it under his foot and broke off a portion. Grasping the shorter part with his trunk, as one would hold a dagger, he scratched the irritated leg.

While driving through the city of Maulmain we noticed a bridal reception of the lower class in a very humble dwelling. The mother of the bride displayed an enormous brass ring worked through her nose and covering her chin, while silver rings encircled her ankles above her bare feet. The fashion seemed to run among the females of using these large and inconvenient ornaments in the noses, ears, and about the ankles. Our native driver described the marriage ceremony. We halted for a moment before the house and watched the wedding feast.

The King directed the driver to call the bride. She came forward modestly, and the guests followed her to our carriage. The King handed her an English sovereign. She took it, looked at it with surprise, bowed to the ground, and returned to the house with a dowry from a king.

We returned to the steamer, and now were transferred to the steamer " Pemba," which was about to leave for Rangoon and Calcutta. A Sikh soldier, in a white turban, brought a message from Colonel Duff, the Civil Commandant of the province, stating that he had heard of the King's presence and wished to pay him an official visit. He arrived shortly afterward. The King relieved him from embarrassment by stating that he had for the time assumed his incognito character, and he alone was responsible for any neglect to tender civilities to himself.

After leaving Maulmain the steamer anchored for a few hours in the Irrawaddy, at Rangoon. The British Commissioner, Mr. Barnard, took us ashore in his launch, and offered to the King the usual military reception, which he declined; but we had tiffin in the Commandant's residence. We drove to the Buddhist pagodas on the rising ground above the city; the domes of the temples glittered in the sunlight; their large number was the evidence of the thriving condition of Buddhism. By the side of these temples are English houses, English street signs, and everywhere the deep prints of the British trail. In the public schools the English language is taught, and the Burmese children, now British subjects, take Western ideas and learn something of the great nations.

Those who advocate the "emancipation of women" will find in Burmah the most advanced thought. Here it has reached giddy heights, for custom and law decree that a woman shall choose her own husband. I could obtain no explanation of the rise of this practice, which clearly dethrones the sovereignty of man. The men who appeared on the streets did not have an abject look, and it is possible that this reversal of the order of things has promoted domestic happiness. Occasionally we saw men with signs on their foreheads, produced by ochres; these we assumed to be members of the despised class who never had an offer of marriage.

We remained in the Government Residence for one night, and on the next day left for Calcutta. It was the anniversary of the Queen's birthday. All Asia knew it. The wings of the morning had taken the news to the uttermost parts. On the Irrawaddy was the noise of guns, and dense clouds of smoke from salutes, as on the Thames or the Mersey. One reflects that the empire of Alexander the Great was a kitchen-garden in comparison with these vast possessions of the Queen.

The British Commissioner in this place was also a quiet, kind, plainly dressed man, and yet, with the touch of his finger on a button, he could summon fleets and armies. He and the other men of the admirable Civil Service are content to rule millions of people without "squeezing them," as the Chinese say, and in middle life they retire on their pensions to the beautiful homes of England.

A British wag had told the Burmese that the foreign King was a cannibal, and on his departure from home had eaten a fat Chinaman for whom he had paid three hundred rupees. At the landing a large crowd gathered to see one of the anthropophagi, and no doubt the story will pass down for generations, of the appearance in Burmah of this well-dressed man-eater, the sultan of some country beyond the sea, but so renowned that even the British saluted him with many guns.

The steerage or forward deck of the steamer was

occupied by many types of the Eastern races, Chinese, Malays, Mohammedans, and Hindus. The most picturesque character of these was the Mohammedan at his evening prayers; grand in his devotions, but perhaps with a Pharisaical conceit in his own impressive gymnastics. As the Koran forbids him a closet, he takes space wherever he is and fashions an effective environment. An American would say he preferred a five-acre lot for his communion with Allah. As the sun went down in a ball of fire, an Islamite stepped to a clear space on deck and carefully laid down his cheap blanket, slowly adjusted his fez cap, and faced the setting sun, which was in the direction of Mecca. Raising his arms high, he was motionless for a moment; then, slowly kneeling, with his eye fixed on the sun and his lips in motion, he again stood like a statue. He then touched the deck three times with his forehead, and remained in this suppliant attitude while he repeated some ritual. Raising himself again slowly to his full stature, with his eyes closed and his hands clasped on his breast, he stood motionless, muttering his Arabic prayer: "God is great! God is great!" Once more, grandly, gracefully, leisurely, he prostrated himself, rose again slowly, repeated in Arabic, "There is no God but God, and Mohammed is his prophet!" then gathered up his blanket, glanced around at his audience, and "closed the show." Perhaps there was more of heredity than sincerity in his devotions; perhaps his motives were mixed and beyond analysis. Did Longfellow interpret his supplications:

> "Allah gives light in the darkness,
>   Allah gives rest from pain;
> Cheeks that are white with weeping,
>   Allah paints red again."

The Chinese, Hindus, and Malays looked with indifference upon the Mohammedans at their prayers. A century before, these men of different religions would have been at one another's throats, with their intolerance and hatred. But at the masthead was the flag which they all knew too well meant law and order. If it were written in the Gospels, " Go ye and keep the peace among all nations," the British were surely filling the commandment.

We entered the muddy waters of the Hooghly on the third day. As the ocean blue shaded off into the water of the earth-coloured stream, there was a sudden cry from the Hindus on the forward deck, " Ganga! Ganga!" (" The Ganges! The Ganges!") They stretched out their arms toward the sacred river which flows by the sacred city of Benares.

CHAPTER XVIII

BEFORE we were anchored off Calcutta, Mr. Macaulay, a relative of the historian, and one of the Secretaries for the great Province of Bengal, with Mr. Kirch of the Civil Service, boarded our steamer bearing an invitation from Sir Astley Eden, the Governor, to the King, asking him to be his guest at Darjeeling, some distance from the city of Calcutta. At this season of the year the Viceroy removes his residence to Simla, in order to avoid the heat of the plains, and the British residents remove to the mountains. The vice-regal court is also transferred to Simla, and the social life of the court is suspended in Calcutta. As our stay in India would be brief, it forbade our accepting any special hospitality from the Viceroy, though it was cordially tendered. The King was already tired of Oriental life and was anxious to see Europe. He did not take any interest in the great problems of the Orient. The scenes and incidents of the tour were merely toys, and he was now a little tired of them unless he secured decorations of the military Orders, which he could exhibit when he reached home.

We were therefore provided with lodgings in a hotel in the city. The King declined the usual royal salute and a military parade, which were offered. The weather was warm, and he preferred to be in his pajamas. The representatives of the government treated him with much courtesy and maintained as much ceremony about him as he would permit.

These quiet, able, well-trained, and unassuming Englishmen in plain clothing, members of the Civil Service, were the rulers of the sixty millions of inhabitants of the Province of Bengal. They were capable of the vast responsibilities which form the English inheritance in India. The time had passed for the making of vast fortunes out of the people by arbitrary exactions. Indian rulers had now become voluntary exiles from England, who expected, after a sufficiently long and honourable service, to retire to quiet English homes; though if they chose they could be petty despots over two hundred and fifty millions of people. Around our table were seated these strong, incorruptible men, close students of political science, familiar with the native languages. Yet this British rule rested on a mine of physical force which, if the natives knew how to explode it, would not leave a vestige of British power. I asked Mr. Macaulay how fifty thousand British soldiers kept these two hundred and fifty millions in order. He replied, " They cannot agree among themselves; if they did, our rule would end instantly." Caste and religion with these millions is above loyalty to a common country. Mohammedans and Hindus cannot keep step to the same national anthem. The organising brain of the Briton, who knows the force of these racial antagonisms, thus keeps one fifth of the human race in order with little more than a policeman's club. Americans say that their own negro civilisation is one of the chief problems of the century. The eight millions of American negroes speak the English language, outwardly conform to Christian doctrine, and have the habit of subservience to the stronger race, which is more effective than the force of law. The task of controlling and moulding these eight millions of simple blacks, important as it is, is a bagatelle in comparison with the greater task of reconstructing the defective civilisation of two hundred and fifty millions of people whose thought and literature are full of force, but are suffering from the dry rot of ancient and unchangeable customs and habits.

We were driven by the representative of the court to the pagodas, the forts, the prisons, and the public square, where in the afternoons the English and native residents meet on foot and in carriages. Here we saw the reign of the " plug hat." Neither heat nor other climatic conditions can dethrone it. It goes all over the world, strapped to the wings of British commerce. It is respected as profoundly as the Flag itself, or the Parliament. It is said that a Malay pirate once appeared before a British magistrate, with naked body, but covered with a silk hat, which he claimed was unanswerable testimony to his loyalty to the British crown.

The King had been advised by some one in Singapore to visit the palace and menagerie of the ex-

King of Oude, in the suburbs of Calcutta. This deposed King, with an income from the British government of $500,000 per annum, lived in much splendour with about three hundred wives, but was disreputable and vicious; his pleasure was in collecting wild beasts and in riotous living. Our King wished to see him; but there were political reasons for preventing it. A call by an acknowledged king, with the assent of the British, would, in the minds of the Hindus, be regarded as homage to their own deposed sovereign. The British government would not prevent a call by the Hawaiian monarch upon his deposed brother, but they preferred that he should not honour him. We, the suite, advised the King not to visit him, but his curiosity to see the magnificent establishment made him obstinate, and he resolved to go. We therefore, with a subterfuge, prevented it. We contrived that a message should be brought to us stating that the measles had broken out in the palace of the ex-King. Our royal master recalled the fate of his predecessor in London, the incidents of death, — Sandwiches, etc., — and he yielded. The success of this subterfuge led us to try another, the story of which will appear later in this memoir. It is a maxim of the Anointed that they are above all law; from this is forced a corollary that those who deal with kings are above all conscience. We confessed our iniquity on reaching home and received the royal pardon.

To me, the old residences of Clive and Warren Hastings, the empire-builders, were the fascinating spots of Calcutta. These men were the commercial travellers who had taken up the sword as a mere incident of trade, and had opened the way for the expansion of British power over such an enormous portion of the globe as it has since dominated. While George III and Lord North were, through a foolish policy, casting away the American colonies, these soldier-traders were replacing them with a vast empire.

Several Hindus who had been educated in the English schools applied to the King by letter for appointments in his islands. One of their letters, we were told, was a fair sample of Babu literature:

"CALCUTTA, May 29, 1887.

"YOUR MIGHTY EXCELLENCY AND SULTAN:

"I debase myself to Your Excellency's greatness, to be magnanimous sentiments, to recognise in me capable of labour in mercantile house. I clutch your blessed hand to be encouraged for post of service in your great Empire, to be discharged gloriously by me. Admiration for me is monotonously expressed in letters. I will be honoured to lay with bended knees before your Majestic Excellence.

"Your most obedient

"SERVANT."

A similar example of Babu literature is cited by Lady Dufferin. One of these worthies writes:

"You are kind to me. May Almighty God give you tit for tat."

Robert was again the cause of annoyance to us. He made another struggle in Calcutta to rise to his level. He had registered himself in the hotel as "Baron von O———, Equerry in Waiting," and without our knowledge was assigned to fine apartments. A place was made for him by the attendants at the King's table, but, as he did not appear, one of the government staff asked for an explanation. I took him aside and frankly told him the rather romantic story of the valet. During the evening, after the King had retired, I related to these gentlemen our many tribulations with Robert, and they were greatly pleased with the humours of the situation and the fortunes of the Feather Cloak. They admitted that even in the vice-regal court there were incidents equally ludicrous. The genteel appearance, tall figure, brilliant complexion, and excellent speech of the valet had impressed and puzzled these gentlemen.

We left in the vice-regal car for a journey across India to Bombay by way of Benares. It was plainly furnished; in one of its co-apartments was a large tub into which water was let from a large tank in the roof of the car. Into the window frames were fastened wheels of straw called *khuskhus*. The wind caused by the motion of the cars caused them to revolve very rapidly. Water trickled down over them in small streams from a tank above, and the resulting evaporation cooled the air within the car. A box filled with ice was stored with the luggage, upon which some Babu had written a direction, —

"H. M. KING, ESQ.,
    KALAKAUA."

For some hundreds of miles our course was through arid land, for the monsoon had not come. If irrigation works are constructed through this vast area, and proper fertilisers are used, the population of this portion of India, it is said, may be trebled, and still find sufficient support from the soil. So far as we could see, for a thousand miles, there was nothing but parched fields and no green thing.

Although we were now travelling in a land where, it is said, famine and misery are the lot of the common people, I recalled the speech of the Nawab Medhi Ali, of Hyderabad, a distinguished Indian statesman, who had recently returned from a visit to England. He spoke with admiration of the industrial power lying in the " two hundred millions of iron men," the steam force of British machinery in the manufacturing districts, and compared it with the conditions of India; but, he said, " so far from widespread happiness in England, there is an appearance of poverty more pinching, and a misery more distressing, in a single quarter of London, than can be found in all the Deccan, — yes, it might be safely said, more than in all India." Is, then, the evolution of Christian civilisation in England abnormal and monstrous, or is it essentially the civilisation of France before the Revolution of 1893? I was not surprised, therefore, when the King, with his simple Polynesian mind, remarked from time to time that his own native subjects were as happy as any people he met in his travels.

During the trip through this part of India the King became tired of gazing out of the windows, and for occupation invented a new Order of merit, which he styled the " Order of Kapiolani," his Queen. He said that he desired to confer distinction on several ladies who were famous in literature; he mentioned Miss Bird and Lady Brassey. He had been greatly annoyed by the innumerable requests for his Orders wherever we had been, and he thought a new Order would enable him to make those in existence less common. So, by a stroke of the pen, it was established, and the decorations were at once made in Paris. These he subsequently conferred upon many persons, some of whom received them as just marks of distinction, and some with much gratitude.

Mr. Dannell, the British Collector of the Province of Benares, met us at the railway station at Benares and invited us to be his guests in the Government House. This invitation was declined, together with his offer of a parade of troops and royal salute, and we lodged in a hotel. The official staff, with some noted natives, called, and during that day and the succeeding one drove us about the sacred city; through the fine grounds of the Maharajah's palace, through narrow streets smelling of all abominations, where multitudes of women of the poorer classes squatted before hovels, with rings of silver or brass around their ankles or riveted through their noses; to the pagodas, temples, and sacred wells, where stench and dirt abounded; to the cow temple, where thirty sacred cows chewed their cuds without prejudice against a religion which filled them with rich provender; to the pen of the blind and sacred bull, who thrust out his tongue for food as the blind beggar holds out his box. We then moved up and down the Ganges in a barge, just beyond the line of the pilgrim bathers, who for a mile along its banks were motionless in the sacred water. Rising from the banks and on the hills above it were the gaudy temples, and on the low brink of the river the crematories, from which the ashes of the dead were flung into the stream. As we rested on the river, before a landscape within which lies the hope and redemption of all Hindu-land, I recalled a fierce debate of my college days, under the elms of Yale, over the question, " Should a Hindu mother obey the dictates of her conscience when it directs her to cast her child into the Ganges? " I was now actually looking upon the banks from which innumerable infants had been flung. If the Hindu mother obeyed her conscience, where was the sin? If the sin lay in her ignorance, was she responsible for light that for her had never shone? The theologists of those early days confidently consigned her to everlasting torments; the theologists of the " higher criticism " now suspend judgment, with less confidence in their knowledge of the moral mystery of this world.

At the monkey temple, within the city, a priest received us and humbly asked alms for the benefit of these consecrated simians. " If a monkey be the god, what must the priest be? " asked the cynical Frenchman. The one who stood at the gate of this temple as the medium between man, the worshipper, and the monkey gods, was a shrewd-looking person, and, no doubt, could advance conclusive reasons for the truths of simian theology. He led us within, where a thousand chattering divinities were climbing pillars, swinging from the rafters, or picking the meat out of sacrificial nuts offered to them by the crowd of worshippers. Nor did they hesitate to drop upon the shoulders of believers and seize fruit from their hands.

A venerable goat stood alone in the court-yard; what his part was in this " divine comedy " we were not told; whether or not in this intricate religious system a scapegoat was needed, no one knew. But his patience was indeed divine. Three active young monkeys sat on his back; another sat between his horns; another pulled his tail, but he stood imperturbable, chewing his cud with the resigned air of one who had suffered much tribulation, with a hope of eternal bliss in a Paradise of rubbish. These mischievous divinities swarm over the city, pounce on and carry off, without resistance, the food of the poor, which is the simian method of assessing for church dues, and they are not punished. An attempt was made by the British authorities to place them on the farther side of the river, but they swarmed back on the river boats, for no boatmen dared molest them. When they are old and feeble they are placed in an asylum; this " retreat," the German poet Heine said, was the model for the French Academy of Science. One can imagine the consolation of a devout Hindu who in his last hour, when all other consolation is gone, grasps this flower of faith in immortal monkeys, and refreshes himself with its fragrance in the last darkness.

I asked the British " Collector " whether he reasoned with the worshippers about their belief in this simian divinity. He replied that he did, but that a cute priest " turned all his points." This belief was based on the writings of the sacred books; if you questioned their authority, the priest replied, " What you need is faith; if you have that, you will believe: you have faith in your own religion, therefore you believe it: have faith in ours, and you will believe as we believe."

British rule, which is flexible and adroit, must tolerate and protect this institution as well as that of polygamy. These are fixed in the customs and ideas of the people, as human slavery was fixed and protected in the political constitution of the American Republic.

Of this wonderful city one hundred books have been written. There was nothing which we saw that has not been told in them by many pens.

We travelled, without rest, to Bombay. The heat was great, and the King had " sucked " up all he cared to know about the Orient. He was the typical tourist, who wished above all things to cover the ground.

Sir James Ferguson, the Lieutenant-Governor of the Bombay Province, received us at the railway station and invited the party to his summer residence in Mahabheshwar; but the invitation was declined, for the King preferred to remain in Bombay during our short stay.

The Civil Service officers, the Consular Corps, distinguished natives, both Indians and Parsees, called upon the King, and for three days made him welcome. He saw the docks, the stables of Arabian horses, the silver wares of Cutch, the singular caves of Elephanta with their immense stone images of the three-headed gods, Brahma, Vishnu, and Siva, and the seven Towers of Silence. The towers are on the brow of a promontory high above and over-looking the ocean. To these the Parsees consign their dead. In the temple at the gateway is the per-petual fire of the Fire-Worshippers.

The Parsees are said to be the Jews of India; followers of Zoroaster, they are able and shrewd men who hold the money power of Bombay. One of them, Sir Jamsetjee Jeejeebhoy, the only native baronet in India at the time of our visit, and a millionaire, called upon the King, who, in order to see his great residence, assumed his incognito and returned his visit. The large hall in which he received us was an art gallery with a great number of pictures by foreign and native artists. By the side of rich European furniture were pieces of delicate Indian workmanship, and the grounds surrounding the place held all the rare plants of India. When we rose to leave, wreaths of jessamine were put about our necks, and bouquets of lily blossoms put into our hands. Sir Jamsetjee pressed the King to attend a banquet, but his invitation was declined for lack of time.

Before leaving India the King proposed that we should take home some souvenir of the country. I suggested that we take back the custom of the faithful Hindu who raises only a single tuft of hair on the very top of his head, by which the Divine hand draws him up to Heaven. The King promptly rejected this Ministerial advice, but selected a striking image of Buddha, for the purpose, I afterwards learned, of showing to his own people that nations with some high civilisation used a variety of idols as well as the Hawaiians. His people, he said, were not the beastly pagans that the travellers and missionaries had represented them to be.

CHAPTER XIX

From Bombay to Suez — Some Modest British Heroes —
Anecdotes of the Candahar Campaign — The Valet's Re-
lations to the King Explained — Aden — No Trace of the
Lost Lenore — Black Arab Boys with Red Hair — Diving
for Coins; an Old Trick of the King and His Suite —
Mount Sinai — An Englishman's Comments on its Pos-
sessors — Surprised by the Khedive's Officers at Suez —
The King Invited to Be the Khedive's Guest — The Suez
Canal — "Sandwiches" at Zigazag — Mohammedan Absti-
nence — Mussulman Comments on Christianity.

WE embarked on the "Rosetta" for Suez, with
royal salutes from ships and forts.

We had rapidly travelled through a vast empire
and had seen as little of it as one sees of the moon
through a small telescope. This was, however, a
royal tour, and "the King does as he pleases."
Not even the splendid mausoleum at Agra, the
"dream" of India, tempted my royal master to delay
his journey. The edge of his curiosity was dulled,
and he was satiated. As to the troublesome problems
and stupendous questions which confronted the British in India, he thought that the British had foolishly
gotten into a scrape and would have to get out of it
the best way they could; they had, he thought, meddled in other people's affairs, and their fingers were
burned. This much he had "sucked" out of his
travels. No doubt there was some wisdom in his
reflections.

The southwest monsoon set in on the second day.
In these dense clouds and strong winds were the airy
cargoes of rain which fall in showers of gold over all

India. Our vessel was crowded with British officers who were returning home after the Candahar campaign. They were simple, rugged men, modest, and full of that supreme pluck which has won empires. They talked of battles in the mountain passes as if they had been trifling skirmishes; there was no magnifying of their office. They recited no heroic stories, though the campaign was filled with brave acts. A colonel told us an incident of their retreat. While falling back through a gorge in the mountains he commanded a force protecting the rear of the column. It was annoyed by the rifle-shots from scattered bands of Afghans on the mountain sides. With his own force were men of a tribe who fight for hire on either side. One of his officers saw a hostile tribeman on the mountain side " potting " British soldiers, and he called to one of his own tribe-men, " Do you see that man firing at us? " " Oh, yes," he replied, " he is my father. I've had three shots at him; I'll kill him next shot." The British force had also taken some Afghan prisoners, but there was not force enough to hold them. They were released on promises not to fight against the British. One of them replied : " My religion compels me to fight you always." " Then we must hang you," said the British commander. " Can't help it," the prisoner replied; and he was hung. Prisoners were often taken and released; the next day they became loyal teamsters in the British service and were excellent foragers. It was said by these British soldiers that the Asiatics were indifferent to death from cannon and gun shots, but that they could not stand a bayonet charge; the personal presence and energy of the British enemy upset their equanimity.

From letters which we received from home, in Bombay, the suite now discovered the curious and rather mysterious relations which existed between the King and Robert. The versatile editor of a local paper had secretly urged the King to keep a record of his travels, which, in the hands of the editor, would be transformed into a brilliant history of his tour. As the editor was politically opposed to the suite, he had recommended that Robert should add to his duties of valet that of keeping a faithful diary of events. The King assented to this without the knowledge of the suite, as it was an assurance of a flattering account of his " ever-glorious " tour. Robert's frailties embarrassed the King; he felt, however, that to discharge him would be to prevent the making of a most valuable record, and he submitted with patience to his irregularities. The sequel proved that Robert, though pretending to keep a faithful diary of events, neglected to do so because he was not relieved from his menial service.

When the steamship anchored at Aden (the spot where it never rains) the British Governor came on board and invited the King to land and lunch with him. Aden stands as a sentinel guarding the waterway from England to India. On the beach were tethered camels, and Arab peddlers offered ostrich feathers at London prices. Here in this " distant Aden " I suppose we should have seen " a fair and radiant maiden whom the angels name Lenore," but neither telescope nor eye could discover her. In her place were some shrivelled women crouching on the sand, not one of whom had ever heard of her, but suggested that she might be a resident of an interior village. Groups of Arab boys, with black skins and reddish-yellow hair, were lying on the sand. This peculiar colour of the hair is obtained by covering the head with a thick paste of clay and lime, the acids of which convert the black into reddish yellow. Many of the small boys were walking about with heavy and dirty caps of mud in order to comply with this fashion.

While the King, from the deck of the steamer, was looking at the swarms of black and artificially red-headed boys who were swimming about the vessel, the British Governor said: " Your Majesty, please notice the great skill of these black chaps, who dive deeply and bring up from the bottom any coin you pitch into the water." He tossed some silver coins into the sea, and they were quickly brought to the surface by the urchins, who sank like lead toward the bottom. The King replied, " It is very clever;" then, turning to his suite, he said in his native language: " Thirty years ago you and I did it just as well in Honolulu harbour." He referred to our childhood days, when our incomes were limited, and we also plunged into the water and brought up coins which American whalemen tossed from the docks. The explanation of this trick is that a coin cast into the water sinks in a moderate zigzag course, and a skilful diver, sinking more rapidly than the coin, turns, looks upward, and catches it as it descends and before it reaches the bottom.

Steaming up the Red Sea, parched in the hot air which flows over it from the Arabian Desert, the shores gradually narrowed into the Gulf of Suez. Mount Sinai loomed up through the transparent air far to the eastward. One who accepts the faith of Christendom, and for the first time actually sees the rugged and bare peaks from which the Law was given to man, is awed in its presence as if there still remained some of its supernatural wonders; even undying sparks of the Fire in the Bush. An Englishman standing by the King said:

"It's a beastly shame that Sinai is in the hands of a lot of rascally and thieving monks who swindle the Christian visitors; and Jerusalem too, — the blasted Turks hold all the sacred places."

The King asked his English acquaintance why Christendom did not seize the holy places and hold them as sacred memorials of the most memorable event in the history of man. His plain-speaking friend replied: "Can do it, you know, just as easy as a mastiff throws up a rat; but all that's sentiment, — no trade in it; if you found gold mines on Sinai or in Bethlehem, Christendom would clear out those devilish Turkish beggars in a jiffy; if Nelson or Wellington were buried there, we'd have them now."

In this way was the royal Polynesian instructed in the moral sentiment of Europe toward the Holy Land. He had read about the Crusades, and he asked this stranger why they were abandoned after they had been prosecuted for nearly two hundred years. The stranger told him the Mohammedans said it was God's will that they should keep those places, and he fancied they were right about it; the Christian nations, if they got possession of them, would only make a dog-fight over the ownership.

My royal master was much impressed with the statements of this stranger. He said the people of Christian lands seemed to be more indifferent than even his own people toward sacred places; at any rate they did not show as much respect for them as he had believed.

Our steamer anchored near the town of Suez late in the evening. We were told that she would enter the Canal at three o'clock in the morning. We made our plans to leave her and land at that early hour, and take the railway train for Cairo.

We had sent no notice to the Khedive, or requested any to be sent, of our intention to visit Egypt, but pursued our safe policy of inviting no repulse or snubbing. We suspected that his Highness had never heard of the Hawaiian Islands; moreover our kingdom was without any treaty with Turkey, and we were not entitled to any courtesies.

The King was asleep below in his stateroom, and I was dozing in a deck chair about two o'clock in the morning, when one of the vessel's officers woke me with the statement, "An embassy, sir, from the Khedive." I stood up, rubbed my eyes, looked into the darkness, and by the dim light of the hanging lantern saw six persons in full uniform, with fez caps, standing before me. I was surprised and confused at this apparition of gold lace and fez caps. One of the party introduced himself to me as Sami-Pasha, and his companions as Abbati-Bey and Ali-Saroudi-Bey, and others, who had been directed by the Khedive to proceed from Cairo to Suez and invite the King to become his Highness's guest as long as he remained in Egypt. Sami-Pasha had formerly represented the Khedive in London, and spoke English fluently, and, though he was no longer in active service, had been requested to join in receiving the King. Abbati-Bey was another noted member of the vice-regal court, and Ali-Saroudi was the Director of Railways.

I roused the Chamberlain, who directed the valet to wake up the King, who was soundly asleep on a sofa. After several minutes' shaking the royal personage awoke, and was told that an embassy from the Khedive was on deck. The valet dressed him, and he reached the deck, though not fully awake. In the dim light he stood leaning against the sides of the saloon while the members of the embassy were presented to him and gave him the Khedive's invitation, which he graciously accepted, though he was too drowsy to understand it. He began to take a nap in a standing position, but we all entered the dining-saloon and some coffee woke us up. The chief of the embassy said that they had just arrived from Cairo on the Khedive's private car, and they asked the King to breakfast in Suez and then take the train, which would be kept waiting for him. We thereupon boarded the yacht of the embassy just as it began to dawn. As it was now three o'clock in the morning, and breakfast would not be served for several hours, we steamed into the Canal for a mile, and then returned. In the clear morning air the ranges of mountains on both sides of the Red Sea loomed up barren and desolate, with Sinai towering in the middle range to the eastward. Suddenly a flash of light from the rising sun shot across the sky, and the mountains of the African range were tinted with purple. The King, now well awake, wished to know where the Israelites had crossed the Red Sea. He was told that many men had studied the matter, but could not agree on the route; that Napoleon, in his expedition to Egypt, had tried to follow it under the direction of his savants, but came near being swamped. According to the Arab story he was fished out of the water in a very sad plight; according to the French account he had been saved by his own fertile genius.

The desert, like a great sea, stretched away until lost in the horizon. Not far off was a camp of Bedouins, the camels tethered around the tents. At some distance toward the east were the two green spots known as " Moses' Wells," and over all was the silence of centuries.

On landing in Suez an elaborate breakfast was served in the hotel by cooks and servants who were brought by the train from the Khedive's palace in Cairo. We entered the vice-regal car, which was furnished in silk and embroideries, and to which was attached another car containing the servants and luggage.

As we ran for many miles on a line parallel with the Canal, there appeared the strange phenomenon of huge steamers ploughing their course through the sands of the desert; for the water of the Canal was below the plane of the sand and not visible.

When we reached Zigazag an amusing incident occurred. It was arranged before we left Suez that at this station we should have luncheon at one o'clock. Entering a private room, we saw upon a table a large tray upon which was a mountain of sandwiches. His Excellency Sami-Pasha was enraged. Calling for the keeper of the station, he shouted: " What does this mean? I ordered lunch for his Majesty the King; you give us sandwiches, bah!" The station-master trembled, bowed low, and, when our vice-regal escort would listen, explained that he had received a telegram ordering sandwiches. " Where is it?" Abbati-Bey shouted. It was brought. The despatch dictated at Suez was: "Prepare lunch for the King of the Sandwich Islands." The telegram received read:

"Prepare lunch for the King. Sandwiches."

In the angry discussion over this error, which was carried on in the Osmanli or Egyptian tongue, we heard "Allah" repeated several times; but the occasion required something more vigorous, and the rugged strength of the English language, now the imprecating language of the world, was mustered up, and a "Damn" was heard in the land where Pharaoh had ruled. The embassy apologised to the King, and the traffic of the railway was suspended during the delay of the train while an excellent lunch was prepared. Had Death a grudge against this Polynesian monarch? He had demanded "Royal Sandwiches" in London nearly sixty years before, and now he had wickedly instigated the guileless Egyptians to put before him a pile of sandwiches as a solemn reminder that he was stalking behind him, even at the foot of the Pyramids.

Looking from the window of the car, as we again rode through the desert, several points appeared just above the horizon in the western sky. "You see the Pyramids," said Sami-Pasha. "They are curiosities only," he said: "if you compare them with mountains, they are nothing; but they are grand because man made them. You will visit them to-morrow."

While we rested on the silk-covered divans the obsequious Egyptian servants tendered us, as usual, champagne and whiskey. The embassy did not touch them. If temperance be a virtue and drunkenness a vice, Islamism has absorbed all the virtue and turned over to Christendom an undisputed title to the vice.

Sami-Pasha said that while the Koran forbade the use of wine, there was a prevailing reason for the abstinence of the Mohammedans in the poverty of the people and the lack of material out of which cheap spirits could be made. He continued:

" If the Arabs could raise potatoes like the Irishman, or grain like the Russians, the command of the Koran would not be kept as well as it is. But," he continued, " Europe will make drunkards of the Mussulmans within a century. When I see a tipsy Mussulman I know he is free from all religion and is a renegade, though he calls himself a Christian. We are Unitarians and do not believe that God forgives sin; if a good Mussulman gets tipsy and does mischief, he can't pray and be forgiven; but a Christian can get drunk a hundred times and he is forgiven each time if he repents. There may be no limit to his sin, but he is always forgiven if he repents; the Christians have the easiest religion of the world."

I asked him if he thought Christianity would not benefit the races who accept Islamism.

" There is much good in Christianity," he replied, " but if it prevailed in Asia, it would free the people from direct responsibility to God. Do the Christians of Europe obey the teachings of Christ? I have lived in England, and I have not seen obedience. There is more wickedness in London than in all Asia Minor or Arabia and Egypt; more drunkenness and immorality and crime. If the English people were forced to practise the teaching of the Prophet for twenty years, as we are, there would be such sobriety and temperance among the people that you would not recognise them. Christianity suits them, but Islam-

ism is best for our people. I do not deny the
greatness and wisdom of Christ. I believe in his
teachings; the Koran does not condemn him; but
Mohammed gave us a religion better suited to our
people; it was the will of God. If Christianity is
better for us, God will send it here; he knows best
what we need, and he gives us what is best for us."

These were the thoughts of an educated Mussulman who had seen the world. In another conversation he said: "The Europeans do not understand
us. It is impossible to separate religious from political faith; they unite Church and State, but Christians ask us to separate them. We do not proselyte;
we tolerate all religions; but the preaching of the
Western religion in our countries disturbs allegiance
to the government. The Sultan is the leader of our
faith and rules through the obedience of the people
to him as the leader; the missionaries and the Americans say he is not a true leader, and that makes
political treason."

I remembered that Chancellor Kent, in his "Commentaries," which form a text-book for lawyers, declares that the American government is founded on
the principles of Christianity; the conclusions of this
great American jurist and of this Mussulman statesman were the same, — that political and religious
faith are interwoven and cannot be separated.

CHAPTER XX

AFTER a journey of one hundred and forty miles
we reached Cairo. We stepped out of the vice-
regal carriage upon carpets laid over the stone pavements. The Minister of Foreign Affairs greeted the
King and presented to him some of the high officials. Among them was General Charles F. Stone,
an American soldier, who, after the Civil War in
America, took service in the Khedive's army. I had
known him in the early days of that war, when the
political generals of the American Senate meddled
in the military campaigns and had caused his arrest
and imprisonment, without charges or trial, for many
months; he was finally discharged and restored to
service, but under this gross humiliation, had abandoned his native land and taken service with the
Khedive. He was also most considerately assigned

by the Khedive to attend our party.   Passing through lines of Egyptian troops, we were taken to the palace of Kasr-el-Moussa, which had been closed for the season, but was reopened for the royal guest.   The Khedive was spending the summer in Alexandria and had assigned a palace to the King whenever he should reach that city.

I asked General Stone why the Khedive was so hospitable to the King of a small domain of which he certainly knew little if anything.   He replied that the reception of the King in the Orient was known to the Khedive's government, and though it had no diplomatic relations with Hawaii it would not refuse the courtesies which other nations had shown.   We were again in the best of luck, for we did not expect it.   Our travels in Asia had taken the edge off our curiosity to see the courts of the world, but we were now with another race and in the land of the Nile and the Pyramids.

We drove the next morning over a splendid highway to the Pyramids.   Napoleon's battle with the Mamelukes interested the King more than the Pyramids; from a rising spot General Stone explained to him the movements and strategy of the battle; pointing out the ground over which the Mamelukes made their reckless charge upon the French infantry.   The King thought that the generalship of the Mamelukes was open to criticism; General Stone agreed with him.   The ride from the Pyramids to the Sphinx was made, as it is usually made, upon very small donkeys.   The large frame of the King, with his clothing, so covered his donkey that its identity was lost; the King's legs nearly touched the ground; it appeared at a short distance as if a new and queer animal, more of man than beast, was moving about, supplied with two heads, six legs, and a tail. While in front of the Sphinx, the little donkey brayed, with his companions who carried the suite; the Sphinx did not smile, but a close observer might have noticed a slight cocking of an eye as he looked upon the new member of the zoölogical world.

In the streets of Cairo our vice-regal carriage had the right of way. Two Arabs dressed in white, with embroidered jackets and turbans, and legs bare below the knees, ran in front of it with long graceful steps, and struck those in the street who were in the way with long, slim poles, crying to all with loud, harsh voices to open the way for the Khedive's carriage. We saw what tourists usually see in the old city; the dreamy, weird life of the Arabian Nights; laden camels picking their way through narrow streets with their heads high in the air; deformed beggars, and almost naked water-carriers; maniacal-looking dervishes tossing up their arms; veiled women in shrouds gliding by; and in the narrowest streets, crowded with donkeys and camels, great disturbance and frantic efforts to make way for our carriage. At the grand alabaster mosque on the citadel, overlooking the city, holy men received us at the entrance; servants placed on our feet cloth overshoes, which protected the polished floors. We were led through deep, shadowy archways, and between graceful alabaster columns, with rich colouring, to the ancient citadel. We stood on the quadrangle where the tragical massacre of the Mamelukes took place by the order of the perfidious Mohammed Ali. Fearing these aristocratic soldiers, whose ancestors had once ruled Egypt, he invited all of their great chiefs to a banquet of reconciliation in the citadel; they came on their splendid Arabian horses, and while they sat at a gorgeous feast the curtains suddenly fell from the sides of the great hall, and Mohammed Ali's soldiers opened fire on the guests. Only one daring young Mameluke escaped; he sprang from the table, mounted his horse, dashed through the inner gate as they were closing it, reached the parapet, leaped from it into the deep darkness below, rose from his steed's crushed body, and fled.

After we had dined and the King had retired, I followed General Stone to his headquarters. Here was an American, of a nation not a hundred years old, teaching a race that had been involved in wars for fifty centuries, how to fight. While the Egyptian sentinel slowly paced the stone pavement the General described the political disturbances and the immediate danger of insurrection.

We visited the Museum. The celebrated Curator was eloquent in his description of " mummies and things." His life, his joy, was in rummaging in the débris which the old centuries had packed away in decayed temples. What was musty gave him inspiration; the discovery of an ancient dish which the infant Rameses used five thousand years before gave him more pleasure than the regeneration of Egypt; the discovery of an embalmed rabbit was of more importance than the conservation of the waters of the Nile; he was enriching our knowledge of the past while the Egypt of to-day was in darkness; like the Chinese epicure, who finds his best dish in stale eggs, he found pleasure in nothing unless it was ancient.

The next morning we left for Alexandria in the

vice-regal car, reaching the station at eleven o'clock. Carpets were laid on the stone pavements, and when the King stepped out of the car the Khedive, Tewfik, who succeeded to the vice-regal throne, a year before, took the King's hand, and led him to his carriage. This was driven, with a bodyguard of cavalry, to what is known as " Number Three Palace," or the Palace of Mahmondieh, situated about three miles from the city,. in extensive and well-kept grounds. The Khedive led the King to a large reception-room, and after a brief conversation committed him again to the care of Sami-Pasha and Abbati-Bey. The floors of the palace were of marble; the furniture was mainly European; divans of rich material lay against the walls. About fifty feet from the palace was a large, plain building, several stories in height. The shutters of its many windows were closed, and there was no sign of life within it. Before the doors sat large, fat eunuchs. Here lived about three hundred women, it was said, who were the wives of the former Khedive. We watched the shutters, and from time to time could see many of them open slightly, for the inmates were as curious to see the King as he was to see them. We warned the King that an unbridled curiosity might bring him to the bowstring and the deposit of his body in the Nile. Our distinguished companion, Sami-Pasha, told us that the Khedive was a monogamist, and these women were a legacy not altogether desirable; good faith forbade that he should turn them out in the streets. I asked him, as he seemed to invite discussion, about the life of the women of the harems. He replied that there was no hardship in it; that it was eagerly sought for; the harem was a condition of social life; these women, like birds born in captivity, were contented, for there were no contrasts of life in their experiences, which created a desire for change. "No doubt," he said, "they might become restless and miserable if they were allowed for a time the freedom of European life, but they know nothing about that freedom and are satisfied." I asked him if the thinking Mohammedans favoured any change in the institution of the harem. He replied that it was God's will that present conditions existed, and God would change them if it was best. His placid belief in predestination was as childlike as that of a stern Calvinist. He said he had seen much of life in Europe, and especially England, particularly the condition of women; Christendom had much to boast of, but more to be ashamed of; it immeasurably surpassed Islamism in its debaucheries. "The European women," he said, "did not appear to be happier than the Mohammedan women, and the lot of the wives of the poorer class was certainly not better than the lot of the wives of the poorer classes in Constantinople or Cairo; indeed, he said, he believed, and some intelligent Europeans held the same opinions, that Mohammedan women were in some respects better off. Monogamy, he said, might be one of the best forms of civilisation, but God knew what was best. He had allowed the best men, by the records of the Old Testament, to practise polygamy, and if He approved of it, why should men contradict Him?"

At five o'clock we returned the Khedive's visit. The State carriages, with Arabic crests on the door panels, took us to the palace within the city. The cavalry escort was unusually large, for it was said that the outskirts of the city were still open to the incursions of Bedouins.

The Khedive met his royal friend at the door with a very cordial manner. He led us through several large chambers, with furniture of a European rather than an Egyptian fashion, but extremely rich; divans were evidently more popular than chairs. As soon as we were seated in a group, servants placed before each of us a long pipe, with a bowl studded with diamonds. At each bowl a servant kneeled, filled it with tobacco, and lighted it. Coffee was served in gold cups also studded with diamonds. The Khedive was short, rather stout, and dark in feature; his smile was genial; there was no evidence of his father's stern and cruel nature. A physiognomist might call him irresolute and easy; the roaring sea of political troubles about him did not disturb him; he was outwardly as tranquil as the goat among the sacred and mischievous monkeys of Benares. He spoke the English language with ease and directed his questions to the King's travels in the Far East. The presence of two white men in the King's suite led him to ask if they were Hawaiians. The King replied that they were born in his kingdom and were his subjects, but were of American descent. The Khedive asked if he had any of his native subjects in his Cabinet. He replied that he usually did have at least one native, but generally he selected white men. The Khedive nodded to this answer and made no reply; his thought, I suspect, was this: "There now, even at the ends of the earth the Anglo-Saxons are grabbing everything." He was restless himself under English dominance.

When the King said he intended to leave shortly

for Italy, the Khedive invited him to a State banquet in the evening, and to a State ball on the following evening. The conversation drifted into a comparison of the customs of the Egyptians and the Hawaiians. The Khedive asked if polygamy was practised in the Hawaiian kingdom, and when he learned that it was not, he said, "I have only one wife; I believe it is the best way. The people of Europe think it is best for us." He is, however, a true Mohammedan. His father Ismail, who was a cruel, cold, and extravagant despot, squeezing the life out of the *fellahin*, said to him when he was young, "Why do you remain a Mussulman? Go over to the Europeans. Be like me. I am now a Christian." He said that his children were receiving education in the English language. I knew that while he spoke the paw of the British lion rested on Egypt, and he was without the substance of power; no doubt he was more contented under that great paw than if he were exposed to the teeth of the European wolves that howled around the Pyramids. The King said he had been in the Suez Canal for a short distance. "Yes," said the Khedive, "it is a great work, but it has made much trouble for us." I asked him if he was proud of the wisdom of his uncle Said, who, when Khedive, built the Canal under the guidance of De Lesseps, though the English engineers said it was an impracticable scheme. He replied that the English did not believe in De Lesseps because he was a Frenchman. He turned to the King and said, "You must see De Lesseps when you are in Paris; he is a very able man."

When we had returned to our palace, and had cast ourselves on the divans, and were smoking the fragrant tobacco brought by the attendants, the King began to display his knowledge of Egyptian history. He said the Egyptians, like the Japanese, the Chinese, and the Siamese, traced the origin of their sovereigns to a divine source. I asked him if he believed that his own origin was divine. He said that though he was elected King it was quite probable that he was selected for reasons which were peculiar. This vague statement indicated to me that his mind was working on the subject. I told him that he was perhaps on the very spot occupied by Alexander the Great when he selected this site for the city; it was here that he fell in doubt about his own origin, and so he pushed out into the desert to the Temple of Ammon to get out of the priests a declaration that he was divine. Here was an excellent opportunity for him, the King, to take the Feather Cloak, Robert, and a donkey, push out into the desert to the same temple, and " suck " up some information about his own origin; he could bring back some of the hieroglyphics, which might be deciphered so as to declare his own divinity, and no doubt the Khedive would certify to its correctness. He would then return to his own people, not with some base information about useful things, but with the precious discovery that he came down from the gods. He made no reply to this, but afterward told his Chamberlain that the Minister trifled with very important matters. It had touched a subject on which the royal mind was reflecting from time to time.

In the evening we dined with the Khedive. About forty guests were present, men of different races, his own Cabinet, and intimate friends, the diplomatic representatives of England, France, and Austria, who had substantially taken the political power out of his hands. The table service was of solid silver, with, of course, flowers in profusion.

There were at this time symptoms of political unrest among the Egyptians, owing to the joint domination of the European Commissioners, since the recent accession of Tewfik to the vice-regal office, — some rumblings of far thunder; but the Viceroy said he hoped that there would be no disturbance. Within about a year from the time of this banquet, Arabi-Pasha rose in insurrection, the city was bombarded, and the very splendid hall in which we dined was burned. Looking back upon this event, I recalled the men of many races who quietly sat around the table, under the lights of the great chandeliers, amid vases filled with flowers, and music in the court-yard; the Khedive helplessly in the grasp of the Great Powers, but chatting pleasantly with the King of the little islands at the cross-roads of the Pacific, which were as important to the commerce of the Pacific as Egypt on the highway to India, and a king as helpless too, before the manifest destiny of America; two rulers over weak nations lying in the way of the Anglo-Saxon march.

I asked the Medical Director, who was also a devout Mussulman, about the condition of women in the harems. He replied that they thought their condition was superior to that of the married women of Europe, who insisted on their husbands remaining at home, without giving them liberty, which put them in a sort of domestic slavery; the women believed in the Koran, and therefore were contented. He said, too, that God had willed polygamy, and it was difficult to make the devout believe that it existed in defiance of the will of the Almighty.

The Viceroy of Egypt (1881).

The guests were placed at the table according to rank; but having now had much experience in dull table companions at royal banquets, I had asked our good friend, Sami-Pasha, to ignore my own rank and place me near some person who was familiar with Egyptian affairs. I was placed next to the Medical Director of the government, who at once spoke of the leprosy which prevailed in Hawaii and had given our earthly Paradise a bad name. He had his theory about the mysterious disease, but it failed to fit the facts within our own experience. He knew every guest at the table, and for three hours described to me, with diplomatic reserve at times, the crisis which was approaching, though he hoped that it would not end in insurrection.

After the banquet, coffee was served in jewelled cups. The coffee-bearer wore a rich uniform over his shoulder, like a Hussar's jacket. In one hand he carried a gold salver on which were the cups; with the other he held a gold frame containing a deep gold coffee-urn which nearly touched the floor.

The following day we visited the Khedive's stables of Arabian horses. The King and Chamberlain found much delight in the superb animals. They were brought out one by one for their inspection, and the master of the stables declared that few persons more quickly detected the fine points in the animals. When the Khedive heard of this, he offered one of them to the King, who would have, if we had consented, taken him with us to America and Hawaii.

In the evening we went to a grand ball at the palace of the Ras-el-Tin, which was bombarded and destroyed by the British during the next year. Arriving at eleven o'clock, a grand usher received us;

we were led up a broad marble stairway to the first
landing, where we passed through two lines of
officials to a room in which two more lines of higher
officials were drawn up. Passing these, we entered
the grand reception-room, which was in the form of
a great dome, with marvellous frescoes. Around it
were divans, and strips of rich carpet ran around its
sides on a wood floor polished in black. Massive
chandeliers cast a brilliant but soft light through
the great hall. We approached the Khedive, who
shook our hands and placed us on his right. Here
we could see the guests as they entered and were
presented. All the world was there; but the Italians
and Greeks were the most numerous; many of the
Turks appeared in European dress, but retained the
fez cap. The middle-aged Italian women were not
handsome, and the Grecian women were homely, but
all of them had graceful manners.

The belle of the ball-room was, however, a Grecian,
the wife of the Greek Consul. She had a clear pink-
and-white complexion, and her Parisian dress was
rather picturesque from some distinctive Grecian
ornaments. As no ladies of the court were present, the King, on the Khedive's invitation, selected a walking partner from the foreign women.
He naturally chose the beautiful Greek, but their
promenade was a silent march, as they found no
language which they could use in common, and the
few pantomimic expressions which they exchanged
were quite spiritless.

It was a Mussulman fête-day. From the high balcony of the palace there was an excellent view of
the harbour illuminated by the light of the Egyptian
warships and the rapid bursting of rockets. The

British Consul pointed out to me an old coal-receiving hulk lying in the shadows across the bay. It was, he said, the frigate " Resolution," in which Captain Cook sailed when he discovered the Sandwich Islands. This was another curious incident which connected our little kingdom with places we visited. From her deck, as she lay in Kealakakua Bay ("the pathway of the gods "), the great Captain had landed, and his head had been fatally punched with the spear of the King's predecessor. Here she now lay, rusty, dismantled, and dirty, with the Sphinx winking its sympathetic eye toward her. Yet she was among " the first that ever burst into that silent sea " of the Pacific. I called the King's attention to it, and with the beautiful Greek he came to the balcony and looked at this old fighting-ship in a marine almshouse.

One's fancy could picture a pretty scene. The King stood on soil more famous in history than any he had yet visited. He could "toss a biscuit," no doubt, to the spot where Alexander the Great stood while he watched the flight of ducks which alighted here and fixed the seat of the city of Alexandria; over yonder Julius Cæsar received Cleopatra rolled up in a mattress; he stood within a few steps of where Pompey's head was brought to him on a platter. Here Mark Antony, governing one third of the world, " reeled through the streets at noon," drunk with his love of the enchanting Queen, and then fell on his own sword because he was conquered; near by was the mausoleum where the "matchless dark beauty " barred out Octavius Cæsar, the ruler of another third of the world, and in her robes and beneath her crown untied the knot of her life " with the teeth of an asp." And looking down over this place of grand tragedies stood a Polynesian king with a beautiful Greek on his arm, perhaps a lineal descendant of Helen of Troy, while over across the bay lay the hulk of the old ship which once bore the discoverer of his kingdom. I noticed at the time these curious coincidences for the use of our poet laureate, but they gave the King no inspiration. I tried to impress on him the romantic character of the events which happened here. But he replied with simplicity and most directly: " Those Romans you are talking about only made asses of themselves for a woman." I replied most respectfully that making asses of themselves by sovereigns were the prominent facts of history as it was written, and if the Recording Angel graciously permitted him to inspect the records when he got into the next world, this opinion would be confirmed. He believed that I had cast a slur upon the brotherhood of monarchs, and resented it by saying that Ministers of monarchs were often asses too. This proposition I candidly assented to, but it only proved, I urged, how poorly the world had been governed, and how prudent and wise it would be to suck some wisdom out of the events which had taken place on the spot upon which we stood. The Khedive joined us. We pointed out the old " Resolution " and repeated to him her story. Cook's voyages and discoveries he had not heard of. The tragedy of his violent death led him to ask whether the British ever punished his slayers. The King said: " Let us drink a toast to the old ship." The wine was brought, and on the grand balcony, with the harbour lighted with rockets and lanterns, the King raised his glass and said, " Here's to the ' Resolution.' "

At one o'clock in the morning we left this palace of the Ras-el-Tin, and as the steamer left early in the morning for Italy the King bade the Khedive good-bye. Both walked slowly together through the splendid halls, between rows of bowing courtiers and attendants, to the Viceroy's carriage, and there they parted.

We returned to our palace, the Mahmondieh, with the troop of horse galloping with us. We lay down on the divans for several hours, and at five o'clock in the morning were served with coffee, for the hour of leaving the city was seven o'clock. We left our palace with the usual ceremony; many of the shutters of the great silent house near by moved slightly, for the harem was still curious to see the King. At the early hour of six we found the officers of the marine service waiting for us. Our constant companions, Sami-Pasha, Abbati-Bey, and General Stone, were with us. We stepped into a large barge in which sat twenty-four oarsmen in red shirts and fez caps. Over the stern was a silk canopy with gold tassels. The cushions were of blue velvet embroidered in gold. Rich Turkish rugs covered the floor. The stroke of the twenty-four oars was slow and stately; it expressed a royal dignity. Perhaps the ancestors of the oarsmen had in these very waters pulled the oar when the Egyptian Queen sat under a like canopy, and her barge, " like a burnished throne, burned on the water."

CHAPTER XXI

Comments of Egyptian Press — The King's Masonic Rank —
Voyage to Naples — A Comet — Catalonia — Volcanoes of
Hawaii and Sicily — Divine Stoppage of Lava-Flows — An
Italian Adventurer in Honolulu — He Reappears at Naples
and Abducts the King — Pursuit and Recapture of His
Majesty — Visit to the King and Queen of Italy — The
Adventurer Dismissed — Italian Poems of Adulation to
Strangers — Ex-Khedive Ismail Calls — Troubles with
Hotel-Keepers Begin — News of Attack on President
Garfield.

THE captain of the Italian steamer received his
royal guest at the gangway. Sami-Pasha and
Abbati-Bey bade us good-bye, and the forts and an
Egyptian frigate fired royal salutes. The old " Resolution," lying on the other side of the harbour, stared
at us out of her " dead-eyes " and seemed to mutter :
" Just a hundred years ago, less two years, I discovered your kingdom, my royal friend, and here
I am, a naval coal-scuttle."

The French and English papers of Egypt highly
commended the King's appearance and behaviour ;
one of the French papers placed him above some of
the European monarchs in intelligence and education ;
others said, he was " a man of noble presence, with
a benevolent expression " and " with distinguished
manners."

The Masonic Fraternity of Alexandria paid the
King great attention, because he held high rank in
that body. It was said that he delivered an address

before them and surprised them with his knowledge of the history of their Order.

The voyage toward Naples was over a glassy sea. Late one day the island of Sicily loomed up on our left, but as the night came on a comet appeared in the cloudless sky; at first a large star with a dim white trail which became denser as the darkness deepened until it had the shape of a half-closed fan. It pointed toward the earth, with its tail flung back to the zenith. Under it, in the clear sky, the outlines of Ætna were faintly drawn. We anchored in the port of Catalonia, and in the early morning visited the vaults of the old Aragonese kings, the chapel and tomb of St. Agatha, the Roman baths, and the monastery of the Benedictines. The lava-flows of Ætna were quite similar in form to those of the Hawaiian group. We were told a legend of an eruption which had its counterpart in our own kingdom. It was said by the believers of the Roman Church that when the molten lava of Ætna reached the monastery, the monks, in a suppliant procession, holding before them the veil of St. Agatha, offered up prayers, and the flow was stayed within fifteen feet of the building. While we were on this tour a stream of lava over half a mile in width from the vast Hawaiian volcano, Mauna Loa, reached the outskirts of a settlement about thirty miles from its outbreak. Christian prayers besought the Almighty to arrest it, but they did not avail. Thereupon an old native Princess of the royal line, with some superstitious natives, placed themselves in front of the molten mass and made the ancient orthodox offering of a white pig to the goddess of the volcano. The flow stopped, — conclusive evidence to the superstitious natives of the power of their own gods, and the contempt of the goddess Pele for the prayers of the white people. It was a simple reasoning from an apparent cause to an apparent effect.

In the upward slope of the land, the belts of verdure at different altitudes, the cones on its flanks, and the cloud-capped summit, the contour of Ætna resembled that of the vast extinct volcano of Hale-a-ka-la ("house of the sun") upon the island of Maui, one of the Hawaiian group. But the Hawaiian crater, with a depth of two thousand feet and a diameter of nine miles, surpassed Ætna, and, indeed, every other volcano of the earth, in grandeur.

Before we reached Naples the Chamberlain and I anticipated some annoyance when we should land. A few months before we left our kingdom, an Italian adventurer, one Signor Moreno, quietly arrived in Honolulu by a tramp steamer from Hongkong, and had, without the knowledge of the King's advisers, placed before him a brilliant and fascinating scheme for the " development " of his country and the exaltation of the throne. It involved the securing of a large loan of money from the Chinese and an overwhelming Chinese immigration, the building of railways and steamships, and, above all, the suppression of the missionary and foreign influence in the government. The King disliked the conservative ways of the whites, and any scheme that supplied him with large sums of money would relieve him from dependence on them. Signor Moreno's scheme, therefore, captivated him; his Polynesian mind did not see that it was utterly visionary and impracticable, and, if executed, would be disastrous to him. He suddenly dismissed his reputable Ministers, and selected

Humberto, King of Italy (1881).

a new Cabinet, with the adventurer as Minister of
Foreign Affairs. The white population, having the
wealth and intelligence of the kingdom, rose up, and
with the aid of the foreign diplomats, who discredited
Moreno, peremptorily demanded of the King his dismissal. The King unwillingly consented, and formed
a new Cabinet, of which I became a member. The
adventurer was driven out of the kingdom, but he
retained the King's confidence. He took with him to
Italy, at the King's request, three native youths, to
be educated in the military and naval schools of that
country; these, when educated, were to be placed in
charge of the King's forces, to aid him in suppressing
his white subjects if they were troublesome. We
learned in Alexandria from the valet that letters had
been received by the King from Signor Moreno,
stating that he would meet him in Naples, and he
had arranged for his presentation to the King of
Italy. The King, though on the most cordial terms
with his suite, knew that they would oppose any intercourse with the Italian, and he therefore resorted to
some "diplomacy" without their knowledge. Moreno had also foolishly advised the King to secure
from the European sovereigns a guarantee of the
perpetual independence of his kingdom; it would
prevent any encroachments by the United States on
his sovereignty. While the King had, through pressure, discarded the clever adventurer, who was without standing in any community, he still had faith in
his wild schemes and had determined to renew his
acquaintance with him. Even if there should be no
practical results from their intercourse, it would
show his white subjects that he was personally quite
independent and that he resented their interference.

As we anchored at Naples, the Italian admiral, the general commanding the forces, and the mayor of the city, with many officials, led by Moreno, appeared on board. Instead of seeking a presentation to the King through his Chamberlain, the adventurer, after he had been cordially received by the King, assumed charge of him, and presented to him the distinguished visitors, who understood, we afterward learned, that the King still retained the Italian in his service as a private adviser and a guardian of the Hawaiian youth. The King did not wish openly to discredit his ex-Minister, while the suite, unfortunately, were unable to speak the Italian language. Signor Moreno privately presented the Italian officials, and the Mayor of Naples cordially welcomed the King to Italy. The suite stood at a short distance, contriving means to grapple with the nerve and audacity of the adventurer, who impudently smiled upon them, for he was now the master of ceremonies and acted as interpreter.

A written address was now read to the King by some friend of the ex-Minister; it pronounced the King to be a wise and far-seeing monarch and thanked him for having appointed a noble-minded Italian to the office of Cabinet Minister, and it expressed the profound regret of the Italian nation that wicked men had forced him to remove such an able counsellor.

The King was bewildered, and allowed himself to be taken on shore by the adventurer to the Hôtel des Étrangers, leaving his suite alone on the deck of the steamer, kingless and dumfounded. The King believed, when he left, that they were in a boat closely following him.

Margherita, Queen of Italy (1881).

There was something rather comical in the departure of the suite from the steamer, in a boat, alone, without knowing the Italian language, without acquaintance, and in pursuit of an abducted monarch. We suspected, however, that the King had been taken to the Hôtel des Étrangers, and drove there. We found him with his ex-Minister in his private parlour, and at once asked the King whether he desired our presence. He asked us to remain in the room, and as we did so the adventurer soon left. We told the King that if we should send to his kingdom the story of the events of the preceding hour his throne would be in immediate danger. He replied that he did not realise the compromising situation in which he was placed. He then left to us the disposition of the affair, and we excluded Signor Moreno from the King's apartments unless we were present at all interviews. He claimed that he needed funds for the education of the Hawaiian boys; this we provided for by putting them in charge of the King's Consul-General at Hamburg.

The King and Queen of Italy were temporarily in the city, and the King sent an aide requesting his Hawaiian Majesty to call informally at the palace the next day. We called at two o'clock. There was a parade of troops and the music of bugles. We entered a reception-room from the windows of which was a view of the great bay, and of Vesuvius with a spiral smoke curling up from its summit.

King Humberto and Queen Margherita entered, received our sovereign cordially, and led him to an adjoining room, where they conversed for half an hour. Both Humberto and his Queen were plainly dressed; they had come to Naples for rest, and were pleased, they said, to meet the King of Hawaii.

While the sovereigns were conversing, the suite engaged in conversation with the ladies of the court. When we spoke in English, they were surprised, for they expected we would speak in Hawaiian and that an interpreter would aid us. The Queen's sister said it was believed that the King of Hawaii had come to meet his natural sons, who were in the military and naval schools, and it must give him great pleasure to do so. We replied that the young men were not related to the King, which surprised them. We now detected the adventurer's game; he was securing consideration from the Italian government as the guardian of those who, he had confidentially stated, were the natural sons of the Hawaiian King.

Their Majesties now returned to the reception-room and joined in the general conversation. The Queen was not a handsome woman, but the aureole of royalty about her person, like well-adjusted lights, set off her features to good advantage. She was not stately, nor had she an impressive presence, but was gracious and simple. By her side was the little Crown Prince; she seemed to have a pathetic expression as she took and held his hand. Their Italian Majesties knew something about the Hawaiian group through persons of the court who had visited them; they asked about their countrymen who had settled there. The Queen was greatly pleased when she learned that many of the Hawaiian subjects were good Catholics.

We then retired. King Humberto walked to the steps of the carriage with our King; the bugle sounded, the troops presented arms, and we returned to our hotel. Within an hour King Humberto returned the visit. He said that the Minister of Foreign Affairs in Rome would show our King the attention due to his rank, and regretted his own absence from the capital. After he left, our King informed us that his Italian Majesty, in their interview in the drawing-room, had assumed that the native youths were his sons, but he had corrected his error and regretted that the adventurer had misled him.

Moreno now abandoned his scheme of connecting himself with the King, but he asked to be permitted to accompany him to Rome as an old and faithful friend. The suite advised the King not to compromise himself further with him, and his request was denied.

The following day we visited the ruins of Pompeii and the spots which usually attract tourists.

The Italians have a custom of addressing poems of admiration to their friends or to distinguished visitors; the inspiration of the poet, in many cases, being stimulated by the hope of some substantial reward. Numerous Italians eagerly sought decorations from the King. One devised a plan of securing one through his Minister, by addressing him in verse, —

> " All Egregio Signore
> Sua Eccellenza —— "

The poet asked excuse for his boldness in offering spontaneous words of praise to the Minister's noble merits and his splendid virtues; he declared that all Italy breathed through his words as he struck his lyre in honour of one who was the glory of Hawaii and one of the honourable men of the earth. It was an infinite pleasure to address one who was entitled to adoration; the Minister was kindly asked to accept the loyalty of the song.

It was signed by one Beneduce, who called the next day, sent up his card, and, after some preliminary conversation, humbly asked the gift of a decoration. The King, as well as the Chamberlain, received many fervid effusions. A large number, perhaps the most of them, were not followed by applications for decorations, but were only harmless ways of gratifying the Italian emotions.

During the next day Ismail, the ex-Khedive of Egypt, and the father of the present Khedive, called on the King. He was short, fat, blear-eyed, and had reddish hair. When he was deposed by the Powers two years before this time, because he was extravagant beyond control and oppressed the *fellahin,* he selected forty of his wives, gathered the richest furniture of his palace, took the state jewelry, and moved to a residence near Naples. During his reign he had invested vast sums in the cultivation of sugar-cane and in factories for the making of sugar. He said that he had heard of the sugar-production of the Hawaiian group, and asked many questions about the labour used by the planters; he believed that Egypt would become one of the largest sugar-producing countries of the earth, but he had no longer any interest in such matters, as he had been sent away. He asked the King to make him a visit, but, he said, he was now only a private citizen and not entitled to a visit from him.

Our troubles with the rapacious hotel-keepers of Europe now began. We were charged exorbitant prices without mercy. In the Orient royal gratuities

The Crown Prince of Italy (1881).

to servants in the palaces which we occupied were
expected, and largely exceeded the expenses of hotels.
The lists of servants who expected such gratuities in
one Eastern palace numbered over one hundred, although there were only three in our party. But we
were having a royal dance and paid the pipers royally.
The European hotel-keepers took merciless advantage of us. Their most effective and cunning way
of doing it was by withholding our accounts until we
were on the point of leaving, when it was awkward
for the Chamberlain to review or dispute the items of
the bills. The Chamberlain, who attended to those
matters, looked upon the hour of leaving as one of
great annoyance. Apartments were charged to us
which we did not occupy; the prices for those we
used were excessive; quantities of wine were charged
which we never had; charges for meals and service
were made sufficient to maintain a large retinue.
The valet had declared that he was well capable of
preventing these extortions, but in no instance did
he aid the Chamberlain. The King was not aware
of these gross impositions. Perhaps it should not
have been expected that a king would be treated as
a common guest, though he received only the same
accommodations. When the ex-King of Spain,
Joseph Bonaparte, received a bill from an innkeeper
of a hotel in Bordentown, New Jersey, which contained a charge, " Miscellaneous, $300," he inquired
for the items; the innkeeper promptly informed his
secretary that it might be read, " For kicking up a
damned fuss while you were my guest." The European innkeepers were without even this excuse in
charging our royal party.

Just before we left Naples we were informed of

the shooting of President Garfield, in Washington, by Guiteau. This was the second assassination of a ruler since we began the tour. Revising these notes of travel, I recall the incident of King Humberto's taking off twenty years after our interview with him. I had known General Garfield from early days, and was one of his friends who regretted his election to the Presidency, which withdrew him from occupations which were better suited to his talents and temperament.

CHAPTER XXII

Rome, Cardinal Jacobini — Interview with the Holy Father
— Pleasant Conversation — Cardinal Howard — A Pictur-
esque Scene — The King Prevented by His Suite from
Visiting St. Petersburg — Leave for England via Paris —
A Scheming Hollander — Ride through Paris and Leave
for London — Violation of French Etiquette.

WHEN we arrived in Rome, by command of
the King, I addressed a note to Cardinal
Jacobini, the Papal Secretary of State, asking for
an interview with the Holy Father. He replied at
once, fixing four o'clock as the most convenient hour.
We accordingly, in evening dress, drove to the Vatican. An officer led us to a corridor through which
we passed and were taken by other officials through
other grand corridors to an upper chamber. At the
rest on the broad stairways, Swiss soldiers, armed
with spears and lances and clad in rich uniforms,
stood on guard. Cardinal Jacobini, short, fat, jolly,
and shrewd, received us, and led us through several
chambers, with ceilings richly frescoed, to a room
which was comparatively small; this was the audience-room. It was exquisitely frescoed, and a soft
light entered the stained windows. The Cardinals
silently entered; among them Cardinal Howard, an
enormous Englishman, about seven feet in height,
with ruddy cheeks, a humorous expression, and a
living proof that these high prelates did not always
mortify the flesh.

A door opened, and his Holiness, Leo XIII, a thin and spare old man with an extremely pale face, entered and slowly moved across the room, while all bowed in reverence, to a chair on a daïs raised a few inches from the floor. In front of him another chair was placed for the King; around the Holy Father the Cardinals were grouped, and we of the suite stood near the King.

The Pope began the conversation at once in Italian, which was interpreted by Cardinal Howard. He asked many questions about the Hawaiian kingdom. The Cardinals joined, and soon showed that they were well informed about the condition of the native Catholics in Hawaii, of whom there were almost as many as there were Protestants. The Holy Father said to the King: "Will you present your companions?" The King presented us. The Pope asked: "Are they natives of your country?" The King replied that we were, and the sons of Protestant missionaries. Cardinal Howard laughed, and said, "Then they are in the opposition." The Holy Father smiled. There was no solemnity in the interview; it was only a pleasant chat.

"Do my people in your kingdom behave well?" asked the Pope.

"Yes," said the King, "they are good subjects."

"If they do not behave," said the Pope, "I must look after them. Why do you have a white Minister in your government?" he continued.

The King could not make a brief explanation and turned to me. I answered, for him, that the kings of Hawaii chose educated white men, who were better able to deal with the foreigners, who held most of the wealth of the country.

Pope Leo XIII (1881).

Cardinal Howard asked: "Are there any Catholics in your government?"

I answered: "No, the American Protestants entered the country before the Catholics did, and have kept control of public affairs; but no efficient Catholic is excluded from high office by reason of his faith."

There was often a pleasant twinkle in the Holy Father's eye, and he smiled while he spoke. I then recalled his humour in the naïve blessing which, it was said, he had given to the Oriental bishops during the Œcumenical Council. They were, as a rule, not very clean in person. He raised his vicarious hand when they knelt before him, saying, *sotto voce*, "Dirty as ye all are" (then aloud), "I give ye all my blessing."

After an interview which lasted twenty minutes we kissed the Holy Father's hand and rose. He said to the King: "Your country is far away. I shall pray for your safe return."

The scene was picturesque. On the slightly raised daïs sat a slender, quiet man, with a kindly eye, holding supreme power over nearly two hundred millions of people, their faith in him qualified by no conditions, reservations, or distinctions; in another and in its best sense, "the strongest business corporation of the world," or, as Cardinal Pacca, the Prime Minister of Pius VII, said of the Pontifical government, "a masterpiece, not of divine, but of human policy." Here was the solitary man to whom these millions looked for guidance in life and for salvation beyond the grave. Before this stupendous power in the moral world sat the king of an insignificant group of islands; the great mountain and the mole-hill were confronting each other.

Though Heine had called this great Church the " Bastile of the Spirit," it was for centuries the conservative power which, through its influence over the State, maintained whatever order existed; it was the police force of the civilised world for a thousand years, whatever the truth of its religious doctrine might be.

We were then taken through many rooms of the Vatican, and from them went to St. Peter's, where so many kings had humbled themselves before the awful power of Rome.

We made an agreement with Cardinal Jacobini by which the Holy Father would confer on the King and suite some Papal decoration, and the King would confer his own Orders on the Holy Father and the Papal Staff.

The King had not given up his intention to visit St. Petersburg, for he hoped to exchange decorations with the Tsar. His suite opposed such a visit for a number of reasons; not only would he fail to be in London during the " season," but he might find the Tsar had left St. Petersburg, and his time was limited. He was obstinate, and inclined to push on at once to Russia. The suite then resorted to a trick which caused him to change his mind. While taking our coffee in the morning I opened a morning Italian paper and pretended to read it. The Chamberlain, according to a prearranged conspiracy, asked for the news. I therefore read to him from the paper, composing or improvising as I read, this item: " There has been a fresh outbreak of the Nihilists in St. Petersburg, and there is great fear of an attack on the Tsar. Ten thousand troops are ordered out to protect the Palace." This was not read directly to the King, nor did we call his attention to it, but he listened. I then handed the paper to him, saying, " Perhaps your Majesty wishes to look over this paper." I knew that he could not read it. The Chamberlain remarked: " If his Majesty goes to St. Petersburg, the Nihilists, in their hatred of all sovereigns, may attack him; better for him, before leaving, to sign papers containing his wishes in the event of any trouble." We said no more; but within an hour the King told us that on reflection he would not visit the Tsar.

We left Rome in a direct and unbroken journey to London, in order to be there before the season closed.

During the journey to Paris, a clever Hollander, who had visited our kingdom for a few hours while on a voyage to New Caledonia, introduced himself to the King when he was alone. He adroitly placed before him a specious financial scheme which, he said, would be of much personal benefit to him. He had opened large beds of nickel ore in New Caledonia; he proposed to furnish his Majesty's government with nickel coins of small denomination, for which his Majesty's government should pay the sum of $200,000. The cost of the coin would not exceed $50,000, and the profit, he proposed, should be equally divided between the King and himself. This simple scheme of forcing a base coin into our kingdom for personal gain captivated the King, and he favoured it, and did not display any more lack of moral sense in this affair than the majority of rulers and statesmen. The Hollander subsequently caused samples of the nickel coin to be made in Paris and sent them to his Majesty after he had returned home; but the King's white advisers were again obstinate and refused to execute the scheme. The suite suspected the nature of the transaction, and warned the Hollander that it would fail to bring him any profit; but he believed that the King was an absolute monarch in his own country and refused to abandon it. The King's justification for engaging in it was that the largest capitalist in his kingdom, a white man, had secured a great profit by introducing silver coin into the kingdom in a similar manner, and there was no reason why the King himself should not take advantage of a business opportunity.

We reached Paris at five o'clock in the morning and were met by the King's Vice-Consul and suite. We drove for several hours through the streets until the departure of the train to Boulogne. On passing through the Place Vendôme, the Vice-Consul pointed to the site of the grand Column of Napoleon, which was destroyed during the Commune. "There," he said, "stood the magnificent column; it was torn down by the vicious Communists." I replied, "I was here, and saw it destroyed. I saw the workmen boring holes in its base." "How extraordinary," he said; "is not this the first visit of the King and his party in Europe? Do people travel from your country to Paris?" By a mere chance, in 1871, I had been assistant bearer of despatches to the American Minister in Paris during the Commune, and left the city just before the attack and massacre of the Communists by the Versailles troops.

We left for London, but ignorantly committed a breach of courtly etiquette which subsequently annoyed us. Though only in transition through the city, the King should have directed his Chamberlain to call at the palace of the Élysée, and leave his card with the President of the French Republic. This omission was regarded by the Foreign Office as a breach of etiquette, as we soon discovered. The King had no minister at the French court, although he had a Consul-General in Paris without diplomatic power. It was our purpose to visit Paris later in the season, and exchange courtesies with the French President.

We had no love for the French nation. Its diplomatic agents and warships had made hostile visits to our Islands on several occasions. Under threat of bombarding our capital they at one time had extorted unjust commercial privileges from our government, and at a later period had, in spite of the protests of the representative of the United States, landed an armed force, destroyed a large amount of government property, spiked the guns of the fortress, and carried away the King's yacht to the South Seas.

CHAPTER XXIII

London, Claridge's Hotel — Royal and Ministerial Callers —
The Duke of Edinburgh's Visit to Hawaii — The Prince of
Wales Makes a Social "Lion" of the King — The Royal
Family Takes the King up Without Reserve — The Queen's
Carriages at His Service — Patti at the Royal Italian
Opera — An Old Schoolmate, General Armstrong — The
Houses of Parliament — The "Plug" Hat the Symbol of
British Power — Volunteer Review in Windsor Park —
— The Crown Prince of Germany — Novelty of Our Situa-
tion — Westminster Abbey — A Trip on the River with
Lord Charles Beresford.

WHEN we reached London the King's Consul-
General for England insisted that his Majesty should lodge at Claridge's Hotel, where all
visiting monarchs reside if they are in good and
regular standing and are not invited to any of the
palaces.

The Gladstone government was in power, and Earl
Granville promptly called on the King, and was followed by Lord Charles Beresford, who, with the
Duke of Edinburgh, had visited the Hawaiian kingdom in the warship "Galatea" some years before.
After them came Sir Thomas and Lady Brassey,
who had also visited the kingdom in the "Sunbeam."
By the King's command our Chamberlain called on
Mr. James Russell Lowell, the American Minister,
with the deep regrets of the King for the deadly
attack on President Garfield. Mr. F. R. Synge, of
the Foreign Office, was directed by Earl Granville
to attend the King so long as he remained in Lon-

The Duke of Edinburgh (1881).

don. He was a clever man, familiar with royal etiquette, knew everybody, and, moreover, had lived when a child in Hawaii, where his father at one time resided as British Commissioner. Mr. Synge at once relieved us of all anxiety about matters of etiquette, and managed with great skill what we in private called the "royal circus with a Polynesian lion in the cage."

Though we had arrived in London at the height of the season, for it was now July, we did not anticipate any unusual courtesies from the Queen, but hoped to get a glimpse of high life, a formal presentation at court, and invitations to some social functions where the "swells" of England might be seen. But a bit of bread which the King had cast upon the waters ten years before now floated back to him as a very large loaf. While only a Hawaiian prince he had received the Duke of Edinburgh and Lord Charles Beresford on their visit to the islands mentioned above. The chief entertainment was a feast served in the native style in one of the beautiful valleys near the city, with the mountains rising up on either side, which cast deep shadows over it. The exquisite beauty of the place, the wilderness of native flowers, and the dancing of the native girls, fascinated the Duke, and on his return to England he told the Royal Family, some of whom repeated his story to us, that of all the visits he had made during his long voyage in the "Galatea" the one to the Sandwich Islands was the most charming, so delightful that it was reported in the press soon after his return that the Prince of Wales declared that if he ever made a long cruise his first visit would be to these islands. The Duke, when we arrived, was in command of a warship in the Baltic; but he telegraphed his congratulations to the King on his arrival, and, we were told, had requested the Royal Family to make the King's visit a pleasant one.

The Prince of Wales, as the social chief of the English people, representing the Queen, gave the "tip," or, more decorously speaking, fixed the measure of his reception, and the King at once bounded into the glittering arena as a social lion. This was accepted with excellent humour by the aristocracy, who are always charmed with some new sensation. The King's use of the English language gave him a great advantage over some visiting monarchs; besides, he did not exhibit the habits of the Shah of Persia, who, while occupying Buckingham Palace, turned one of the drawing-rooms into a slaughter-house for chickens, because it was the custom in Persia to kill and cook in the presence of the ruler, in order to remove the risk of being poisoned. Instead of staying only three days in London, the King remained sixteen days, during which time he was most royally entertained, and, if a lion fattens on attentions, he finally waddled out of England "as fat as a poodle dog."

The Prince of Wales called at once and greeted him pleasantly; the Duke of Albany, the Duke of Connaught, the Duke of Cambridge, Prince Teck, Prime Minister and Mrs. Gladstone, Lord Kimberley, Colonel Teesdale, Equerry to the Prince of Wales, Earl Spencer, the Earl and Countess of Clarendon, the Earl and Countess of Breadalbane, the Earl and Countess Dalhousie, the Right Hon. George and Mrs. Cavendish Bentinck, Baroness Burdett-Coutts, the foreign Ambassadors and Ministers

The Prince of Wales (1881).

resident in London, and many other distinguished persons also called and gave the King a cordial greeting. His movements were recorded daily in the " Court Circular " along with the doings of the British court, and with the same conscientious fidelity to detail as that with which the last moments of a criminal on the morning of his execution are described in American newspapers.

Until we left, one of her Majesty's carriages was at the King's disposal at all times; the driver and footman in red livery during the day and in black during the evening. A card was also given to us on which was inscribed an order granting the right of way in the streets.

On our first evening we attended the Royal Italian Opera, and the King, with his keen sense of good music, enjoyed Patti's singing. It was an event in his life, and when he intimated a wish to visit her she promptly invited him behind the curtain; he handed her a bouquet, which she received " graciously," and no doubt soon tossed on the heap of dead flowers which Crowned Heads had cast at her feet for twenty years. Although a thousand glasses from all parts of the house were directed to her Majesty's box, in which he was, the King paid no attention to them while Patti sang; it was for him a supreme hour, and he recalled it often with much satisfaction in later years.

The next morning, General S. C. Armstrong, of the Hampton Normal Institute of Virginia, called upon the King. In early days they had been not only schoolmates but collaborators in the publication of a newspaper in the Hawaiian language; the " lion " and his friend roared in the Hawaiian language, the British court passed out of sight, and they were again under the cocoanut palms of Hawaii.

With Mr. Foster, the Secretary of State for Ireland, I visited the Houses of Parliament, the cradle of British liberty and the home of silk hats. The hat is worn during the sittings as a badge of power, and it stands as a perpetual invitation to the King and the Lords to knock it off and arouse the slumbering energy of the people. While the Chinese indicate rank and power by a peacock's feather, and the wild Indian shows it in that of an eagle or rooster, the British citizen selects the silk hat as the emblem of his supreme power under the Constitution. If a local whirlwind found its way into Westminster during a session of Parliament, and carried off the sacred hats, the empire would tremble on the verge of anarchy. Still, under these hats are the heads that rule one fourth of the people of the earth; were it a rabbit's foot, instead of a hat, it would remain an awful emblem of physical force. Under these hats exists more power than any body of men have held since the beginning of time; a power which, until America has reached the full measure of her dominance, is the best hope of pushing civilisation to the uttermost parts of the earth. In its weakness and strength, in its glory and shame, the British empire presents all the virtues and vices of men. It has seized territory without right, overthrown weaker governments, bombarded defenceless cities, butchered women and children, despised and overthrown the rights of many communities. On the other hand, it has established law and order and the wise administration of justice over one fourth of the globe, and opened a safe commerce with the world to all nations; without reserving special privileges to itself, it puts the Frenchman, the German, the Russian, and the American on the same footing as the Briton in all countries, where, through the prodigal use of its own blood and treasure, it has made commerce safe. These considerations I put before my royal master while we took our breakfast tea; but he, like Tolstoi's tiger looking at the world from his own standpoint, asked, "What is there in all this for me?" The British and the Americans were, after all, one people, and how soon would his monarchy be reorganised out of existence by their hard and restless race? There was no comfort for him in the reflection that he was a grasshopper in a procession of elephants.

The Queen, on the day of our arrival, sent to the King an invitation to attend the review of the volunteer forces next day in Windsor Park. On nearing the Park, we were met by a royal carriage and driven to the tent of Lord Brassey, who commanded a regiment of volunteer marines, where we lunched with a large company and listened to a clever but brief speech from Lady Brassey, who responded to a toast. We were then driven within the grounds of Windsor Castle, from which all others, including the nobility, were excluded. The Duke of Cambridge, the Commander-in-Chief, saluted the King, and assigned to our carriage a place in front of the seats which had been placed, with rising steps, for the nobility of England. The Royal Family, in carriages, escorted by a detachment of the Royal Horse Guards, now appeared, and were so arranged that our carriage was the last, and the only one which contained persons

who were not members of the Royal Family.   With
the Queen were the Princess of Wales and the Crown
Princess of Germany.   At the flagstaff her Majesty
received a royal salute, and the volunteers, numbering over 50,000, marched past her carriage.   His
Imperial Highness the Crown Prince Frederick of
Germany was the honorary commander of a regiment, and as soon as it had saluted and passed the
Queen, he left his regiment, rode up to our carriage,
saluted, and gave his hand to the King, saying, —

"Your Majesty, I am the Crown Prince of Germany.   I shall call upon you to-morrow; but permit
me now to thank you for your hospitality to my son,
Prince Henry, when he visited your kingdom.   My
father, the Emperor, is at Gastein, but you will be
received, if you visit Berlin, by my son, Prince
William" [now Emperor].

He then returned to his place by the side of the
Queen's carriage.   The Prince of Wales, when his
own regiment had passed, also rode up to our carriage, chatted with the King, and told him that he
hoped to receive him at a garden party at Marlborough House on the following Tuesday.   At the
close of the review the Queen's carriage turned and
passed us; the Queen had not then received the King,
but she bowed to him as she went by.   There were
cords drawn in front of the seats occupied by the
nobility, so that no one could enter the ground where
the carriages stood.   We then drove back to London.

I had visited England before this and had gazed
from curbstones on the nobility and the Queen; I
had, by tipping a half-crown to the guard, ridden in
a first-class railway coach with a lord, so that I might
look upon a creature unknown to American insti-

The Prince Imperial of Germany (1881).

tutions. I had, from the depths, looked up at the beautiful feet of the aristocracy upon the purple mountain tops; but now, by a singular fate, I was permitted (for this occasion only) actually to stand with them on these lofty altitudes; aye, even to breathe the rare and perfumed air in which these social and patrician gods were dwelling in the devout adoration of the British public. Like the gods of Homer, they had many defects, but still they were gods, and the beloved fetish of a great people.

As we entered the city after the review, our carriage got into a jam of waggons at a crossing. A drunken cabby, pointing to the King, who sat with dignity in the royal carriage, shouted: "There goes me father, hit's the big one!" A policeman cried out, "Make room for the Queen's carriage!" and directed cabby to turn aside. The cabby turned on him with a drunken leer and answered: "I belongs to this ere royal party."

On the next day, Sunday, we attended the services in Westminster Abbey. Dean Stanley was unable to be present, owing to illness; but he sent to the King a kindly message and directed that he should be taken to the interesting parts of the Abbey.

The King looked reverently on the effigies and tombs. "Those who are buried here," said his friend, "take all the fame just now. But when the 'Society for the Propagation of the Names of the Deserving Dead, Which Have Been Omitted,' reconstructs the Abbey, five hundred years from now, and publishes a revised list of Immortals, some of them will go into the rubbish heap."

In the afternoon there was a trip up the Thames in a small yacht belonging to Lord Beresford, the

King's genial friend, filled with a party of high-born people whose conversation instructed the King greatly in the use of colloquial language and idiomatic terms. "Lord Charles," as he was called, was a humourous Englishman, and his strong, healthy spirits made him the staunch friend of the Prince of Wales. After dining at Lord William Beresford's place in Maidenhead we returned to the city.

The Princess of Prussia (1881).

CHAPTER XXIV

AN interview with the Queen was now arranged. Accordingly, the next day we took luncheon with Earl and Lady Granville. Mr. Gladstone, Sir Charles Dilke, Lord Kimberley, and other members of the Cabinet were there. With due observance of etiquette the Prime Minister of the greatest empire of the world and the Minister of the smallest kingdom of the world were placed opposite each other. Mr. Gladstone said little. No startling aphorism sprang from his lips. But much pudding went into his mouth, which, by the mysterious transmutation of nature, was converted into a brief and admirable speech on the Transvaal, in Parliament that evening.

After luncheon with Lord Granville we drove to the Paddington station, whence we went to Windsor by train. There we were met by royal carriages and a detachment of the Horse Guards, and taken to the castle, where we were to be presented to the Queen.

Gentlemen-in-waiting received us at the entrance and led us into a room where there were basins and looking-glasses, wherewith we could prevent dirt from offending the august eye. We were in morning dress. After passing through several chambers and galleries we entered the Green Drawing-room. The King and Lord Granville stood alone; we of the suite, with Mr. Synge, stood aside. There was silence for a moment, as if we were on a trap door and about to be launched, like criminals, into eternity; then the doors were suddenly thrown wide open, and the British Queen entered the room, advanced toward the King, and shook his hand. With her were the Princess Louise and Princess Beatrice, the Duke of Albany, and the Duke of Hesse. It is at this moment of introduction to the royal presence that fear and tremblings distress many who are presented, much like the " buck fever " in America, which affects an amateur hunter when he tries his first shot at a deer. But we, now well acclimated in the atmosphere of royal splendours in the Orient, were not stricken with it. The King stood, large, impassive, graceful. Her Majesty and the King were then seated, and she at once spoke of the visit of the Duke of Edinburgh to his Majesty's islands, and declared that they must be very beautiful, for the Duke often spoke of them.

After a few moments of conversation her Majesty arose, presented the King to the other members of the Royal Family, and, turning toward the suite, received us with Lord Cranville's presentation. She

Queen Victoria and the Princess Beatrice (1881).

said to me: "His Majesty speaks our language easily; how did he learn it?" I replied that he learned it in the missionary schools when young. She asked about Queen Emma (the Queen Dowager, the widow of one of the King's predecessors; she had visited England, and was a guest at Windsor for some days), saying, "She is a charming young woman; I was very fond of her." She then asked the King if he would walk about the castle, or drive to Virginia Water. He said he preferred to see the interior of the castle. She said that she hoped his Majesty would enjoy his visit; she had always been much interested in his kingdom; he might feel assured that he was very welcome in London. She then retired.

With the Duke of Hesse and the Duke of Albany we then sat down in another room, overlooking the park, to luncheon. We were taken through the many rooms of the castle, and the Dukes repeated the story of each apartment. Again taking the royal carriages, surrounded with Horse Guards, we returned to the station, where we took the train for London. We learned, soon after this, that the Queen had been in excellent humour during the King's visit; it pleased her especially that he spoke the English language so easily and with an English accent; no other foreign sovereign who had visited England spoke it as fluently.

As a project for an alliance between the royal families of Japan and Hawaii was still pending, it was not practicable for the King to propose one between the Royal Family of Great Britain and that of Hawaii. The suite were therefore not to be surprised by a sudden and secret visit of the King to Windsor

Castle with intent to put a British steel rod into the uneasy throne of Hawaii.

Our days and nights were now spent in constant intercourse with the superior beings who constitute the highest class of British social and political life. But at times there came to us evidence of the fact that exaltation of rank does not remove the unpleasant environments of life; that the prince and the pauper have much in common; in fact, one who was familiar with the court life told me that it was full of annoyances and tribulations in spite of the sweet air of adoration which pervaded it.

The Crown Prince of Germany called in the morning, and again thanked the King for his kind services to his son, Prince Henry. We quickly returned his call at Buckingham Palace, where we were received also by the Crown Princess, who, though born in England and the daughter of the Queen, spoke with a slight German accent. She spoke as if she had an active mind and was by no means indifferent to public affairs; the Crown Prince we admired almost above all men we had met in our travels; his face was an open one, and in his blue Teutonic eye was kindness and warmth.

We called upon the Prince and Princess of Wales at Marlborough House; their children were present, and the Princess spoke of the beautiful islands of which she had so often heard. Standing near her, it was easy to understand how Tennyson wrote that the English were

"All Danes in our welcome of thee."

The Prince took the King in his carriage, with the suite following, to luncheon at Lord Charles

Prince Henry of Prussia (1881).

Beresford's in Eaton Square, where we met the clever American, Lady Mandeville, now Dowager Duchess of Manchester, whom I had met before in the United States, — a woman with the rare gift for telling a story well; also Mrs. Sands, one of the American beauties of "the Prince's set." After luncheon, while we were smoking in the balcony, the Prince again spoke of his brother's visit to the King's country and of his desire to see it. Lord Beresford, at the time of his brother's visit, was a midshipman on the "Galatea," and in one of his frolics on shore had removed at night the sign of the American Consul to the front of a Chinese junk-shop; for his indiscretion, which had greatly incensed the people of the town, and had stirred the local American Eagle to frantic screams, he duly apologised. We did not dream that the political unrest in Egypt which we detected at the banquet of the Khedive would in the next year invite the bombardment of Alexandria, the burning of the great palace in which we were received, and be the occasion for the signal daring of Lord Beresford in fighting his warship at close range to the Egyptian forts.

The Prince of Wales in his eighteenth year, with the Duke of Newcastle, had visited the United States in 1859. The grandest and most ambitious ball ever given on American soil up to that time took place in the Academy of Music in New York City. I was present, and now recalled to the Prince one of its unique features, which, he said, embarrassed him greatly at the time. The young ladies were eager to dance with him, but the Committee of Managers could not select his partners without giving great offence to hundreds who would be neglected. A shrewd merchant, who was a member of the Committee, therefore proposed that " the Prince be turned loose among the girls and left to select his own partners." This plan was adopted, and he modestly moved through the lines of beautiful girls, who opened the way for him, — a very apple of discord, — and made his own selections, which could not be charged to the Committee.

At six o'clock in the evening we again visited Marlborough House, where a garden party was held on the lawn. Many carriages of the nobility were in a long line at the entrance, awaiting their turns to discharge their occupants, but the royal carriage containing the King and suite took precedence. The Prince and Princess received their guests near the door. Tents had been erected on the lawn, under the venerable trees. The Queen was announced; it was the first garden party she had attended since the death of Prince Albert. The Prince led her to a tent, where she was attended by the Princesses Louise and Beatrice. The King entered it, and, after a few moments' conversation, moved to one of the old trees, and under its branches held a reception of his own. While " the best blood " of England was there, the most attractive person on the ground, it seemed to me, was the American Minister, Mr. Lowell. It seemed as if here was the source of a pretty historical picture. As he slowly walked amid the members of the British court, among the descendants of those who had driven the Puritans out of England, and of those who for lack of foresight had called into being a great and independent republic beyond the seas, he seemed quietly to say:

The Princess of Wales (1881).

" I represent the crew of the ' Mayflower,' returning to you in their splendid transformation into a
nation of your own blood."

Yet it was an informal gathering. The Princesses
Louise and Beatrice, the Crown Princess of Germany, the Princesses Sophia and Margaret of Prussia,
the Duchess of Connaught, the Princess Mary of
Cambridge, moved from group to group and joined
those who gathered around the King. If an intelligent traveller had been present who was entirely ignorant of the rank of the persons composing this
garden party, he would have described them as good-
natured people with simple manners and direct speech,
and in all respects differing in no way from well-bred
people in any land. The ruler over one fourth of the
people of the world took her cup of tea with the same
enjoyment, neither more nor less, than Mrs. Gup-
pins, an East side washerwoman, takes hers. The
conversation was confined to pleasant gossip; in no
case did I hear the winds of exalted thoughts playing
about the heads of these distinguished people. There
were no formal introductions to the Queen, for the
guests were her acquaintances and friends. I over-
heard, sometimes, the quiet comments of the guests
upon my King. They were in every case pleasant;
for his large size, the quiet repose of his manners, and
his excellent command of the English language commended him; his colour seemed to bring him advantage among these people, who have no prejudice
against it, and who cannot understand why, in the
United States, the presence of a negro in society
agitates it, like a rat in a ball-room.

The following day we were driven to Lord's cricket
grounds, the Tower, St. Paul's, and through Hyde

Park, in the Queen's carriage, and closed it with attending a garden party in Lambeth Palace, the residence of Archbishop Tait, of Canterbury. The Archbishop led the King and suite through its rooms, and revealed the splendour in which the spiritual lords of England lived, — a manner of living which had been reversed by the spiritual leaders of the same Church in their residences beyond the Atlantic, where the English race had created, "a State without a King, a Church without a Bishop."

In Albert Hall there was an afternoon concert. The King and suite sat in Lord Granville's box. The King was delighted with a duet sung by Patti and Albani.

At eleven o'clock in the evening we went to a reception given by Earl and Countess Spencer to the Prince and Princess of Wales in the Kensington Museum. We were received by Lord Spencer, who led us to a small chamber where his royal visitors gathered before they formally entered the large hall to meet the fifteen hundred guests who had been invited. There we found the Prince and Princess of Wales, their royal Highnesses the Princesses Louise and Beatrice, the Crown Prince and Princess of Germany, Princess Mary of Cambridge, and the Duke of Cambridge. We were in this small chamber for a few moments, and the intercourse was informal.

Lord Spencer, who had been engaged in receiving his royal guests and had spoken briefly to the King, now entered the chamber rather hurriedly and approached our Chamberlain, who had, I have said, a very dark complexion, saying: " Will your Majesty please take ——— " when he was interrupted by our

Chamberlain, who, seeing the mistake, replied: "I am not his Majesty; he is over there." This slight error was greatly enjoyed by the Princess Mary of Cambridge.

The Earl spoke to the King, who then took the Princess of Wales on his arm, and led a procession, followed by the Prince, and by Princess Louise and the rest, including the King's suite, to the large hall, where many hundreds of noble and distinguished persons awaited them. This royal body moved slowly through lines formed by the guests, and after this ceremony was over there began the functions of a *conversazione* which, so far as I could see, was substantially a close watch of the movements of the regal party, with subdued conversation.

There was an atmosphere of seriousness, as if all were engaged in anything but a frolic; the high-born women seemed to be anxious to get near to the Royal Family, who were in a group, informally chatting with acquaintances. A lady, covered with magnificent diamonds, whom I had met at the garden party, but whose name I could not recall, kindly offered to point out the grand people to me, and as we moved about we heard the comments made upon the King: " I am told he has thirty wives." — " He carries himself well." — " The Prince has taken him up." — " Where is his country; is it near America? " — " Was his grandfather a cannibal? "

There was a supper-room, to which only the Royal Family were admitted with their attendants and close friends. My clever escort, who knew every one, pointed out the statesmen, the men with great lineage, the soldiers who were in London to-day at the clubs, and to-morrow were fighting in the mountain passes of the Himalayas, or chasing savages in the African jungle; the beautiful women of the aristocracy, not at all numerous, and with the reputation for personal charms, created by the accidents of public opinion; men of great rank, many of whom descended from ancestors whose characters were now protected from review by a statute of limitations which protects the memories of the dead. Upon the tables in the supper-room were salads, ices, cold meats, and champagne, the same foods and drink which are consumed by the vast majority of English people who are called the commonalty, and who accept without murmur, even with pleasure, their social inferiority. I said to my patrician escort that having been born with the traditions of American democracy, though holding for a time some political rank, I desired to know from one, like herself, who occupied those rare social altitudes, whether there were any ecstatic sensations connected with such life; were there sensations pervading it which were not permitted to those of low rank. She replied that life was a great bore, and the aristocracy found it as monotonous as other people found it. It was nothing but a chasing of baubles and shadows. She inquired, "Is your party in ecstasies because you have seen so many new countries, and courts, and kings and queens?" I replied that instead of being in ecstasies we were counting the hours which would bring us to the cocoanut groves and the valleys of our islands.

I was then summoned to attend my royal master in the reception-room from which we had started; from it we returned to our lodgings. It was now four o'clock in the morning, and in an hour kings and princes, noblemen and great soldiers, princesses and beauties, were in their night-caps, with heads full of foolish dreams, restoring themselves for a repetition of the same pageantry the following days and nights.

CHAPTER XXV

Ball at Hyde Park Barracks — Grand Decorations — The
Prince of Wales, as Colonel of the Second Life Guards,
Receives the Guests — Colonial Banquet at Guildhall —
Builders of the British Empire — The Prince and King
Make Speeches — The King Offends the Irish — The Con-
sequences — Entertained by Lord Brassey at Normalhurst
— Lunch with Prince of Wales at Sir Christopher Sykes's
— Dinner at Trinity House — General Grant's Mistake —
Places of Interest — Handsome Jewish Women — Dinner
with Baroness Burdett-Coutts — The King Decorated —
He Also Decorates the Queen and Prince of Wales —
" Punch " and the King — Ball at Marlborough House
— Lunch with the Duke and Duchess of Teck — The
" Lion " Leaves England — The King and the British
Government.

THE following evening we attended a ball at
the Hyde Park barracks, given by the Second
Life Guards, of which the Prince of Wales was
Colonel-in-Chief. The decorations of the great ball-
room rivalled in splendour, but not in delicate taste,
the displays of the Orient. Around it was a crimson dado, and above it the polished helmets of the
Guards, silver kettledrums, and standards; fountains surrounded by groups of rare exotics and
flowers; with eight magnificent Louis Seize cande-
labra on ebony and ormolu pedestals. The royal
supper-room was decorated with fine old tapestries,
the floor covered with Persian carpets; and the table
decorated with white flowers.

The Prince, as the Colonel Commanding, received
the King and suite and the members of the Royal

Family. One would suspect that the members of this family would become weary of meeting each other constantly in these public parades. This was, however, their mission in life, and no doubt they received the same satisfaction from the discharge of duty which Providence had imposed upon them as the priests of the ancient Jewish nations were consoled for the discharge of their arduous duties by selecting and eating the choicest parts of the animals which they sacrificed.

Two lines of the Guards, tall men, with polished helmets and glittering cuirasses, stood immovable as statues while the guests passed between them. The dancing was without life; the British frame is too heavily built for graceful motion; its best action is in endurance, in taking ditches and fences, or in fighting its way over mountains or across deserts. The women were thick-set and heavy, rarely graceful or willowy, but with the beauty of high colour and the repose of great physical strength.

The next evening we attended the Colonial banquet given by the Lord Mayor at the Guildhall, at which the prominent men connected with the Colonies were brought together. The Lord Mayor, in gorgeous trappings, received the King at the door and led him into a reception-room where the Prince of Wales had just arrived. The attendants were in ancient and grotesque livery. One of them announced in a loud voice, "Your Royal Highness, your Majesty, my Lord Mayor, dinner is served." The Lord Mayor, with the Prince on his right and the King on his left, entered the great banqueting-hall, in which three hundred guests stood to receive them. Many of the foremost men of the empire were there. If you had mentioned any accessible spot on the earth and had asked if any one present had been there, some one would have replied, " I have." These men were the coral insects, who were building up the atolls of British Empire out of the seas.

At the close of the formal part of the banquet a choir of male and female voices, in a high balcony, chanted the Lord's Prayer. The Lord Mayor then rose and said, —

" Your Royal Highness, your Majesty, my Lords and gentlemen, charge your glasses."

He then proposed the health of the Queen. The Prince of Wales responded. Much practice had made him an adroit, pleasant, and even a model after-dinner orator, who, indeed, must speak in public, but by the inexorable rule of the British unwritten law, must say nothing. As firmly as Prometheus was fastened to the rock is the Prince, as the representative of the Queen, fastened to the top of the political fence, which he must invariably straddle, for he can take no side in political matters. The costermonger may, as a British freeman, be a violent partisan, but under the strange contrivances of the British Constitution the King must remain as impassive in political life as the image of Buddha in the Hindu religion; the nation elevates him, adores him, kisses his hand, but stands with an ugly club in its hands, with which it hits his head if he dares even to enlighten the thoughts of his subjects.

The Lord Mayor again rose, and said, —

" Your Royal Highness, my Lords, and gentlemen, charge your glasses! " He then proposed the health of King Kalakaua in a brief speech in which he said that in his travels he had visited the kingdom of

Hawaii and found all things there which were a credit to civilisation.

The suite had selected this occasion as the one on which the King might properly express his thanks publicly for the favours he had received from the Colonial Governors and the Royal Family. What he said would, through the press, reach all of the colonies he had visited. At his request I prepared the outlines of a speech which he attempted to memorise while dressing for the banquet; but late hours had made him sleepy, and his excellent memory was sluggish. I noticed that during the banquet he closed his eyes several times. At this time there was intense feeling in England against the Land Leaguers of Ireland, — a matter which the King did not understand. He had intended to visit Ireland before leaving for the United States. When he arose to respond to the toast, he began, —

"Your Royal Highness, my Lord Mayor, and gentlemen — "

Then he hesitated; he had forgotten the prepared speech, and was adrift in an open boat on the squally and dangerous sea of an impromptu talk. He looked around the room, at the ceiling, at the three hundred guests who watched him, but was imperturbable as usual. He began by thanking the Royal Family and the Colonial Governors for their hospitality, and declared that no event in his tour around the world had given him more pleasure than his reception in London. Upon this there was much applause, and he instantly took courage for more speech.

"I have," he said, "no political parties in my own country; there are no Land Leaguers there [his open boat began to rock in the dangerous sea], I would not permit such men to trouble my people."

The applause was great, for he had touched the right chord. But a well-known statesman sitting next to me whispered, " I fear he will hear from the Irish about this." He continued for a few moments longer, and sat down with much satisfaction to himself and amid loud applause. His Royal Highness nodded pleasantly to him across the broad form of the Lord Mayor, who sat between, and the King looked at me as if he said: " You see, I am able to take care of myself."

It was not until many years later that Kipling wrote that song of " The Native-Born," which was most fitting for this occasion in Guildhall:

> " I charge you charge your glasses —
>   I charge you drink with me
> To the men of the Four New Nations,
>   And the Islands of the Sea. . . .
>
> " To the hearth of our people's people, —
>   To her well-ploughed windy sea,
> To the hush of our dread high-altars
>   Where the Abbey makes us We ;
> To the grist of the slow-ground ages,
>   To the gain that is yours and mine —
> To the Bank of the Open Credit,
>   To the Power-house of the Line ! "

The loving-cup was now passed around, and the Prince, with the Lord Mayor, walked with the King to the royal carriage, which having entered, he fell asleep at once.

At our tea the next morning I advised the King to abandon his trip to Ireland unless he was ready to face showers of decayed vegetables and an Irish mob of the Land Leaguers. He said the British government would protect him. I replied, " It may give you some money satisfaction, but you will get the contents of a hundred swill-pails. You have unintentionally insulted those people; if you are willing to be the target for dead cats, I am not." Mr. Synge agreed with me. The trip was abandoned.

A few days later, while we were in Berlin, Mr. Synge forwarded to me a copy of a Dublin newspaper which contained an editorial from which the following is an extract: —

" QUASHEE ON HIS LEGS.

" The nominal ruler of Hawaii, who is a lineal descendant of Ho-Ki-Po-Kia-Wua-Ki-Frum, King of the Cannibal Islands, is on a visit to England in quest of subjects, and has been entertained at the Mansion House by that rabid nonconformist, Mr. Lord Mayor McArthur; this great grandson of the Anthropophagi indulged in a sneer at Ireland. We must take the liberty of giving him a figurative rap over the knuckles."

These words were followed by a column of invective comment on the King's speech at the Colonial dinner. I showed this article to my royal master, who declared that it was " Irish mud." I replied, " Your Majesty, you are doing well by Lord Bacon's advice, for you are sucking much knowledge of foreign countries; Irish mud comes up with other stuff."

Sir Thomas and Lady Brassey, by reason of their pleasant visit to the King's islands in the " Sunbeam," tendered to him their hospitality in their fine country seat of five thousand acres at Normalhurst, near Hastings, and he remained there one night. It was a large residence, in which scores of guests could be entertained at the same time; a principality in itself, covering gardens and forests and lakes. The municipal authorities of Hastings presented him with an "address," which is the common and rather dreary form of expressing municipal good-will in Great Britain.

The following day we had luncheon with Sir Christopher Sykes, and again met the Prince of Wales, with several of the charming beauties who were described as the members of his "set." In the evening we attended the Board of Trade banquet in Trinity House. It was the annual dinner given by the Board of Trade, which is the most powerful corporation of the city of London, for it superintends marine affairs. The Prince of Wales and the King again spoke; the direct and simple speech of the Prince resembled other speeches which he constantly makes as the spokesman of the Queen, but differing from each other as one human face differs from another. Among the distinguished men who discharged the office of after-dinner orators was Sir William Harcourt, who was most amusing. It was said that General Grant, who attended the annual banquet two years before, had been misled by the invitation to "Trinity House," and for lack of inquiry assumed that it had some connection with the promotion of the interests of the church; he therefore delivered a devout speech on the propagation of the gospel, which surprised the guests, who looked upon their religion as they do upon the water of the Thames, — a most excellent article for certain uses, but not to be served up at a banquet.

After visiting many places, the next day, including

Madame Tussaud's Museum, the Tower, and the National Gallery, the King in the evening attended a dinner at the residence of Mr. Hoffnung, a commercial agent of his government. It was unlike all other banquets for the surprise it gave him in meeting a number of the most beautiful Jewish women in London. At no place in any country did he see so many handsome women gathered in one place as there were here; for their dark beauty was enhanced by the rich colouring which is developed by the English climate.

On the following evening we dined with the Baroness Burdett-Coutts, in Holly Lodge. The house was reached through a covered way of rocks fantastically arranged with shells, rare plants, and coloured lights; so that it was like a grotto of the tropics; the lawns and old trees were illuminated. The Baroness, with a singularly benevolent face and quiet manners, had a talent for drawing out her guests in conversation; she seemed to carry at her girdle a bunch of many keys of different moulds, from which she readily selected one which fitted and opened the lock of the brain of each guest. She opened the mind of the Polynesian King, and he talked with freedom and ease about the traditions of his people. A peeress who was one of the guests asked the King if Tahiti was not the capital of his kingdom, although it is two thousand miles distant from it and is a French possession. Upon this George Augustus Sala, who was a guest, remarked that although the English people traded with the world, their geographical knowledge was most limited, as it was considered a minor matter in the schools.

The King and the Baroness, after dinner, played a game of billiards, the tally of which was kept by the Baroness's young husband.

On returning to Claridge's the King found a letter from the Prime Minister in which he stated that the Queen had conferred on him the Grand Cross of the Order of St. Michael and St. George. He was delighted with this gift, and in turn conferred on the Queen and the Prince of Wales the Order of Kamehameha. While the King was decorated with many Orders, there was none which he sought so earnestly as those of the British Queen. It was not an Order held in the highest esteem among Englishmen, but was used often in doing honour to foreigners of rank.

"Punch" did not ignore the King; among its shots at the flying follies it emptied a barrel at this royal bird of passage. Whatever the merit of this verse may be, it belongs beyond dispute to the Victorian age: —

> "He 's really a most intelligent wight,
> Who 's looked on many a wonderful sight,
> And travelled by day, and eke by night,
> O'er rivers and seas and dry lands ;
> But wrongly, it seems, his name we say,
> And print it too, in a horrible way,
> He ought to be called King Kalakua,
> This King of the Sandwich Islands."

"Punch's" review of the debates in the House of Commons referred to the King, who had visited it with Sir Charles Dilke.

"Sick of civilisation, he sighed for some of those scenes of savage manners among which he had been bred. 'My island home is far off, I will go to the

House of Commons.' Sir Charles Dilke pointed out the eminent men. 'Yes, yes,' said the King, 'but where is Toby?' Dilke did n't like this urgency. It looked suspicious. But Dilke said the King never cared for dog in that way, and besides he had dined."

When the King read this allusion to his inquiry for "Punch's" dog, Toby, he declared the Englishmen had often eaten dog in his kingdom and enjoyed it, in the belief that it was young roast pig.

We attended the last of the dances in high life, for the season, at Marlborough House. It is unwritten law that on this occasion the Prince is relieved from social and political obligations and invites only his personal friends. It was necessary for us to appear in knee-breeches. The unusually large calves of the King's and the Chamberlain's legs, though in just proportion to their size, became the distress of the tailor, for stockings of ample size could not be obtained; those that there were fitted so tightly we feared that through some weakness in their texture they would burst open at an inopportune moment. His Royal Highness wore no decorations but that presented to him by the King. The pretty women of his coterie were, as usual, there, and diamonds were as common as pebbles. Many of these beauties looked tired, as if palled with the sameness of splendour; as if they had been diving all the season, as Balzac said, to the bottom for pleasure, and had brought up gravel. Many noted men of the younger class moved about as if they also had found pleasure the sternest moralist. Still they chatted and grinned like the inmates of the hall of Eblis, where it was mutually agreed that though each of them bore grievous diseases it should be denied by all that there was any suffering. A quiet decorum prevailed; hilarity was forbidden by the unwritten law. There was music by the stringed pieces and some languid dancing. The Princess of Wales moved about with her quiet, sweet smile which is the joy of England; she was a mistress of the art of warm personal recognition. The gardens were lighted with Chinese lanterns, and the supper table offered salads, cold meats, ices, and wine. At two o'clock the King became sleepy, and the Prince of Wales led him to the royal carriage.

We took luncheon the next day with the Duke and Duchess of Teck in Kensington Palace. As they were under no obligation to entertain the King, the invitation was some proof of the estimation in which the Royal Family held his manners and conduct. The luncheon was entirely informal, and was served in the room in which the Queen was born; in the adjoining room she held her first Council of State on ascending the throne. The children of the family were present, one of whom became the Duchess of York. The Princess Mary was in fine humour and related many anecdotes about the Palace and the Queen.

Royal banquets are seas, and conversations the winds that pleasantly ruffle them. We often found them dead seas, or subject to doldrums, — seas on which the guests floated like painted ships — blazing oceans of silence — without a ripple from the " cat's paw " of a story. But the Princess made it sparkle with her stories of incidents connected with this palace.

The children, who were allowed to be present at

the luncheon, were interested in the dusky monarch. There was no expectation at that time that the young girl who sat silently watching him would be the future Queen of England. We were told, afterward, that the Princess wished her children to see a Polynesian king with attractive manners.

We had now extended our visit to sixteen days, and still the King, as a veritable " lion," was overwhelmed with invitations to luncheons, balls, and receptions. Several which he did attend in great houses I do not mention, because they were repetitions of those I have described. There was now some danger, in my opinion, that the King might outlast his welcome; it was wise to leave before the " lion " became a sucking dove or the Royal Family began to yawn. But we had been thrice fortunate in that we had been in actual, living touch for so many days with the family which crowns that vast political fabric which has been erected in these islands, lying off the coast of Europe, after centuries of revolutions, wars, abdications, dethronement, beheadings, — the fabric which rules one fourth of the people of the globe.

By the King's command I now sent to Earl Granville a letter in which the thanks of the King were conveyed to the Royal Family for their gracious hospitality. We were informed at the last moment that even our expenses in London had been paid by the direction of the Queen.

Although it was now late in the season, we determined to make brief visits to Belgium, Germany, Austria, France, Spain, and Portugal.

We accordingly took the train for Dover *en route* to Ostend and Brussels. We also adhered to our plan of not giving to the monarchs of these countries any formal notice of our intention to visit them.

While still in England, and on the way to Dover, I again tried to enforce a moral on the King's mind from the incidents and experiences which were fresh. The kings of Hawaii did not understand the nature of ministerial government as contrasted with kingly or personal government. In their simple minds, if there was a king, he should rule. The fiction of a kingly figurehead as it existed in Great Britain, which was essentially the rule of the Commons, or people, was an intricate arrangement which was beyond their understanding. The white subjects of King Kalakaua, though able to destroy the monarchy because they possessed the brains and wealth of his kingdom, cordially assented, though the majority of them were Americans, to its rule, but insisted that it should be ministerial rule. By refusing to submit to this form of government the King had already put his throne in great jeopardy, and if the offence were repeated he would again be in peril.

I explained to him the eccentric growth of Parliamentary rule, but I was invariably met with this simple inquiry: " What is the use of having a queen if she cannot rule? " My explanations of the evolution of the British Constitution confused him. The gradual modification of traditions and political habits arising out of many circumstances he could not comprehend. I cautioned him against trifling with the Anglo-Saxons, who were his most powerful subjects. Within five years from that time he was forced to establish ministerial rule by a bloodless revolution, and within twelve years his monarchy was extinguished, as the sequel will show. I said to him on this occasion, while describing the growth of the English government, " the British nation has a prehensile tail," as an essayist, Emerson, says: " it clings to traditions and old forms, but it improves their substance." " Then," said the King, " it is a monkey government, is it? I don't want anything of that kind in my country." The tube through which we had hoped he would suck wisdom of the world was defective; all that rose in it filtered upward through Polynesian ideas.

CHAPTER XXVI

Belgium — Consular Offices — The Battlefield of Waterloo — Civilised and Pagan Warfare — Visits from and to King Leopold — Berlin — Visit to Prince William and Other Princes in Potsdam — Dines with Prince William — Military Reviews — The Skeleton Dances — The Royal Hawaiian Band — Dinner with the Red Prince — Krupp's Gun Factory.

A T the railway station in Brussels, early in the morning, the Count de Cannart d'Hamale, in a brilliant uniform, received us. He was the Hawaiian Consul-General for Belgium, and with him, in a uniform less imposing, but with a large portfolio under his arm, was the Chancellor of the Consulate.

Consular offices are eagerly sought in Europe by European residents, although they are not salaried, are without income, and even cost the occupant some outlay. These offices give a certain social standing to the holder, and entitle him to public recognition in local entertainments and to the privilege of wearing a uniform, which may be as expensive as the vanity of the owner chooses. Often the Consul receives some decoration from the little government he represents, which enables him to claim some social distinction among his friends. Among the annoyances which now confronted us during the tour through Europe were the applicants for consulships in places where there was no foreign trade with Hawaii, and the earnest requests for decorations or Orders.

The King of Belgium (1881).

We took lodgings in the Hotel Belle-Vue. King Leopold of Belgium was not in the city; but one of his aides promptly called and told us he would be at home the next day and would call.

King Kalakaua had looked forward with great pleasure to a visit to the battlefield of Waterloo. So at once, guided by an aide of the Belgian King, we drove to it, but unfortunately in a deluge of rain (an item recorded in the royal jest-book as a waterloo). From the top of the great earth mound which the British have built on the field in commemoration of their victory, under umbrellas, and before a driving rain, the King looked down upon the grain fields and the greenest of grass, and upon the objective point in that stubborn fight, the details of which were clearly fixed in his memory.

"Your Majesty sees," I said, as the moralising Minister of State, "that the Christian nations settled their differences in the same way that your savage ancestors did, with the advantage on the side of your ancestors that they made their wars economical by eating the bodies of their enemies instead of letting them rot and waste as they are wasted in Europe. Besides, in killing and eating their prisoners, your warlike ancestors avoid a vast amount of suffering which arises from wounds, disease, and broken limbs." This, I said, was a view which a certain English moralist named Carlyle had taken on the subject, and it was an eminently practical one, for beyond pepper and salt for seasoning a victorious army need carry no rations.

The King asked me why the great nations engaged in war, and why they did not resort to arbitration. I replied that the explanation of this strange condition of affairs could not be easily explained while we were standing on the top of the mound in a rainstorm, but I would repeat to him a remark made by John Bright in Parliament, that "all the wars England had been engaged in could have been avoided if wisdom and prudence and patience had governed."

My royal master, like a good military critic, did not approve of some of Napoleon's strategy; but the details of this criticism I will not repeat here, as it is only a fragment of the discussion on the merits of that great warrior which will be carried on for the next thousand years.

The next day the King of Belgium returned to Brussels and promptly called on his Hawaiian Majesty. Though his palace was next door to the hotel, he appeared in his state carriage, with footmen, outriders, and an escort of cavalry. He asked King Kalakaua many questions about his own country and about the Oriental courts he had visited. After an interview of twenty minutes he left. Within half an hour his state carriage, with its escort of cavalry, came to the hotel, and we entered it, drove into the court-yard of the palace, which was, as I have said, next door, and returned the visit. It was singular that our little and distant kingdom had so many relations with foreign lands. We told the Belgian King that it was only by what is called an "accident" that the group of Hawaiian Islands was not a dependency of Belgium at this time. In 1840 some enterprising Americans obtained from one of the King's predecessors a lease of nearly all the public lands of the group, and had entered into contracts in Brussels for the emigration of large numbers of Belgian peasants who should become settlers upon

The Queen of Belgium (1881).

these lands; but before the contracts were concluded
the British seized the islands and defeated the project. His Hawaiian Majesty said to King Leopold,
" If this plan had been executed, I, instead of being
the king of the islands, would be one of your subjects
visiting his sovereign." This incident the Belgian
King had never heard of.

As we could not remain longer in Brussels our
King declined the offer of hospitalities, and the next
morning we left for Berlin.

In Berlin we were met by aides and officers of
the German court and taken to the Hotel de Roma.
The Emperor William was at Ems. The next day
we went by train to Potsdam, where a state carriage
met us, and we were taken to the summer residence
of Prince William (now the Emperor). Both the
Prince and Princess received the King cordially.
They spoke of Prince Henry's visit to Hawaii, and
invited us to dine with them at noon the following
day. We then called upon the old Prince Charles,
and his son Prince Frederick Charles, known as the
Red Prince, who also invited us to dine with him.
We were driven to the Emperor's summer palace in
the forest, with the lake before it, and the stillness of
the place unbroken save by the sound of the artificial
cascades.

At dinner the next day Prince William appeared in
a simple military uniform; both he and the Princess
admired the King's use of the English language; one
could see in the manner and discourse of the Prince
that he was somewhat nervous and impetuous. After
dinner, which was simple in comparison with the
heavy feasts of the English, we were led about the
grounds and smoked on the lawn. The Prince re-

gretted the absence of the Emperor, which was due to the hot weather, as well as the absence of his father, the Crown Prince, who had requested him from London to make his Majesty's visit pleasant. He asked if there were any objects that he especially wished to see. Now the King, with all his military studies, was anxious to see military manœuvres, but did not like to say so; he said, however, that he regretted that he was not in Berlin at the time when the parade took place, for he had heard and read much about the German army. The Prince replied that during the hot weather the grand exercises did not take place; but if his Majesty would be pleased to see some of the troops, they would be paraded next day.

The next morning one of the aides called with carriages, and drove us to an open field about four miles from the city. We had hardly drawn up on one side of it when we noticed dust in the distance, and within a few moments eight batteries, each of them having six field guns, dashed over the stumps and broken ground with the horses at the very top of their speed. Halting instantly at a certain point, the horses were detached, the guns unlimbered, and in a moment forty-eight guns filled the air with thunder and smoke in their discharges at targets a mile and a half distant. The terrible rapidity with which this was done seemed the very essence of masterly fighting. The artillery then passed in review before the King, and we were taken some distance to the field of cavalry practice. Seven thousand mounted men passed the King in review, and then practised evolutions over the field. Finally, forming a line nearly a mile long on one side of the field, our car-

Prince William of Prussia and Princess Augusta Victoria
of Schleswig Holstein (1881).

riage being in the centre of it, a charge was made. The double line came down toward the carriage like a whirlwind; it was almost upon us, the speed of the horses was not slackened, and in spite of our absolute safety, as the charge seemed to be upon us we rose in the carriage as if we would jump out. The charge, which seemed to be utterly mad and headlong, stopped with the noses of the horses at the wheels of the carriage. The King recovered his martial spirits, the Emperor's aides smiled, and, I have no doubt, made a capital story of the incident. We had luncheon in the officers' barracks while the military band played the Hawaiian anthem. Its leader sent word to the King that Berger, the leader of the Hawaiian band, was a graduate from this Berlin band. Thereupon the King asked that he should be presented to him, and after it was done the bandmaster declared that the King's band had now a European reputation; this opinion was confirmed during this tour. When we retired there suddenly rose from the band the plaintive music of some of our native melodies; the fine-looking German officers rose; the King was toasted, and he left as " Hawaii Ponoi " was repeated with " The Watch on the Rhine."

An invitation was received from the King's Consul-General of Sweden and Norway, to enjoy a yachting excursion about the North Sea, but it could not be accepted. One of the Swedish illustrated papers represented the meeting of the British Queen and the Hawaiian King, in which the ancient royal etiquette of kissing was observed. The letterpress was: (The Queen), " Sire, you are a bad fellow; you bit me." She hesitates, then continues: — " but you are such a sweet thing you may kiss me again."

The King reviewed a large body of infantry the next day, but the little skeleton in the royal closet rattled incessantly, for he was repeatedly asked, "How large is your Majesty's army?" But this time, in the presence of the magnificent German force, he faced the truth and meekly replied, "I have no army."

At noon we went to Potsdam again and dined with the Red Prince, and called upon Prince William in order to take leave. The King thanked him for directing a review of the artillery, cavalry, and infantry; the Prince replied that he regretted that the Emperor, also his father, and his brother, Prince Henry, were absent, and urged the King to remain and visit some of the German cities. We visited Krupp's gun factory at Essen. Many persons were presented to the King in the office of the gun factory. He desired to decorate Mr. Krupp, but in the multitude of presentations he mistook an old gentleman for Krupp and conferred the honour on him; this was an embarrassment which was subsequently relieved by correspondence and explanations.

Franz Joseph I, Emperor of Austria (1881).

CHAPTER XXVII

WE left for Vienna without hope of seeing the royal family, as it had left the city for the summer season. One of the Emperor's aides, and a captain of the navy who had visited Hawaii, received us, together with the King's Consul-General residing in Vienna. At the Imperial Hotel many officials called, among them the Archduke Albrecht, the only member of the royal family in the city. Mr. William Walter Phelps, the American Minister at the Austrian court, and Mr. Eugene Schuyler, the American *chargé d'affaires* at Bucharest, my old college friends, also called, and were presented to the King. After their presentation was made with due ceremony, they retired to my apartments and we had a Yale jubilee. It was a singular incident that three friends, intimate in college days and afterward, should suddenly meet in the capital of the Austrian Empire: one as the Minister of the United States, another already distinguished as a diplomat and scholar, and the third as the Minister of the Polynesian ruler of about the smallest kingdom of the world. We discarded for the time, however, all earthly distinctions, and when, later, the King asked what song we were singing in my apartments, I replied, " It 's a Way We Have at Old Yale." For the purpose of recalling our old associations we converted the large centre table of the apartment into the old fence in front of ancient South College, and were once more boys of Old Eli. I, the oldest of the three, have outlived them, for these splendid men died at the noon of their lives, before they had even cast shadows.

That evening the King dined with Mr. Phelps and then occupied the Emperor's box at the Royal Opera. The next day he reviewed the Imperial troops stationed in the city; it was said that he quickly and intelligently distinguished the difference in the drill tactics of the Austrian and German armies.

There were rumours published in the press that the King intended to sell his islands to some European Power; but these were mere jests. To one of the newspaper correspondents, however, he said, while denying these rumours, that the European Powers should unite in a joint guarantee of the independence of his kingdom. He was still under the influence of the Italian adventurer, although, aside from it, he had a vague feeling that he was confronted with the " manifest destiny " of the United States. Any active movement at this time toward obtaining such a guarantee would have involved us in trouble, as the United States would have firmly declared to the European Powers that the King's islands were within " the sphere of American influence," and such a guarantee would have been resented as an unwarrantable interference. Mr. Phelps and

Elisabeth, Empress of Austria (1881).

Mr. Schuyler, on my suggestion, quietly but earnestly, in a conversation with the King, urged him not to make any effort to secure such a guarantee, and he abandoned the scheme.

The King unfortunately, with the Austrian gentlemen attending him, visited one of the noted music and beer gardens, the Prater, and was placed in a conspicuous place; he drank wine and beer, and, while walking about the place, was approached by a pretty Viennese girl who bowed to him and asked him to dance with her. He instantly assented, and was soon waltzing, and surrounded by a large crowd, who watched him with much interest. The reporters of the Viennese newspapers were the most persistent and impudent news-gatherers we met in Europe; they swarmed in our hotel, noted and published the names of the dishes of which the King ate and the number of glasses of wine which he drank, his manner of holding a napkin, and the smallest details regarding his dress. A legion of them followed him to the beer-garden. The following morning the newspapers published picturesque and exaggerated descriptions of his dancing in the Prater; and these were sent by telegram to many cities of Europe, including Paris, to which place we were next to go; and with these was sent a statement, without foundation, that the Emperor of Austria had requested him to leave the empire.

The people gathered in the Prater, however, approved of the King's democratic manners, and when the band rendered the Hawaiian national anthem they rose and uncovered. The press editorially spoke of the King as a good-natured, enlightened, and liberal monarch, a suitable model for a European ruler;

the correspondent of the London " Times " reported to his paper that the Austrian government had gone out of its way to make his visit an agreeable one.

When we reached Paris no representative of the French government met us; for the first time in the tour we met the cold shoulder, and we were without knowledge of the reason for it. The King was much aggrieved at this want of hospitality, for the French Foreign Office had sent him a telegram, while we were in London, inviting him to attend the Fêtes of July in Paris, as the President's guest. I advised the King to assume his incognito and pay no attention to the French court. He was, I suspected, anxious to get the decoration of the Legion of Honour, and insisted on an explanation, as his government had a treaty with France, and a French diplomatic commissioner resided at his own court. As I now had some experience in the ways of royal etiquette, I resorted to a very simple plan of finding the reason for this apparent discourtesy. I called upon the Minister from Portugal to the French Republic, who was an old and kindly man with large experience in public affairs. He received me cordially, upon which I frankly told him what the situation was and asked his advice. He advised me to call at the Foreign Office at once and inquire. I called, with some feeling of humiliation, but believing that it was wise to do so under the circumstances. I was courteously received by the *Chef du Cabinet,* who in a polite manner, without any arrogance, said that the King " had not reciprocated the courtesies of the French government," for he had failed to notify it of his presence in Paris while in transit to London, and, moreover, had declined to accept the invitation to the Fêtes of

President Grévy of France (1881).

July; he had even neglected to inform the government of his intention to visit Paris. I replied by stating that we much regretted any neglect of the requirements of etiquette; it arose from our residence in a distant part of the world. He then said that these errors would be overlooked, but President Grévy would leave the city within an hour, and it would be impossible to arrange an interview. M. Mollard, the introducer of ambassadors, he said, would call upon the King, but there were no longer any court entertainments, as the season had closed and everybody was out of town.

I reported this interview to the King and his Chamberlain, both of whom were dissatisfied with it, and especially the intimation that we were ignorant of the forms of royal etiquette. This sudden suppression of modesty by our royal party certainly amused me. I believed that it might be due to some vanity inspired by our gracious reception in London, Berlin, and Vienna.

I then said if the King would make no concession the acts of the French government might be regarded as offensive and would justify a prompt declaration of war. As we were already within the city, the Chamberlain, as Colonel commanding, could represent the army itself, and seize the heights of Montmartre, and then work around and spike the guns of Mont Valerien; while his Majesty, with the maps before him, could direct the general campaign; and I, as a diplomat, could at the proper time negotiate the terms on which we would accept the surrender of the city.

The King refused to resort to harsh means, but described the French Foreign Office as a " mean lot."

He then took a drive in the Bois de Boulogne and visited the Hippodrome. On his return, M. Mollard, the introducer of ambassadors, called, and, after courteously discussing our errors, placed the President's box in the Opera at the King's service, and asked him to visit Versailles and the porcelain works at Sèvres. This interview closed the incident; the prices of stocks on the Bourse were not disturbed; a State paper placing before the world our reasons for declaring war against France was not written.

Trivial incidents, like small matches, may explode great magazines. Had the incident not been closed at this time, six months later the Hawaiian fleet of sixty double war-canoes would have appeared off Havre, and Europe been cast again in convulsions. I take to myself much credit for avoiding this catastrophe.

M. St. Hilaire, the Minister of Foreign Affairs, called upon the King. He spoke of the unbroken amity which had existed between the two countries. This was not true, for reasons which I have before stated. The Minister regretted, he said, that the President had been unable to meet the King, but would receive him if he remained in Paris for another week. Not at this time, but after his return to his own kingdom, decorations were exchanged with the French government.

I had told the King of an incident of the massacre of the Communists by the Versailles troops in 1870, of which I was aware because I was in Paris just before and after it occurred. He wished to see the spot on the Heights of Montmartre where it occurred, and we visited it. A boy twelve years of age served one of the Commune field-pieces with great skill, while it was planted behind one of the street barricades. By a flank movement of the Versailles troops the few remaining Communists, with the boy, were captured, and at once were placed in line to be shot. "Mon capitaine," asked the boy, "give me three minutes to take this watch to my poor grandmother in the next street; it is all she has left." "Yes," replied the captain, thinking that he would never return. Within three minutes the boy appeared, took his place before the muskets, said, "Captain, I am here," and fell with the next volley.

At this time Colonel George Macfarlane, who was a member of the King's staff, arrived from the Hawaiian kingdom and continued with the royal party until it finished its tour. He reported to the King that there was tranquillity at home, and that his Majesty's subjects awaited his return with schemes of prosperity which would make their idle lot still more idle.

After brief visits to the former site of the Bastille, the Conciergerie, the site of the ancient Hôtel de Ville, the galleries of the Louvre, the Palace of Versailles, and the porcelain works at Sèvres, the King was quite ready to leave, as the weather was so warm.

During the few days we were in Paris numerous requests were made for decorations. Merchants, politicians, and idle men about town wished to secure some of these distinctions given by royalty. One who claimed to be a savant desired an Order because he had discovered some new bugs; another claimed that he had served on a warship which had visited Hawaii; another, that he was the author of a great book; another, that he had killed a ferocious tiger in

Algeria. While the decorations of the Spanish republics of South America could be readily obtained, they did not have the seal of monarchy on them and were much discredited. But these were refused by the King, as he now held them in much esteem, since he had secured high standing in the courts of Europe.

The Count de Lesseps called on us, and asked his Majesty to dine at his residence in Passy. We there met the Countess, a young and charming woman with nine children. After the dinner there was a reception to which many people came; it was the only occasion on which the King met Parisian women. He noticed their vivacity and faultless dress; no doubt they had much amusement at our expense, for the majority of them did not know where the King's country was situated; one of them placed it in the Gulf of Mexico, and another near Patagonia.

The Count said that a canal would at some time be constructed across the Isthmus of Darien; but he did not then foresee that he would himself promote it, and that the scandal attending it would for ever cloud his great reputation. He hoped that the Hawaiian Islands (*Îles de Sandwich*) would become the great free port of the Pacific.

During the rendering of " Aïda " at the Opera the King visited the green-room, and the *ballerines* showed him the exercise which kept their limbs supple. They were told that the King was a very proper person; he was not *un roi pour rire,* and had a *corps de ballet* of his own numbering a hundred. Whereupon one of them asked him how they danced. He replied, like the nautch-dancers, and one of them then fell to a clever imitation of it, closing with a cancan which nearly put the King's nose in jeopardy.

With the recent example of the Prince of Wales before him, he visited the office of " Figaro " and became a subscriber. " This," said one of the reporters, " will enable him, when he comes here to live as a subsidised monarch, to speak French and understand the *chansons* of the *opéra bouffe*."

The Ministers of Spain and Portugal called on the King, and told him that he would be officially received in Madrid and Lisbon, but that the King of Spain was at a watering-place and would not be able to meet him.

CHAPTER XXVIII

At the Spanish Frontier — The Escurial — Reception at Madrid — Our Car Derailed by a Cow — Portugal — The Royal Car — Received by the King and Queen — The Little Skeleton Again — Mutual Decorations — Dom Fernando — Portuguese in Hawaii — Cintra — Pena — A Magnificent Outlook — Dinner with the Portuguese King — A Narrow Escape for Vasco da Gama as Told by His Descendant — A Bull-Fight — Good-Bye to Portugal — The Monarchs Embrace — Negotiating a Treaty — The King Starts for Home via Spain, France, England, Scotland, and the United States — The Valet's Estimate of His Position.

AT the Spanish frontier we were received with some ceremony; we left the train for a brief visit to the Escurial. The Governor of the place met us, and led us down to the vaults where the bodies of the dead kings and queens were laid; through the rooms of the palace, with its fine tapestries; and then, with a guard of honour, we returned to the train. At Madrid, carpets were spread in the railway station for the royal feet, and a large crowd, which was there to see a Polynesian king, was kept in order by a detachment of troops. The Governor of Madrid took us in state carriages to the palace, through which we strolled, and thence to the Plaza. Afterward we dined and drove to the station. The Governor asked the King to revisit Madrid on his return from Lisbon; for he said he had been instructed by the Regent of Spain to entertain his Majesty.

As there was no sleeping-car on the train which took us to Portugal, we dozed in chairs and on the

The Queen of Spain (1881).

floor. At a station we passed a train in which were
two of our Hawaiian white compatriots travelling for
pleasure, and we ended a miserable night by the de-
railing of the car by a cow. The trainmen first spent
half an hour inspecting the mangled beast; and then,
with infinite talk and the smoking of many cigarettes,
devised plans for restoring the cars to the rails, which
was finally done after much delay.

At Badajoz, on the Spanish frontier, the Portuguese officials placed us in the royal car of their King,
which they had brought from Lisbon, at which place
we arrived early in the morning. The Portuguese
Chamberlain met us, with the royal carriages, and
with an escort of cavalry we went to the Hotel Bra-
ganza, before which stood a battalion of infantry.

In the afternoon, in the royal carriages, we called
upon the King of Portugal. The drive was along the
Tagus to the Palace of Adjuda, situated on high
ground overlooking the river. At the gates of the
palace men armed with ancient halberds lined the way
to the entrance, where we were met by Dom Luis,
"King of Portugal and the Algarvies, without and
beyond the seas, in Africa, Lord of Guiana, and of
the Navigation and Commerce of Ethiopia, Arabia,
Persia, and the Indies." He and his predecessors
had been robbed of many of these possessions by an
envious and thieving world, but he retained the titles
as certificates of the past glory of his throne.

The monarchs walked beside each other through
several chambers to the reception-room, where the
Queen, with her ladies, was standing. Her Majesty
Maria Pia, a sister of Victor Emmanuel of Italy, was
tall and graceful, but extremely homely; an excellent
rider on horseback, a good shot, quick in retort, the

owner of costly jewels, and withal most charitable and fond of botanic study. Dom Luis was short and stout, and with something of the bluffness of a sailor; he was in command of the warship " Bartolommeo Diaz " when his brother died, and from the deck he ascended the throne.

After a brief conversation the King presented me, and then his Chamberlain and Col. Macfarlane, his new aide, and Mr. Abram Hoffnung, now an *attaché*. The Portuguese King, looking up at the Chamberlain, who towered above him in his military uniform, said, " Ah! you belong to his Majesty's army? How large is it? " The little skeleton rattled again in the royal closet; but the Hawaiian King, relieved from taxing his brain for an answer, smiled as he saw his own Chamberlain in the pitiless bog, and left him with a free hand to extricate himself. The reply, as usual, referred to volunteers and regulars, but neglected figures, and adroitly changed the subject by a statement about the navies of the world which protected our independence, — a matter which greatly interested his Portuguese Majesty.

We retired with the usual ceremony, and within an hour Dom Luis returned the visit. He presented to the King the insignia of the Grand Cross of " Our Lady of the Conception," and the decorations of a lesser rank to each of the suite; and in return he and his Ministers received the promise of Hawaiian Orders, which were later sent to them from Paris.

Following the Portuguese King, Dom Fernando, his father, who had been Regent during the minority of Dom Luis's brother, called. He had been a conspicuous figure in Europe. He had refused the

Dom Fernando, Regent of Portugal (1881).

crowns of Greece and of Spain, on the ground, he said, that they would only be crowns of thorns. His suggestion of placing Prince Leopold, a Hohenzollern, who had married his daughter, upon the throne of Spain, was the immediate or ostensible cause of the Franco-Prussian war. For his third wife he had married Miss Hensler, of Boston, Massachusetts, an opera-singer, who was an attractive person, but who was not, at the time of our visit, in favour with the court. This refuser of two crowns, and the apparent cause of one of the great wars of the world, was to us a most interesting person. He was a good linguist, promoted the arts, and had wide knowledge of affairs. He was extremely simple in manners, and plied us with questions about our own country and its Portuguese inhabitants.

Again appeared the curious relations of our little and remote kingdom with the European countries. At this time several thousands of Portuguese subjects had emigrated from the Azores and had settled in Hawaii as labourers on the sugar plantations. They remained Portuguese subjects, but were in fact joint subjects of the two kings. I was authorised to initiate a treaty between the two countries which would enlarge this emigration. Within three years from this time the Portuguese had emigrated in such numbers to Hawaii that under a good military leader they would have been able to have taken possession of the country and made it a Portuguese colony, provided the American star of empire did not rain a " ghastly dew " upon the scheme.

We visited Cintra the next day. From the palace, which was the Alhambra of the Moorish kings, rose two lofty cones, visible at a long distance and most

impressive. But on entering the building it appeared
that these impressive cones were vast chimneys, ex-
panded at the base, and invented by some eccentric
architect to discharge the smoke and odours of the
kitchen into the clouds. By far the most magnificent
site for a palace which we saw during our tour was
Pena, built near by, on a pinnacle of rock, with a
sheer, vertical descent of a thousand feet from its
bastions to the ocean. A winding road leads up to
this palace on the summit, which is an old castle in
the Moorish style, with Gothic archways, picturesque
drawbridges, great chambers with frescoed ceilings
and innumerable carvings. One may step from the
banquet-hall to the balcony and toss a pebble over
its low parapet into the surf at its base. The land-
ward view takes in Torres Vedras, where, during the
Peninsular War, Wellington forced the beginning of
the end of Napoleon's career; from its towers the
old King, Dom Manuel, daily looked seaward for
many months, in 1497, for the return from India of
his great captain Vasco da Gama. Like the tall
lighthouses against which the flying birds strike in
the dark, it is a cloud-piercing structure against
which angels would scrape their wings unless they
carried lanterns. The views from the highest mountain summits are incomparable with this, because
here are united the grandest views of ocean and
land.

On our return to Lisbon we assumed our uniforms
and went to the palace to dine. After the formal
reception we were taken through its halls, adorned
with pictures and statuary, until dinner was proclaimed by a herald. The King of Hawaii was
seated upon the right of the Queen, while Dom Luis

The King of Portugal (1881).

was seated at the middle of the opposite side of the table, and I was placed on his right with our own suite; other guests, numbering thirty, were arranged according to their rank. As the Queen did not speak English, the flashes of royal silence were prolonged, being broken only by occasional interpretations by Dom Luis. On my right was one of the Queen's ladies of honour, who was a lineal descendant of Vasco da Gama. She spoke English fluently. She asked who was the discoverer of the Hawaiian Islands. I replied, an Englishman, Captain Cook, who had been killed by the people he had discovered. She said that it was indeed fortunate that her illustrious ancestor had passed around the Cape of Good Hope to India, instead of taking the passage around Cape Horn; for if he had taken the Western course he might have anticipated Captain Cook and been killed by the King's predecessor.

The ceiling of the banquet-chamber was superbly frescoed, and its walls were tinted in soft ashes-of-rose colouring; great glass chandeliers, with myriads of candles, lit up the flowers; and the table service was of gold and silver.

The Kings now toasted the Queen and each other. The band on the balcony played the native hymns of Portugal and Hawaii. We then sat for a short time in the balcony, from which we looked down on the Tagus, where so many fleets have ridden at anchor in many wars.

We left with the usual escort of honour. It was the last of the royal banquets which we attended during our tour.

Dom Luis had requested the King to attend a bull-fight on Sunday, the next day; he placed the royal box at the King's pleasure. Unlike the cruel fights which the Spanish people delight in, the one we attended was a respectable affair. It opened with six cavalleïros on noble horses with rich trappings riding around the arena. At a point opposite the royal box and on the farther side of the arena, they formed in line and moved slowly with majestic steps to the royal box, where the riders saluted; then, instead of turning, they backed slowly and in straight alignment to the point from which they started. The bull-fighters, the bandarilha, in rich, close-fitting costumes and cloaks, then approached the royal box, saluted and retired, backing across the arena. Two horsemen entered the ring; a door was opened, and a bull with long horns galloped into the arena, stood bewildered for a moment, and then charged on a red flag. These fights are described in detail in tourists' books, and a description will not be repeated here. The fine horses were too valuable to be slaughtered; they engaged in no serious business, but with much intelligence kept out of the bull's way; they added to the fascination of the scene. Nor are the bulls butchered. When they are tired or cease to show pluck, the audience clamours, and they are withdrawn. Thirteen bulls entered the arena, but some of them were without hatred or malice toward mankind, and refused combat. These Quaker beasts, preferring grass to glory, stolidly looked around the vast amphitheatre and seemed to say: " It takes two to make a fight."

Aside from the wounds made by the barbed darts, which are not serious, the bulls are not injured. Many of them, which show spirit, are, after an interval of some weeks, brought into the arena again.

But even these lose their spirit, or take a reasonable view of the situation, and seem to say, " What is there in this for us?" The excitement of a Portuguese bull-fight, which is somewhat regulated by a Humane Society, does not lie in the cruelty to the beasts, as it does in Spain, but in the fascinating gymnastics of the fighters and the dangerous risks they invite. They fence with opponents who have horns instead of rapiers, and are not governed by any rules of the duelling code. The advantage of the fighter is that he moves with much greater rapidity than the bull and makes an unerring calculation of the value of space. Three inches serves him as well as a hundred feet in avoiding the touch of a horn.

At the close of the exhibition the cavalleïros and bandarilha approached the royal box, bowed to the King, and retired; the chief and most popular of them soon appearing at the hotel for a kingly remembrance in gold.

The next day we went to the palace to bid good-bye to our royal hosts. The Queen placed flowers on his Hawaiian Majesty's coat and handed bouquets to the suite. When we had reached the door of the royal carriage, the two monarchs stood for a moment facing each other; the Portuguese King gave his Royal Brother an embrace, but his head hardly reached the shoulder of the Hawaiian sovereign, and his arms were clasped about his thighs; Kalakaua, towering above him, and unable to embrace him, patted his back.

In order to initiate a treaty between the two countries which would regulate the emigration of Portuguese to Hawaii, I remained in Lisbon for several days. The King, with the remainder of his suite, returned to Madrid for two days, from which place they travelled continually through France and England to Scotland, and from that country left for Liverpool and embarked for New York.

On completing the general form of a treaty between Hawaii and Portugal, I left for Paris, London, and Liverpool, and arrived in New York in advance of the King and waited for him.

As Robert, the Count von O———, was more or less prominent in our tour through the Orient, this memoir would not be complete without including some record of his services in Europe.

After reaching Italy the King quickly saw that any parade of the royal feather cloak would be a grotesque affair; it would be ridiculous even to float the royal standard. Robert was virtually deposed from his office and left to the discharge of his exhilarating menial duties. He also abandoned with indignation his secret office of historian or biographer, because the person who had secured for him this office, and had promised him remuneration, had evidently not put a high financial value on the literary work which he had furnished, and had made him no remittance. As the King treated Robert as valet or friend, as his moods changed, it was not easy for me to treat him as a servant, and I listened occasionally to his grievances. He bitterly criticised the King and his Chamberlain for not recognising his own superior education, for he said to me, " Your Excellency, you and I are the only educated men in this party." I replied to this discrimination, " It is not education which is at issue, but your extraordinary capacity for getting drunk at the wrong time." He

The Queen of Portugal (1881).

continued to serve the King during the rest of the tour, in his own irresponsible way, receiving at times, when the demand for decorations was pressing, some considerations from the hungry applicants for the privilege of seeing the King.

CHAPTER XXIX

New York, Philadelphia, and Washington — On the Cobble-
stones of Democracy — The King Presented to President
Arthur — Fortress Monroe and Hampton Normal School
— The King Buys Horses in Kentucky — Banquet in San
Francisco — Sailing for Home — Casting Up Accounts —
What Wisdom Has His Majesty "Sucked" — He Agrees
with Learned Men — Reception at Honolulu — The Girdle
Around the Earth Is Clasped.

AS the King had visited New York six years
before this time and had been the guest of the
city, we did not remain there, for it was now the
month of August, but went to Philadelphia and
Washington. At the railway station in Philadelphia,
where we remained one day, there was an incident
which illustrated the democratic ideas of the hack-
men. The "boss" of the carriage-stand was asked
to provide a vehicle for the King. As it drove up,
the "boss," smoking a cigar, shouted to the driver,
"Here, Jim, here's your load!" Nor did we find
in any place a willingness to use the term, "Your
Majesty;" the use of it seemed to be an approval
of effete civilisation. Nor were there offered the
carpeted walks which elsewhere protect the royal feet
from dirt; we were on the plain cobble-stones of
democracy.

In Washington the King was received by Mr. R. B.
Hill, the Assistant Secretary of State, by whom he
was presented to President Arthur, who by the death
of General Garfield had become President. I had
known Mr. Arthur for many years in the city of

New York while he was engaged in the practice of law. By the "conjunction of the stars" he was President of the Great Republic; the quiet citizen whom for many years I had seen quietly strolling up Broadway had suddenly become the equal of monarchs; and he smiled as he saw me in this new and strange relation. Both President and King were alike in physical structure and weight; moreover there was some resemblance in their facial lines and deportment. If the President had been a dark or a black man, the resemblance would have been a singular one.

Through the kind services of Mr. Hill the government placed a despatch boat at the King's service, and he visited Fortress Monroe, and the Hampton Normal and Agricultural School, of which his old friend, General Armstrong, was Principal.

In the course of our journey across the continent we visited some of the Kentucky farms where fine horses are bred, and the King purchased some excellent animals.

When we reached San Francisco his Majesty was again entertained at a large banquet. But he was now above democratic simplicity; he missed, perhaps, the companionship of monarchs, the perfumed air of royal courts, the spontaneous reverence which crowned heads command. He attracted respectful attention in the United States, but he did see, though dimly, that he only amused the American populace and excited their curiosity. One of the papers stated that "while he was a good fellow, his throne was only a relic of barbarism," and others likened his court to the royal families in *opéra bouffe*.

We steamed down toward the Southern Cross. The pomp and circumstance of the world were behind us. In our debit and credit account with these we had much to the good; we had taken much and given little; our assets in a little kingdom which appeared, comparatively, like a few bullets rising out of the vast expanse of the Pacific, had been turned over repeatedly and profitably.

As we ran down the latitude and entered the trade-wind belt I once more and finally made an effort to find what knowledge or wisdom my royal master had " sucked " out of these travels in many lands. I asked him what benefit he took back to his people, to whom he had promised much. He replied that his subjects were already better off than the majority of the people in the many lands we had visited; they had enough to eat and wear, and they were certainly happier than any people he had seen; they were never in debt, because no one trusted them; their *kulianas* (little homesteads) brought them a living; they enjoyed music and out-of-door life; he did not believe that one of his subjects ever went to bed hungry; no one robbed them; they had no dyspepsia, which, he said, was common in America. I said:

" Your people are dying out and will soon be extinct."

" Well, if they are," he replied, " I 've read lots of times that great races died out, and new ones took their places; my people are like the rest. I think the best way is to let us be. What good do you think the Europeans and Americans have done them, Mr. Minister? Captain Cook, and the fellows who came after him from New England, filled my people with disease and leprosy, and, besides, they forced rum on us. Where one missionary did good, there were five hundred of his countrymen who debauched our women, filled them with disease, and sold liquor to the people. The missionaries told our people to keep Sunday and stop dancing, but the countrymen of the missionaries called them blasted fools and told us not to mind them." His Majesty admitted that the missionaries were always honest, and were the best friends of the people, and did them good by establishing schools and churches. He read Herbert Spencer's works in a desultory way, and thought he knew more about the world than the missionaries did. So his conclusion was that he had seen nothing which his people needed but some well-bred horses and cattle.

When, on my part, I examined what I had sucked out of this tour, I realised the vast conceit of the nations and their humiliating ignorance of each other's capacity, virtues, and character. This ignorance was lamentable, for it was astonishing. The Englishmen despised all other nations, not excepting the Germans and French. The French looked with contempt on the English, Germans, and Americans. The literature of each nation was filled with untrue and unjust comments upon the character of every other. And all the nations of Christendom were agreed that the Chinese, Japanese, and East Indians were " pagans," without noble traits, and, according to the creeds of Christendom, were incapable of moral and intellectual progress, though they included more than two thirds of the inhabitants of the earth.

And yet there were a few able and broad-minded men who spoke with freedom and observation. I had noted some of their opinions, and I cite them, because they singularly resemble in many respects those of this Polynesian chief, though there was a wide gulf which divided their racial instincts and inherited traditions. In the closing chapter of "The Malay Archipelago," written by Professor A. R. Wallace, the contemporary and rival of Darwin, who for eight years had studied the Asiatic races in their native land, not in the interests of trade or religion, but in that of science only, are these words:

"The mass of our people [the English] have not at all advanced beyond the savage code of morals, and have in many instances sunk below it; compared with our wondrous progress in physical science and its practical application, our system of government, of administering justice, of national education, and our whole social and moral organisation remain in a state of barbarism. Our gigantic commerce creates an army who in this respect are worse off than the savage in the midst of his tribe. Until there is a more general recognition of this failure of our civilisation, we shall never, as regards the whole community, attain any real important superiority over the better class of savages: this is the lesson I have been taught by my observations of uncivilised man."

"General" William Booth wrote:

"More minute, patient, intelligent observation has been devoted to the study of earthworms [in England] than to the evolution or rather the degradation of the sunken section of our people," —

of whom, he said, three millions, equal in number to the inhabitants of Scotland, are in a state of abject destitution and misery.

As I review these notes of travel I may add what our genial friend Lord Charles Beresford has recently written:

" British society has been eaten into by the canker of money. From the top downward the tree is rotten. The most immoral pass before the public as the most philanthropic and as doers of all good works. Beauty is the slave of gold. Our intellect, led by beauty, unknowingly dances to the strings which are pulled by Plutocracy."

Mr. Andrew Carnegie, in his " Tour Around the World," which anticipated ours by two years, wrote:

" The traveller will not see in all his wanderings so much abject, repulsive misery among human beings in the most heathen lands as that which startles him in his Christian home."

Emerson puts the knife into our boastings and forces us to humiliation in these words:

" We think our civilisation near its meridian; but we are yet only at the cock-crowing and the morning star."

So " pagan " King, scientist, philanthropist, rich traveller, and philosopher seemed to have " sucked " the same conclusions from wide observation; the King only was without that abiding faith in the evolution of right which will end in the final establishment of universal contentment and happiness. The King saw only the bald fact; he could not see the final reign of law behind it.

My relations to the King, as a Hawaiian-born subject but an American by inheritance, put me under an obligation to him like that of the apprentice in the " Pirates of Penzance " who was bound until noon every day to an absolute loyalty to his piratical masters, but after that hour and until night was entirely free to circumvent and destroy them. As a Hawaiian Minister of State I was bound, for at least part of the time, to observe loyalty to the King and to Polynesian institutions, however primitive they were; for the monarchy and people were rather more pagan than civilised. In this regard I was under some obligation to take a hopeful view of the future of the race and to magnify its racial progress. But when relieved, like the pirate's apprentice, of the obligations of loyalty by my American inheritance, I was free in some degree to suggest and predict the swiftly coming end of Polynesian rule in the Islands, the causes for which were numerous and adequate. These views I freely expressed before the King.

As we neared our little kingdom in the early dawn, the vast volcanic mountain of Haleakala ("House of the Sun") loomed up on the left. Like the devout Hindus, who shouted "Ganga! Ganga!" when they saw the turbid waters of the Ganges as they approached Calcutta, we shouted, "It is home! It is Hawaii nei!"

The harbour of Honolulu was soon in sight. Arches wreathed in flowers spanned the streets; the "army" paraded, the natives wailed a childish welcome to their King and covered him with flowers. The royal band played "Home, Sweet Home!" the royal palms bowed their "Aloha;" the cocoanut-trees flung their yellow jewels from their tall tufts; the breakers pounded out their loyalty. The little military skeleton which had gently rattled around the world was sealed up for ever in its vault. At the Palace, which was an humble place, though it was soon replaced by an imposing building, the people massed, and again buried their King in a wilderness

William N. Armstrong, after a Dinner given by King Kalakaua.

of flowers and scented vines. One who assumed to
be the poet laureate delivered a *mele,* or ode, which
the outspoken and vicious opposition Press said was
only a part of " the elaborate bestialities of a decrepit
paganism."

MELES, OR SONGS.[1]

KING KALAKAUA'S TOUR AROUND THE WORLD.

(No. 1.)

Arise! O Hawaii of Keawe!
Here is thy Chief of Chiefs!
Thy bud; thy blossom ; and thy flower,
Thy chief indeed; O, Maui of Kama!
The blooming flower of Kakae,
The sacred choice of the Heavens!
Advance, ye shores of Piilani
(Shores of Lanai and Kahoolawe.)
Thou also, O! Molokai of Hina!
Oahu stands forth in the lead,
The loved land of Kakuihewa!
The chosen seat doth greet thee!
Flags wave gently in the breeze,
Cannons blare forth their roar;
And the entrance of Mamala re-echoes
Voices of song, and loud hurrahs;
Voices of joyous Welcome Home!
It was the journey of a great free Chief,
Who glanced at all things,
He stood on the highest of the heights;
And reached the four remote corners.
Come up, O Kauai of Mano!
With thy sun shining on Lehua
Let all bless and honour
Every one; O, ye People!
Join with the heavenly hosts;
Who have joined with us;
With our Sovereign Lord and King,

[1] Translation.

Hawaii's wreathed royal Diadem.
Long live Ka Lani (The King) the Chosen One!
Until the heights of the heavens are reached.

(No. 2.)

To Thee, O Sun, that shineth brightly,
O'er all the skirts of the globe,
Make known his royal worth,
Thy light shall reveal his glory,
He sought his wish with wisdom,
And beheld the hidden things of the world.
He witnessed the beauty of Himala, (Asia,)
The joyous rippling waters bore him on;
He beheld the mountain of great fragrance, (Fusiyama,)
Famed for its splendour and towering crest,
And thou, O Ka Lani, set high above,
Thou didst o'erpass the tabus of Tahiti, (of all foreign Lands.)
Uprose the angry sea,
And smoothed its wild flow for thee!
Reach forth to all the isles of the sea! (the Pacific.)
To be thy companions O Ka Lani!
Whilst thou journeyest, O King!
The spirit of Heaven was thy helper,
The morning star was thy guide.
Thy enemies fled before thee —
They speaking vainly against thee!
　Long live Ka Lani,
　　To the farthest reach of the advancing world!

As we entered the Palace, from which we had departed ten months before, one might have heard the sharp click of the clasp which closed the girdle that, for the first time since the beginning of things, had been put around the earth by a ruling sovereign.

CHAPTER XXX

The End of the Monarchy — The King and His Divine
Origin and Mission — Insists on Coronation — Ministers
Resign — The King Resists Parliamentary Government —
Confronted with the Bayonet and Yields — He Instigates
Revolution, but Fails — Visits California and Dies — Liliuo-
kalani His Successor — She Attempts to Make a New
Constitution, and the Monarchy Is Overthrown — Annexa-
tion to the United States — The Work of the Missionaries.

THESE memoirs would not be complete without
a brief account of the effect of this royal tour
upon the King's reign; for some reader may ask
what became of this daring monarch who put a girdle
around the earth?

There were a hundred causes which contributed
to destroy his monarchy, the most of which were
beyond his control, and there was, it may be said in
truth, not one to preserve it. Its extinction, twelve
years after his return, was due to the cold and inexorable law of political evolution, which even now is
hardly understood. There was a conflict of races,
the stronger Teutonic races against the weaker Polynesian. Although it was aggressive and made acutely
so by the geographical situation of the islands at the
crossways of the Pacific commerce, it was peaceful
and bloodless; for of all weak races which have come
in contact in any land whatsoever with the stronger
races, the Hawaiians have suffered the least from injustice and physical dominance. On the other hand,

they have been cared for and coddled by the whites to an unwholesome extent. The new conditions of commerce and industry created by the Anglo-Saxons overshadowed the Polynesians and caused their decay, as the growth of forest trees takes sunlight away from plants and grasses and withers them.

The King did not understand this law of evolution. He was like the majority of monarchs who have lost their thrones, or gone into exile, or been despatched by assassins. He did not see that his monarchy was indulgently tolerated by the Anglo-Saxons so long as it did not put in jeopardy their rigid ideas regarding the rights of persons and property and the administration of law.

Soon after his return the King began to do those things which would, in his opinion, strengthen his throne. As his native subjects were in a very great majority, he believed that if he increased their loyalty to himself he would be able to check the influence of the whites, whose resources and character he could not clearly comprehend. Beneath this, however, was the racial instinct that unconsciously suspected the whites.

He at once determined to have a coronation, though he had been on the throne for six years. Finding that the members of his Cabinet, who were white men, did not approve of such a useless and very expensive proceeding, he secretly went behind them to his native legislature and asked for $75,000 for a coronation. When I discovered this defiance of Ministerial rule I peremptorily resigned my office in the Cabinet, and the rest of my colleagues followed me.

Thereupon the King appointed as his new Prime

King Kalakaua and his Military Staff.   (*On the Steps of his Palace, 1882.*)

Minister an educated American named Gibson, who had been an adventurer in Sumatra, where he had been imprisoned by the Dutch government for sedition; he had also been a Mormon. He was a brilliant writer, and was full of political dreams regarding his own mission in Polynesia. He had encouraged the King to look upon himself as the Colossus of the Pacific, the one who would unite the half-savage tribes scattered through Oceanica into some federal union, of which he would be Primate.

The coronation now took place, for his new Ministers approved of it and the legislature provided the money. Its forms and ceremonies were composed out of what could be found in European books which described such events, mixed with Polynesian customs. It took place in a large pavilion. There were Bearers of the King's Jewels and Decorations; of the Sword of State, and the Crown, which was imported from England; Bearers of the Robes and the Torch; of the Royal Mantle, similar to the one which had such an eventful history during the tour, but of larger dimensions. The King appeared in a white helmet, and the Queen, an excellent woman, wore a diadem studded with diamonds, and a long train supported by the native ladies of her household. The Princes of the Blood were in glittering uniforms. The King crowned himself and again took the oath of office. The hard-headed white men looked on and smiled at this grotesque pageantry of whitewashed paganism. The natives enjoyed it, especially that part of it which gave them continual feasting and abundance of spirits.

In addition to this the King began secretly to

instruct many of the natives in the dogma of his own divine origin, as a means of increasing their loyalty to him, and he renewed some of the ancient vile and licentious practices of the savage times.

Soon after I resigned from office I left the country, and did not again see the King during his lifetime. We held correspondence with each other, however, from time to time. On leaving him I once more advised him to act with great caution in dealing with the white men. I told him that I feared his conduct in choosing an irresponsible Minister would precipitate a revolution, and I predicted that it would come within three years. He replied that he could "take care of" any of his white subjects. The revolution came, however, within five years.

He had now to reckon with the "missionaries." The American missionaries were a body of men, mostly of New England origin, who landed in the islands in 1820 and gradually increased their numbers by immigration until there were about sixty of them. The majority were clergymen and college-bred men, and some of them were unusually able and wise. They were the Romanticists of the Evangelical Church, inspired with an intense desire to save the heathen from everlasting torments. They accepted the dogma of the churches that the heathen, though ignorant of the Gospel, were doomed eternally unless they repented. They did not claim to be agents of civilisation directly, but promoted such forms of civilised life as aided them in propagating the Gospel. For this purpose they established schools, reduced the savage language to writing, and, under their large influence with the chiefs, gradually established wholesome laws, abolished the feudal system, and intro-

duced the American system of jurisprudence so far
as it was practicable. Their main purpose was not
the establishment of an American colony, but the
conversion of the heathen. Forty-five years later
they believed that their mission was fulfilled, and
they voluntarily ceased to be an organised body.
The children of these missionaries, numbering some
hundreds, born in the islands, became to a large
extent permanent residents, professional men, merchants, and planters; they furnished a larger proportion of college-bred men than any community of
the same number in America.[1] With them were associated by marriage, business interests, and religious
sympathy, a number of Anglo-Saxon immigrants
from the mainland. Those who affiliated with the
natives by marriage, those who found law and order
irksome, those who disliked conservative rule, opposed the " missionaries," as they designated this
class of persons, though the original missionaries
no longer lived. The name stood for a political
class.

The " missionaries " born in the islands had a
strong affection for the monarchy in spite of its
grotesque Polynesian ear-marks. But when the
King, with the assent of his Prime Minister, refused to be governed by the legislature, insisted on
personal rule, and became involved in some discred-
itable affairs, they arose promptly and confronted
the King with the bayonet. He instantly yielded to
their demands and proclaimed a new Constitution,
which made his government Ministerial and subject

---

[1] (As originally written) a larger proportion were graduates of
American colleges than of any communities of like size in the United
States.

to the legislature, as it is in England. But he was indignant at this coercion, and within two years secretly contrived a popular revolution, under the leadership of one of the young natives who had been educated in the military schools of Italy; the object of this revolution being to restore the old Constitution, with its strong royal prerogatives and personal rule. The "missionaries" again rose, put down this revolution with their arms, and, with perhaps unwise conservatism, permitted the King to hold the throne.

Within two years of this event, the King again visited the State of California, where he died of pneumonia, and his sister, the Princess Liliuokalani, took his place on the throne.

It is not necessary to discuss the character of King Kalakaua. It is largely revealed in the incidents of his tour around the world. It was his misfortune to have been a Polynesian who with sufficient excuse failed to understand the character of the Anglo-Saxon. He was as wise as the majority of men who have been rulers, but in thought, inheritance, and instinct he was an alien to his white subjects.

His sister, who now succeeded him, had all his defects of character, and, in addition to them, a blind stubbornness of will which he did not have. She had sworn to support the Constitution, but soon engaged in a conspiracy to overthrow it and establish one which increased her personal prerogatives. The "missionaries" again rose in arms. They were tired of irresponsible Polynesian rule. They were no longer willing to exact new promises from the Queen and preserve the monarchy. They abolished it, organised a republic, and co-operated in the annexation of the islands to the United States.

There are now those living who have seen the little kingdom rise out of savagery and paganism, culminate in Kalakaua's reign, and become extinct within one generation. The naturalists say that the mosquito is born, becomes a father and grandfather, and dies, within a day. Such also was the brief life of this monarchy when measured by the average standards of national life. But it will nevertheless stand in history as the solitary community, of that boundless region of Oceanica, that presented all the functions of a complete government, and was in good and regular standing with the family of nations.

More romantic, however, than the brief history of this little kingdom, is the story of the missionaries. They builded better than they knew. The world has now, in a large measure, outgrown the theological dogmas which prompted them to leave America and go into exile in " the darkness ; " their story of saving the perishing souls of the heathen from everlasting perdition has passed into the literature of curious beliefs. But unconsciously they laid the foundations for a high civilisation in which the natives took little part. They established firmly and permanently in these islands the Anglo-Saxon institutions for the regulation and protection of human rights; the trial by jury and the common law, with an independent judiciary; and the watchwords of political liberty were as common in these tropical valleys as they were at the base of Bunker's Hill.

When annexation to the United States took place in 1898, the American flag did not rise over a community of aliens, but over one of original Anglo-

Saxon force, born under the Southern Cross, which had alone for half a century held itself intact against alien influences. At the tap of the Federal drum it wheeled into line and took up its march to the music of the Union without an awkward step, and is now the advanced picket line of American civilisation in the Pacific.